TESTED BY BOMB AND FLAME
LEICESTER VERSUS LUFTWAFFE AIR RAIDS
1939-1945

AUSTIN J. RUDDY

HALSGROVE

IN ASSOCIATION WITH

Leicester Mercury

This book is dedicated to the citizens of Leicester who were killed by Nazi bombs and never lived the peaceful and leisurely lives successive generations have so fortunately enjoyed.

It is also written to perpetuate the memory of the altruistic men, women and children of Leicester's Civil Defence Services, who braved dark and dangerous nights, in some cases, giving their lives, to help their fellow citizens.

First published in Great Britain in 2014

Copyright © Austin J Ruddy

All rights reserved. No part of this publication may be reproduced, stored in a retrieval system, or transmitted in any form or by any means without the prior permission of the copyright holder.

All images are from originals in the author's archive unless annotated otherwise. Every effort has been made to contact the copyright holders of these pictures and permissions obtained. Any omission it is unintentional.

British Library Cataloguing-in-Publication Data
A CIP record for this title is available from the British Library

ISBN 978 0 85704 251 4

HALSGROVE
Halsgrove House,
Ryelands Business Park,
Bagley Road, Wellington, Somerset TA21 9PZ
Tel: 01823 653777   Fax: 01823 216796
email: sales@halsgrove.com

Part of the Halsgrove group of companies
Information on all Halsgrove titles is available at: www.halsgrove.com

Printed and bound in Great Britain by TJ International Ltd

Contents

Acknowledgements	4
Abbreviations	5
Introduction	7
The ARP/CD Services	**9**
The Fire Services	23
Police	34
Post-Raid Welfare Services	37
The Air Raid Warning System	45
Evacuation	47
The Blackout	50
Gas Masks	51
Shelters	51
Uniforms and Insignia of the ARP/CD	57
Leicester's Military Defences Against Air Attack	**60**
Bomb Disposal	63
The RAF	64
The Luftwaffe	64
Leicester Versus the Luftwaffe War Diary	**69**
1939	69
1940	70
Wednesday, August 21, 1940	72
Saturday, September 14, 1940	80
Friday, November 15, 1940	83
Tuesday, November 19/Wednesday, November 20, 1940: Blitz Night	85
Wednesday, November 20/Thursday, November 21, 1940	126
1941	130
Tuesday April 8/Wednesday, April 9, 1941	130
Saturday, May 17, 1941	133
Monday, July 14, 1941	135
1942	137
1943	140
1944	141
1945	144
The Reckoning	146
Conclusion	147
Appendix A: ARP/CD Awards	148
Appendix B: ARP/CD Roll of Honour	149
Appendix C: Military Roll of Honour	150
Appendix D: Civilian Roll of Honour	151
Appendix E: Leicester NFS, July 1942	155
Appendix F: Vulnerable Points in Leicester	156
Primary Sources	158
Secondary Sources	159

Acknowledgements

Interviewees: Ken Allsopp; Brian Bass; Alan Boot; Joyce Chapman; Arthur Hassall, Margaret Hatton; Pete Hpwe; Joy Iliffe; Mary Maynard; Ken Nicholls; Noel Rudkin; Beryl Springthorpe; Dot Wilks.

Plus: my publisher Steven Pugsley and the team at Halsgrove; Andy Baker; Ulf Balke; Ben Beazley; Kerry Bodycote; Dr Margaret Bonney; Terence Burford; Cartographic Section, National Archives, USA; Clive Cartwright; Terry C. Cartwright; John Collier; Andrew Dally; Cllr Mary Draycott MBE; Ian Franklin; Chris Goss; Friends of Welford Road Cemetery; Robert Kemp; *Leicester Mercury*; Jean Mardon of Leicestershire St John Ambulance Association; Marten Lee; Leicestershire & Rutland Family History Society; Leicester Transport Heritage Trust; Sidney Machin; Wayne Manship; Bill Norman; Roger Miles; Mary Pepper; John Pidgeon; Record Office for Leicestershire, Leicester and Rutland; Sub-Officer Malc Tovey (Ret'd) Leicestershire Fire & Rescue Service; Ray Young and last but not least, whoever discovered strong black coffee.

Through their research, Terry Cartwright and his son, Clive, were determined Leicester's Blitz should not slip into history. I thank them for their valuable assistance.

I also thank the many journalists whose words are quoted.

A Morris Commercial chassis with a Leyland-Gwynne heavy pumping unit appliance, of Leicester AFS, at the Granby Halls sub-station, in February 1940. In nine months, this crew would face their baptism of fire during the Leicester Blitz. [Leicester Mercury]

Abbreviations

To avoid repetition, abbreviations have been used:

AA	Anti-Aircraft	LEM	*Leicester Evening Mail*
AFS	Auxiliary Fire Service (1938-1941)	LM	*Leicester Mercury*
AMPC	Auxiliary Military Pioneer Corps	LMS	London Midland & Scottish railway
ARP	Air Raid Precautions		
ATS	Auxiliary Territorial Service (female Army personnel)	LNER	London North East Railway
		LRI	Leicester Royal Infirmary hospital
BD	Bomb Disposal	M/C	Main ARP Control Centre, Charles St
CD	Civil Defence		
CDR	Civil Defence Reserve	MFAU	Mobile First Aid Unit
CGH	City General Hospital	MOH	Medical Officer of Health
Cllr	Councillor	MoH	Ministry of Health
CWD	Civilian War Death records	MoHS	Ministry of Home Security
DC	Decontamination	NFS	National Fire Service (1941-1948)
Do17z	Dornier 17z Luftwaffe medium bomber	PAMS	Police Auxiliary Messenger Service
		PM	Parachute Mine
DRC	District Report Centre	p/t	Part-time
E/A	Enemy Aircraft	RAF	Royal Air Force
FA	First Aid	RAPC	Royal Army Pay Corps
FAP	First Aid Post	RC	Rest Centre
FAPy	First Aid Party	RE	Royal Engineers
FB	Fire Brigade	ROC	Royal Observer Corps
FB1-6	Regular fire engines/appliances	RP	Rescue Party
FG	Fire Guard	SA	Salvation Army
f/t	Full-time	SC	Special Constable/Constabulary
GCR	Great Central Railway	SC	Sprengcylindrische: German thin-cased, higher explosive content bomb
GDA	Gun Defended Area		
GTC	Girls Training Corps		
HAA	Heavy Anti-Aircraft (3.7" calibre)	SD	Sprengdickwande: German thick-walled, armour-piercing, lower explosive content
HE	High Explosive		
He111	Heinkel 111 Luftwaffe medium bomber		
		SJAB	St John Ambulance Brigade
HO	Home Office	SRO	Senior Regional Officer
IB	Incendiary Bomb	TL	Turntable Ladder fire appliance vehicle
IO	Incident Officer		
IP	Incident Post	UXB	Unexploded Bomb
Ju88	Junkers 88 Luftwaffe medium bomber	V-1	Vergultungswaffe 1: 'Vengeance Weapon 1' (German unmanned flying bomb)
KG	Kampfgeschwader (Luftwaffe bomber unit)		
		WMC	Working Men's Club
LAA	Light Anti-Aircraft (.303"-40mm calibre)	WVS	Women's Voluntary Service
		YWCA	Young Women's Christian Association
LG	Lehrgeschwader (Luftwaffe operational training unit)		

Financial values in [brackets] are 2014 comparative prices.

'And what was one's reaction during the raids? To be conscious one was in the service of the city and ready to help, gave a spirit of assurance and strength that even the heaviest of Hitler's bombs could not shake. Leicester – not the city that is visible, the brick and stone, streets, avenues, highways and parks – these are not the real Leicester that endures. The soul of Leicester is to be found in its people. These are the true Leicester, who, though tested by flame and bomb, found the strength to endure. These are they who kept watch, braved the hours of darkness, exhorted and encouraged, schemed and built afresh on the ruins, a fair city for their sons, who, like their fathers, can say, we are citizens of no mean city.'

**George H. Ingles, Special Constable,
Leicester, 1945.**

'Men and women: I see you will be ready and stand firm if trouble comes. I want you to feel you are doing an important job for your city and country. Civil Defence is, essentially, an army of ordinary people, a united lot, from all walks of life. The defence forces are playing a great and worthy part in these cruel and wicked times. When the history of this war comes to be written, the part played by the Civil Defence units will have a proud place in the story. I congratulate the local authority on the work done in creating Leicester's unit of the Civil Defence army.'

**Herbert Morrison, Minister of Home Security,
Leicester Town Hall steps, 8 April, 1941**

Introduction

When, back in 1992, I first came to Leicester, a guided walk, led by a distinguished local academic, seemed a good way to get to know the city. Whilst Leicester's built heritage was impressive, I was puzzled by its piecemeal survival. Knowing neighbouring Coventry had been heavily bombed, I asked the academic if the same fate befell Leicester. He sniffed and dismissively said only a few bombs fell on the city.

But, was that really it? Pre-war, Leicester was a bustling Midland industrial centre, identified by the League of Nations in 1936 as Europe's second wealthiest city. Surely, the Luftwaffe must have been aware of Leicester's productivity as it drew up its list of targets in 1939?

The defence of Leicester was overwhelmingly left to its citizens. Today, there is a common misconception, largely coloured by the portrayal of Chief Warden Hodges in TV's *Dad's Army*, that the ARP (Air Raid Precautions) services were a bunch of befuddled amateurs. Actually, as this book will show, the ARP services were a structured, well-planned organisation, with numerous, highly-trained branches, centred upon a core of experienced professionals from the regular emergency services.

The result of 15 years' exhaustive research, this book uses a plethora of previously unpublished local, national and international archive records, some only recently declassified, to reveal the full cost of the air raids on Leicester. Confusion of the Blitz, together with varied record survival, mean even some source material is inaccurate. However, the majority of the city's bomb incidents have been identified.

Several published key factual errors, uncorrected since the war, such as dates, locations and numbers of casualties, are corrected and enduring enigmas, such as whether Leicester was accidentally bombed, are definitively answered. Furthermore, important controversies, such as how Leicester was left undefended, at the Luftwaffe's mercy, plus the largely forgotten deaths of 28 ARP personnel who died serving their fellow citizens, are revealed for the first time.

Over 70 years' worth of personal testimonies reveal the very human story behind Leicester's struggle. For some interviewees, painful memories resurfaced, but all agreed their story should be told. To provide an honest and accurate history and to illustrate what the city's ARP services and population faced, as with my previous work, I have not shied away from more graphic or uncomfortable episodes.

Together with many previously-unseen archive photographs, documents and memorabilia, this is the most conclusive history of Leicester's Blitz.

In an age where we barely know our neighbours, amidst the bombing, real human kindness and cooperation flourished between strangers. Writer J.B. Priestley said that during the Second World War, the British people were the greatest they've ever been and this is reflected in Leicester's war. As you will read, it was the acts of bravery, altruism and selflessness by 'ordinary' Leicester men, women and children that challenged and beat the Luftwaffe.

It has been my privilege to tell their important story.

Austin J. Ruddy,
Leicester, 2014

This scroll commemorates

W. H. Pratt
Civil Defence Service

held in honour as one who served King and Country in the world war of 1939-1945 and gave his life to save mankind from tyranny. May his sacrifice help to bring the peace and freedom for which he died.

Official commemorative scroll in remembrance of warden William Henry Pratt, who was killed by a parachute mine at Grove Road, Leicester, on November 19, 1940. [Via Andrew Dally]

The ARP/CD Services

During the First World War, there was no ARP organisation, only the existing emergency services. Although a few bombs fell in the county, none fell on Leicester. Despite the general desire the First World War would be the 'war to end all wars', the rise of extremist political parties, with the development of larger aircraft with greater ranges, meant peace was not guaranteed.

As early as 1924, in response to this growing threat, the Committee for Imperial Defence set up an Air Raid Precautions sub-committee. In 1932, acting Prime Minister Stanley Baldwin warned: 'I think it is well for the man in the street to realise there is no power on earth that can protect him from being bombed. Whatever people may tell him, the bomber will always get through…'

In 1933, the ARP sub-committee, no doubt buoyed on by Adolf Hitler's rise to power, recommended local authorities should start ARP schemes. In 1935, a new department of the HO, the ARP Department, was formed under Wing Commander E.J. Hodsoll. The same year, Hitler defiantly announced that, in contravention of the Versailles Treaty, he had formed an air force, the Luftwaffe.

On November 12, 1935, a regional ARP conference was held in Nottingham, at which delegates from Leicestershire attended. No press or public were allowed. In response, Leicester Free Church Women's Council criticised ARP as 'a deception, that can only create a false security… fear would cause the inevitability of war and make all efforts for peace more difficult.' That month, fascist Italy, under dictator Benito Mussolini, bombed and used mustard gas to subjugate the African nation of Abyssinia (now Ethiopia).

The clash of European interwar ideologies came to a head in July 1936, when civil war broke out in Spain, after General Franco's nationalist military staged a coup against the democratically-elected Republican government. As the war developed, both Mussolini and Hitler sent armed 'volunteers' to assist Franco. In return, the fascist powers were able to test their military forces. The world watched in horror as the fledgling Luftwaffe mercilessly bombed Madrid and Guernica, killing hundreds of civilians.

In January 1937, several Leicester Corporation officials were sent for training at the national Civilian Anti-Gas School at Falfield, Eastwood Park, near Bristol. Leicester's Town Clerk, Mr L. McEvoy, had much correspondence with other towns and cities such as Portsmouth, Blackpool and Grimsby, regarding their ARP measures. By February, the City Surveyor, Mr S.C. Bentley, was preparing the Corporation's ARP Scheme.

In July 1937, Japan invaded the Chinese province of Manchuria, killing thousands of civilians. Again, the unrestricted use of bombing civilians was used as a terror tactic. The following year, the Japanese also used poison gas, and later biological warfare, against Chinese civilians. In some areas, councils forged ahead with ARP schemes, but in others, pacifist administrations boycotted the government's advice.

In August 1937, Wing Commander E.J. Hodsoll, Inspector General of ARP, attended a conference at Leicester and called upon the Surveyor to organise Rescue parties. Charles Waterhouse, MP for South Leicester, stated Leicester was 'more advanced in her preparations than any other city I know.'

In January 1938, the ARP Act became law, compelling local authorities to set up ARP schemes. But by this date, Leicester was well ahead. On February 9, 1938, following a tour, Wing Commander Hodsoll approved Leicester's ARP scheme.

NATIONAL, REGIONAL AND LOCAL ORGANISATION

The key to the success of Britain's wartime ARP/CD organisation lay in its early pre-war inception, allowing 15 years of planning. Often criticised as overly bureaucratic, governmental organisation, in this case, acted early enough and in doing so, saved millions of lives.

At the top of this pyramid was the Minister of Home Security (also Home Secretary), head of the MoHS, based at the Home Office, London. At the outbreak of war in 1939, this was Sir John Anderson MP, replaced in October 1940 by the successful Herbert Morrison MP, for the war's duration.

From February 1939, Britain was divided into 12 CD Regions, each headed by a Regional Commissioner. Leicestershire, together with Rutland, Derbyshire, Nottinghamshire, Lincolnshire and Northamptonshire, comprised **No. 3 (North Midland) Region**. In the event of severance of central control from London, through air raid destruction or even invasion, each of these Regions could become autonomous, operating independently under the authority of the **Regional Commissioner**. The Regional Commissioner for No.3 (North Midland) Region was Lord Trent, based at the Regional HQ, Mapperley Hall, Nottingham. The Regional Commissioner was the direct link between central and local government and it was his role to implement government policy across his region. Alongside him were a Regional HQ staff of technical advisers, drawn from the ARP, police, fire, medical and public utility services. In extreme circumstances, such as the breakdown of local authority control due to heavy bombing, the Regional Commissioner could take direct control of a conurbation.

It was the local authority's responsibility to design and implement an ARP plan, or scheme, at local level. Thus, councils became known as 'scheme-making authorities'. In Leicestershire, there were two scheme-making authorities: Leicester Corporation and Leicestershire County Council.

On October 21, 1939, the head of Britain's ARP paid a visit to Leicester's ARP officials. Standing, from left: Chief Constable/Chief Warden Mr O.J.B. Cole, Regional ARP Officer Mr A.R. Beaumont and Medical Officer of Health Dr E.K. MacDonald. Seated, from left: ARP Controller F. Winteringham, Chairman of the Emergency Committee Cllr C. Keene, Inspector General of ARP Wing-Commander E.J. Hodsoll, Mr D.J. Lidbury of the Home Office. [Leicester Mercury]

Each ARP scheme was directed and overseen by an ARP Committee, with a separate subcommittee, called the Emergency Committee. Leicester's **ARP Committee** and **Emergency Committee**, were under the chairmanship of Labour Cllr **Charles R. Keene**. In the ARP Committee, Cllr Keene was assisted by Cllrs John N. Frears and Charles E. Gillot. Dubbed 'the Committee of Three', they assumed much power and more than once received censure for their 'autocracy'. On September 27, 1939, 'a heated City Council meeting accused the Emergency Committee of 'ARP Nazism'. Cllr Keene replied: 'We have to make decisions quickly and cannot wait for them to be confirmed.' Cllr Keene later freely recalled: 'I was virtual dictator of Leicester. I was not responsible to anyone but the government. I spent money like water in the first few months and there was no one to stop me.'

However, in a bid to make the ARP Committee more pluralistic, on October 29, 1940, the Corporation renamed the group the Civil Defence Committee, enlarging it from 16 to 20 members. Fellow councillor Mark Henig remembered Keene showed 'characteristic clear thinking' as chairman of both committees.

On September 6, 1943, Cllr **Charles Edward Worthington**, chairman of the Emergency Committee and then CD Controller, relinquished his position of chairman, as he considered it desirable the two offices should be divided. The Emergency Committee unanimously appointmented Cllr **F.T. Watson** as their new chairman.

The Emergency Committee masterminded the complicated organisation against air raids, providing shelters for every man, woman and child, billeted thousands of evacuees, prepared for invasion and arranged post-raid aid for the populace.

Chairman of ARP/CD Committee: Cllr C.R. Keene (Sep 1939-July 1941)
             Cllr John N. Frears and Cllr Charles E. Gillot.
Emergency Committee: Chairman: Cllr C.R. Keene (Sep 1939-July 1941)
             Cllr C.E. Worthington (July 1941-Sep 1943)
             Cllr F.T. Watson (Sep 1943-May 1945)
ARP Department: 24 Halford Street & 33 Horsefair Street

Control Service

Due to its sheer size, a separate organisation was needed to control all branches of the ARP services. During an air raid, the ARP Controller would direct operations, mostly from the M/C bunker, or if needed, at major incidents. Due to his important role, he had to be a respected, professional public servant.

Leicester's first Controller was 41-year-old Captain **Francis Winteringham**, with **Dr Ernest Kenneth MacDonald** as Deputy Controller. Winteringham also served as Leicester's Chief Fire Officer. However, much to the ARP Committee's consternation, on December 7, 1940, without consultation and just over a year into the job, in the middle of the Blitz, Winteringham was suddenly appointed Chief of Birmingham's FB. Publicly, it was reported that at a special meeting of the Emergency Committee and a Watch Committee deputation, Chief Constable O.J.B. Cole, had been discussed as replacement Controller. The Watch Committee thought Cole ideal for the job, as he had five years' experience within ARP echelons. Consequently, the Chief Constable accepted the position. However, behind closed doors, Corporation officials had doubts. On December 16, 1940, in a closed session chaired by Major C.A. Ledbury, the SRO, the CD Committee unanimously appointed their chairman, Cllr Keene, as joint Chairman and Controller. This did not please the Watch Committee. The *LEM* reported: 'Storm brewing over City ARP Chief'. A Watch member stated: 'We feel our deputation has been fooled and the Chief Constable badly let down.' Nonetheless, Cllr Keene assumed the position.

To assist him, in January 1941, 50-year-old former Royal Navy Lt-Commander **Maxwell Alexander Christian Ritter**, Chief Warden and Deputy Controller of Willesden, London, was appointed Leicester's **Assistant ARP Controller**. But despite his impeccable ARP credentials, within two years, Ritter's personal affairs began to overshadow his professional life. On October 22, 1942, the *LM*'s front page read: 'Lt-Commander Ritter, ARP Officer for Leicester, was summoned at Marylebone Police Court for arrears of income tax amounting to £99 [£3,600]. The magistrate made an order for payment or six weeks' imprisonment.' The controversy did not end there. Just a fortnight later, again, Ritter made local headlines for all the wrong reasons. On November 10, 1942, the *LM* reported: 'Leicester's ARP Chief of Staff, Commander Ritter, of Gwendolen Road, was fined £30 [£1,100] with 10 guineas [£380] costs, by the Leicester Bench for using petrol other than for which a license was granted. Defendant pleaded not guilty. Mr R. Wright, prosecuting, alleged the defendant had made use of CD petrol for private purposes. On September 14, police detectives followed the defendant's car. There was a woman passenger and in one case, defendant admitted to the police that he made a deviation from his authorised journey.' Petrol misuse was viewed heinously, as supplies were limited and merchant seamen were dying bringing fuel to Britain. On November 11, 1942, the CD Committee were definite: 'The Committee resolved unanimously Commander Ritter's services be terminated.' Five months later, Ritter won an appeal against three of his convictions, but was not reinstated.

On December 21, 1942, Mr **F.G. Bailey**, Chief CD Administrative Officer, was appointed

Maxwell Alexander Christian Ritter, Leicester's Assistant ARP Controller, January 1941-November 1942. [Leicester Mercury]

Assistant Controller, as Ritter's replacement.

In summer 1941, Cllr Keene was called to Whitehall to meet the Minister of HS, Herbert Morrison and invited to take up a new position. On July 8, 1941, the *LM* reported: 'Cllr C.R. Keene has been made a Deputy Regional Commissioner for the North Midland Region, an important appointment, which means he will have to resign his position as City ARP Controller and CD Committee chairman.' Straight away, Cllr Keene stamped his authority on the administration of the North Midlands. Later, he applied his energies to post-war reconstruction, becoming Chairman of Leicester Reconstruction Committee in 1944, but remained Deputy Regional Commissioner at Nottingham. Keene became an Alderman of Leicester in 1945 and Charles Keene College of Further Education was named in his honour. Awarded the CBE in 1950, he was later knighted and became Lord Mayor of Leicester in 1953, receiving the freedom of the city in 1962. Charles Keene is now remembered as one of Leicester's last 'city fathers'.

Keene's replacement as ARP Controller and Chairman of the CD and Emergency Committee was Cllr **Charles Edward Worthington**. Educated at Wyggeston Boys' School, Worthington joined the Royal Flying Corps in 1916, serving as a fighter pilot, credited with two air victories. Afterwards, Worthington became a successful businessman, a founder member of Odeon Cinemas and managing director of one of Leicester's largest grocery chains, Worthingtons Cash Stores Ltd. He was elected to the Corporation in 1936 as a Conservative. In 1940, he became City ARP Welfare Officer, responsible for co-ordinating post-raid aid. Cllr Worthington became Lord Mayor of Leicester in 1945.

REPORT SERVICE

Communications were vital to the functioning of the ARP organisation. Without accurate reporting and communication, the whole organisation would collapse and lives would be risked. In an age before short wave radio communications, ARP relied on the civilian landline telephone network. For reporting purposes, Leicester was divided into seven **Divisions** (City centre A-C, suburbs D-G):

'A' (East City) Division
'B' (South City) Division
'C' (North City) Division
'D' (North Leicester) Division
'E' (East Leicester) Division
'F' (South Leicester) Division
'G' (West Leicester) Division

Each Division contained 16 **Groups**, further sub-divided into **Sectors**. At the centre of one or more sector was a wardens' post. Patrolling wardens would report to their post the details of any bomb incident in their sector. The post would telephone the details to their local Divisonal Report Centre, which in 1940 were:

Division
'A': Lighting Department, 31 Rutland Street (August 1940, moved to Erskine Street)
'B': College of Art & Technology (1942, moved to new Western Park Depot)
'C': Friday Street (1942, moved to new Rushey Fields Depot)
'D': Belgrave House/Cross Corners, Thurcaston Road
'E': Police station, Asfordby Street (1942, moved to new Humberstone Depot)
'F': St Michael's Church Rooms, Welford Road (1942, moved to new Aylestone Depot)
'G': Hinckley Road School.

At the DRC, the officer in charge contacted the nearest ARP depot in his Division and ordered the Squads required. Via direct lines, reports were also fed to M/C, located in the strengthened basement of the Corporation's Municipal Buildings, 24 Halford Street. Here, 15 trained telephonists received the calls.

In the M/C, two map plotting officers plotted every incident with colour flags and pins, denoting the type of bomb, roads blocked etc. UXBs were reported to the military, whilst damage to public utilities was passed on to the relevant departments. Another map indicated where the ARP services had been dispatched to. Also based here were the Controller; the

City Engineer and Surveyor, who was in charge of the Rescue service plus the roads and sewers repair squads; MOH Dr E.K. MacDonald, in charge of medical and FA services; the City Transport Engineer; the Decontamination officer and the Depots officer; representatives of the public utilities, a records officer, 12 messengers and two sentries. Typed incident reports were made and Regional Control in Nottingham was notified of developing situations. After the raid, information was sent to the MoHS Technical Intelligence Officer at the Research and Experiments Department Area Office, Kingsley Road, Northampton, for analysis. He, in turn, forwarded his findings to his HQ at the MoHS Research and Experiments Dept, Princes Risborough, Aylesbury, Buckinghamshire.

Although opened on November 7, 1938, M/C was not fully operational until October 1939. During the 1940 invasion threat, an armed policeman stood outside 'G' Division DRC. Folllowing the Blitz, concerns over heavier Luftwaffe raiding led to the conglomeration of all Leicester's depots and DRCs into four new depots in the suburbs, away from the central target area. The new DRCs at Rushey Fields and Western Park depots were occupied from October 14 and 15, 1942, respectively.

With the diminished threat of raids, the four outlying DRCs closed on October 14, 1944, leaving M/C solely responsible. It closed on June 30, 1945, and finally vacated, together with the CD HQ offices, on March 25, 1946.

Deep in the Main Control bunker, under the Municipal Buildings, off Halford Street, a plotting officer marks imaginary incidents on the ARP map of Leicester during an exercise in 1939. Looking on, from left: Controller F. Winteringham, Chairman of the Emergency Committee Cllr C. Keene, Cllr J.N. Frears and Deputy Controller Dr E.K. MacDonald. [Leicester Mercury]

Messengers

As an additional back-up to the vulnerable land-line telephone system, at the war's start, Boy Scouts acted unofficially as volunteer runners for the ARP. However, such was the importance of maintaining communications, a permanent service was needed. The ARP authorities looked to the most energetic section of society – the young – to act as messengers.

Initially, this was not altogether well-received. The *LM* reported in May 1940 that 'Leicester Education Committee viewed using schoolboys, aged 13-18, as ARP messengers as too dangerous – as bad as sending boys to the front line.' Consequently, ARP Committee minutes reveal the following month, 50-60 volunteer messengers under the age of 16 at Report Centres were 'to be dispensed with.' However, testimonies from former boy messengers reveal they were only too eager to serve.

What probably sealed the issue, was the complaint by ARP authorities after Leicester's first bombing incident at Cavendish Road, that there were no f/t messengers to rely on. The Messenger Service grew very quickly. Boy and girl messengers were attached to wardens' posts and depots. During the Blitz period, the messengers were simply issued with a black steel helmet with the letter 'M', plus an armlet. From 1941, they were issued with proper CD uniform. Key equipment was the humble bicycle, which enabled messengers to deliver messages quicker.

But after the Blitz, the messengers had little to do. The authorities tried to maintain the youngsters' interest by fostering an esprit de corps, so messenger bands, sports teams and efficiency tests were introduced. In early 1941, Leicester had 688 messengers, rising to 815 by the year's end. Manpower cuts from May 1943 reduced the service to 450. Later, messen-

A woman's 1941 'Report and Control' CD jacket. The owner worked at one of the four DRCs. She has a pink Divisional identity triangular cloth badge below her shoulder title and five red service chevrons on her cuff, indicating she had served five years. [Author]

The CD Messengers' band at Charnwood Street School, c.1942. Front row, from left: Hume, Joan Goodacre, Jean Lucas, unknown, Mr Bram Goodacre, Betty Lucas, Beryl Lee, Hayden Hubbard. Second row, from left: unknown, Horace Gregory, unknown, mace bearer Ron 'Stubb' Coltman, drum major Alan Ratcliffe, unknown, Peter Wenlock, Norman Cooper. Top row, from left: unknown, Dickie Cooke, Mattock, Bob Plumb, unknown, Gamble, unknown. [Peter Wenlock]

gers were kept busy assisting the war effort, such as in August 1943, when it was reported: 'What is believed to be the first harvest camp staffed entirely by personnel of CD volunteers commenced "somewhere in Leicestershire," when a party of 40 warden messengers from 'F' Division took over a site for a fortnight's stay.'

Incident Officers

Due to the chaotic nature at incidents, an overall incident commander was needed to coordinate the ARP services. Although the theory of incident control had been studied before the raids started, it was only after the practical lessons learnt from the Cavendish Road raid in August 1940, that the issue was properly tackled. It was realised that to prevent further casualties, incidents would have to be controlled by properly trained incident officers.

IOs operated from an incident post, where they directed the ARP services. Unusually, in Leicester, all elements of the ARP, from the police to the FA services, had their own IOs. However, from August 1941, it was decided only police and wardens were to have IOs, and IOs in the other services were renamed Party Supervisors. As the war continued, with the threat of bigger air raids, the science of incident control developed, with trained IOs awarded 'I.O.' insignia and over 1,500 Leicester wardens trained in Incident Control.

Wardens' Service

The Wardens' Service was the linchpin of the ARP organisation, yet was not formed until March 1937. The wardens' main role was to patrol their Sector and if a bomb fell, briefly assess the incident, fill in a report and run back to their post to report to the control service. However, through necessity, the job developed into multifarious important tasks, including rescue, first aid, UXB reconnaissance and incident control.

Wardens also became the local 'face' of the ARP organisation, advising and training the public in ARP matters, conducting gas mask and shelter censuses and, at times, breaking bad news. However, their public duties were not always appreciated: their maintenance of the blackout, with the cry of 'put that light out', sometimes made them unpopular with the public, who accused them of being 'little Hitlers', with several reported cases of wardens being assaulted.

Wardens were largely more mature in years and mostly male, although there was a sizeable proportion of younger female personnel. As with most ARP personnel, they were an amateur army, but were mostly dedicated and professional: they had to know their Sectors and its residents inside out. They had extensive training, sitting courses and examinations. By December 1938, 1,837 wardens had been recruited. Two Leicester wardens, Charles Alderson and William Pratt, were killed by enemy action during Leicester's Blitz Night.

At the head of the Wardens' Service was the Chief Warden, Chief Constable O.J.B. Cole.

The organisation was based along police Divisions, with seven wardens' Divisions, each headed by a Divisional Warden. The city was further divided into 73 Groups, each under a Group Warden, and further sub-divided into 362 Sectors, most with a wardens' post, controlled by a Post or Senior Warden. All these supervisory ranks wore white steel helmets with corresponding insignia.

At the heart of the local wardens' organisation was the wardens' post. From January 1940, these small posts accommodated a f/t warden 12 hours per day, with a table, chair, electric fire, sets of gas-proof clothing and other accessories, whilst also serving as a shelter for six to ten wardens in an air raid. Due to materials shortages, most posts were located in strengthened and sandbagged front rooms or cellars, offering minimal protection. They also carried safety risks: warden Harry Booth, 28, died in October 1942 at his post on Leamington Street, due to accidental coal gas poisoning. By September 1944, there were 238 posts in Leicester.

Far left: *Wardens outside their post by the 'Pork Pie' Library, Saffron Lane Estate, in c.1940. They have full ARP uniform and equipment.* [Leicester Mercury]

Left: *Wardens study their sector map in their post, G40 (Group 12), in the garage of 1 Meredith Road, Rowley Fields c. 1939. Warden George Smith on right.* [Via Wendy Warren/Gillian Smith]

As war subdued on the Home Front, wardens and other CD services found different tasks, such as distributing ration books. A CD boot repairing depot, in Friday Street, staffed by three wardens, repaired 1,627 pairs of CD footwear. Social activities also developed, with inter-divisional competitions, discussion groups, social evenings etc.

In early 1941, there were 3,993 wardens in Leicester, rising to 4,018 by the year's end. Mid-war cuts shifted the emphasis to p/t service, with only 60 f/t and 4,062 p/t wardens. The 70 Group posts were manned nightly until the relaxation of duties in August 1944. About 100 wardens' posts, out of 238, were closed after November 15, 1944 and the establishment reduced to only 10 f/t and 2,066 p/t wardens.

Some noted Leicester wardens included John Higgott, 54, who was awarded the George Medal for displaying a 'very high degree of courage and bravery', rescuing two children and tackling fires during Leicester's Blitz Night. Wardens Kyle Dawson and Divisional Warden John Garner also received MoHS Letters of Commendation for Bravery for deeds on Blitz Night. William Helps, of Beaumanor Road, a Sector Leader and Head FG in 'D' Division, was, in June 1943, awarded the BEM (Civil Division) for his services, including at the Sudeley Avenue PM incident. He died in 1970, and a memorial to him, in the form of a Portland stone pulpit stand, was erected at St Peter's church, Belgrave.

In April 1944, John Davis, known as 'Old Jack', of 9 Palmer Street, Belgrave, was believed to be Leicester's oldest warden. He was a familiar face in Belgrave, usually carrying his white mascot cat with him when the siren sounded or when on duty. He was one of the first to volunteer as a warden in 1937. However, the *LM* later revealed Leicester's oldest warden was actually Mr John E. Ellis, 81, of The Poplars, Evington Lane, Evington, a warden since 1939.

Chief Warden: Chief Constable O.J.B. Cole
Deputy Chief Warden: J.B. Garner

Divisional Wardens (1944):
    'A' (East City) Division: C.T. Johncock
    'B' (South City) Division: D.S. Smith
    'C' (North City) Division: R. Garner
    'D' (North Leicester) Division: F. Barwick
    'E' (East Leicester) Division: F.B. Briggs
    'F' (South Leicester) Division: J.B. Garner
    'G' (West Leicester) Division: P.R. Hall

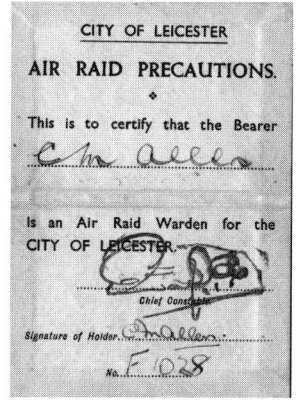

Leicester warden's identity pass of Warden F1028 C.M. Allen. [Author]

Rescue Service

Some of the most physically demanding, yet also careful ARP work was carried out by the Rescue Service. Their job was to rescue people trapped by bombing. This was skilful and painstaking work, as they had to remove rubble without it collapsing on the casualty. Drawn from the building trade, for their knowledge of house construction, Rescue personnel also carried out some of the most dangerous ARP work, tunneling under debris to reach casualties.

Rescue personnel were based at ARP depots until called to incidents, usually in lorries or cars towing equipment trailers. In 1939, under James Fyfe, Housing Department Architect, there were 96 Rescue squads, on a basis of six squads per Division. Each squad comprised two bricklayers, three carpenters, two joiners, one plumber and four labourers. To make buildings safe after raids, the Rescue Service could call upon a pool of 50 men from the Housing Department.

However, later manpower cuts streamlined Rescue squads, becoming six man teams, comprising a foreman and five personnel. Despite their vital work, they also faced budgetary limitations and during the Blitz, some of their transport was defective.

Following reports of experiences in the London Blitz, on November 8, 1940, the City Surveyor organised three-day training in tunnelling for Rescue party leaders at Desford Colliery. In an emergency, the Mine Owners Association also agreed to make 150 miners available for tunnelling work in the city after heavy air raids. Croft Granite Company also volunteered to undertake explosive demolition of dangerous buildings.

After the main Leicester Blitz, it was planned to massively consolidate the Rescue Service. In April 1941, a School of Rescue Instruction was opened in London and three members of Leicester's ARP staff were sent on a five-day course. On their return, they were to lecture ARP units in the City, County and Soke of Peterborough. Four months later, Leicester's Rescue Training School, based in Milton Street School, moved premises at Granby Halls depot.

By July 1941, Leicester had an establishment of 40 Rescue parties, but due to shortages, only 36 sets of equipment. Over 130 miners from four local collieries were available and some wardens were trained in rescue work. Also, it was reported 'The whole of Leicester's building trade is now mobilised for quick action in rescuing trapped people'. By early 1942, there were 193 f/t and 424 p/t personnel in Leicester's Rescue Service, including 160 employees of the Transport Department.

In 1943, there was a major reorganisation, mainly due to manpower cuts and reduced raiding. FAPys were absorbed into the Rescue Service, becoming the Light Rescue Service, whilst the original Rescue personnel were renamed Heavy Rescue. However, unlike elsewhere in Britain, it appears Leicester's Rescue Service was not retitled Light or Heavy Rescue. Photographs show the original 'Rescue' insignia was retained.

With the reduced threat, Rescue personnel found other duties. They assisted in 20 de-training and one entraining operation of injured troops from ambulance trains at Leicester LMS station. From February to May 1944, f/t personnel dismanted aircraft at Granby Halls to reclaim parts for the Ministry of Supply. About 50 personnel also helped bring in the harvest.

Some notable Rescue personnel included Alfred J. Harris, of Stoughton Street, who was awarded the OBE for his work during Leicester's Blitz Night. Similarly, in April 1943: 'Saved Lives in Leicester Raid: For rescue work in an air attack, Squad Leader David Midglow, of Gresham Street, was presented by Controller C.E. Worthington, with a King's Commendation for Bravery badge inscribed "For Brave Conduct".' Midglow also received a letter from the Inspector General of the ARP Services expressing admiration. In 1934, he was commended by Chief Constable O.J.B. Cole for rescuing people from a fire. Another notable Rescue personality was Leicester strongman Gaston, whose considerable strength enabled him to lift heavy debris. In 1954, he performed in Cheapside, lifting barbells.

The Rescue Service also benefited from canine assistance. A Labrador retriever, called Matt, worked for Leicester Constabulary, as one of the first police rescue dogs in Britain. Matt served for six years, including on Blitz Night.

Three Leicester Rescue personnel died in the course of duties. In May 1941, William Jelley, 44, and Archibald Mayes, 52, were killed in a traffic accident on Aylestone Road, on their way to a CD Service at Leicester Cathedral. Ernest Mason, 51, died after falling from a lorry at Melton Road, in June 1943.

City Surveyor: Arthur Gooseman (Sept 1939-Feb 1941)
John L. Beckett (Feb 1941-May 1945)

Gas Identification Service

Following the horrors of the First World War, it was believed poison gas would be a major weapon in future conflicts. As such, much of ARP's pre-war focus was on gas warfare. With several different types of poison gas, decontamination units needed to know what they were dealing with. As such, in 1938, members of the Institute of Chemistry were invited to offer their services to local authorities and several local chemists did. Leicester's Chief GI Officer was Dr Fred Bullock. Fortunately, poison gas was never employed by the Germans against Britain. There were few GIOs for such an important role and they would have been hard-pushed had there been multiple gas attacks. As such, later, some wardens were trained as Gas Wardens to assist in detection. From July 1944, they were issued with pocket vapour detection kits and undertook joint exercises with the GI and DC Services.

Decontamination Service

As 'gas' swirls past, an ARP decontamination squad in full anti-gas clothing demonstrates decontamination using bleach solution, at an exercise in the Friday Street area, on March 31, 1941. [Leicester Mercury]

Drawn from Corporation street cleaning and refuse collection employees, decontamination teams would have had a difficult task. Operating in respirators and full anti-gas oilskin suits following a gas attack, they would use bleach solution and water to decontaminate streets and houses. Under Cleansing Superintendent Hugh Wilson, by July 1941, the DC Service comprised 32 squads, each of seven men. Fortunately, they were never needed and remained ready but dormant. There were six gas cleansing centres in Leicester, either purpose-built or showers in sports changing rooms, for the cleansing of the public contaminated by poison gas. As a back-up, from 1942, the public were encouraged to allow gas contaminated casualties to use their baths for decontamination. By 1944, Leicester's DC Service maintained a staff of two-thirds the authorised 353 personnel. A special solution of war gas was used in training for added realism.

Food Treatment Service

Rationing made food a valuable commodity, so techniques were developed to decontaminate tinned goods and dispose of contaminated stocks. A relatively late CD service, food DC units were not fully developed until mid-1941. Leicester ARP Committee minutes from May 1941, reveal: 'The FTS is in the charge of the Chief Sanitary Inspector. Four senior Sanitary Inspectors have been appointed Food DC Officers. Two FTS depots are to be established, one at Belgrave House depot and the other at Trinity Methodist depot. Twenty personnel will report at each depot when required, recruited from food distribution firms. A building of light construction is to be built on New Parks Estate for Food DC.' After November 1941, a hut was erected at Leicester Cattle Market for food decontamination. In 1942, the Food DC Officer was Mr F.G. McHugh.

Depots

Rescue, FAPy, DC squads, messengers and transport personnel, together with their equipment and vehicles, were all centred at combined ARP aiding depots, on a Divisional basis. Set up during the 1938 Munich Crisis, their last minute nature meant that initially, depots were based in existing public buildings. During Leicester's Blitz, the Divisional ARP depots were:

  A1: 24 Halford Street (from January 1941, transferred to Erskine Street)
  A2: Saxby Street Church Hall. (Destroyed in November 1940, resited to Prebend House, London Road)
  A3: Milton Street School (from January 1941, transferred to Erskine Street)
  B1: College of Art

B2: Granby Halls
C1: Friday Street
D1: Belgrave House, Thurcaston Road
D2: Abbey Park Road Tram Depot
E1: Uppingham Road Baptist church, corner Layton Road
F1: Aylestone Gas Works, Aylestone Road (from January 1941, The Woodlands, Belvoir Drive)
F2: Crusaders' Hall, 64 Clarendon Park Road
G1: Hinckley Road/Westcotes Congregational church, corner Westcotes Drive
G2: Trinity Methodist, Narborough Road Tram Terminus
There was also a depot at Soar Lane/Jarvis Street.

The vulnerability and error in placing these depots in the target area was revealed during the Blitz, when A2 Saxby Street depot was destroyed by a bomb. A major reorganisation of Leicester's depots was undertaken. On May 27, 1941, the SRO wrote to the MoHS, stating:

'After careful consideration, Leicester is reorganising their Depots and Report Centres, and the removal of these from the target area, into the outer perimeter of the built-up area. They propose to concentrate services into four specially-built depots at strategic points on the outskirts, from which they can be quickly deployed to the City.

'At the same time, they propose doing away with the seven existing DRCs and attaching one to each of the four new depots. The reduction of Report Centres has been advocated by the Ministry, but until now, has been met by local opposition. Proposals include:
1. Belgrave House, Melton Road and the majority of Friday Street Depots to new Melton Road Depot, at Rushey Fields. Approx: 6 f/t Rescue Parties, 18 FAPys, 4 p/t Rescue Parties and 5 p/t FAPys. Total: 193 personnel.
2. Erskine Street, Uppingham Road and Prebend House (part) Depots to new Humberstone Road Depot, at Humberstone Park. 6 f/t Rescue, 22 FA staff, 4 p/t rescue, 8 p/t FA: Total: 218 personnel.
3. Granby Halls, Friday Street (part), Crusaders Hall (part) Depots to new Woodlands Depot, at Belvoir Drive/Wigston Lane. 4 f/t Rescue staff, 19 f/t FA staff, 2 p/t rescue staff, 3 p/t rescue staff. Total: 174 personnel.
4. Hinckley Road Methodist, Trinity Methodist and College of Art Depots to new Hinckley Road Depot, at Western Park. 4 f/t rescue, 11 f/t FA staff, 3 p/t rescue, 15 p/t FA. Total: 123 personnel.'

The new scheme was approved in July 1941. But due to manpower and material shortages, it was a year before the first two new depots, at Western Park and Rushey Fields, opened on May 2, 1942. In June, the Controller arranged for aerial photographs to be taken by the RAF, a report was submitted to the CD Committee and they resolved the depots be camouflaged.

The new depots were designed by Corporation architects to standard CD depot specifications. Nissen huts were used for general accommodation. Protected accommodation, consisting of bomb splinter-proof and blast-resistant 14"-thick brickwork was used for dormitories and the integrated DRCs. Asbestos sheeting was used for garage accommodation of 12 cars at each depot.

At Rushey Fields depot, on Melton Road, eight semi-circular Tarran concrete huts formed the main buildings, including stores, a canteen and lecture room. Four protected dormitory blocks, of reinforced brick, each provided sleeping accommodation for 42 personnel, a total of 168 personnel, plus a separate, protected combined DRC and alternative M/C. 24 cars were also garaged. Each depot cost around £10,500 [£400,000].

Due to continuing manpower and material shortages, the remaining new depots at Humberstone and Aylestone were still under construction. By November 1942, there were only two large depots (Rushey Mead and Western Park) and two small depots (Crusaders' Hall and Trinity Methodist church), plus Prebend House. Due to continued 'labour conditions', it was hoped to finally occupy Aylestone depot on December 21, 1942 and Humberstone depot eight days later.

With the end of the war in Europe, it was announced in June 1945 'the acquisition of the three CD depots at Humberstone, Western Park and Wigston Lane for educational purposes is recommended by Leicester Education Post-War Development Sub-Committee.' Rushey Fields depot was transferred to the Highways Committee.

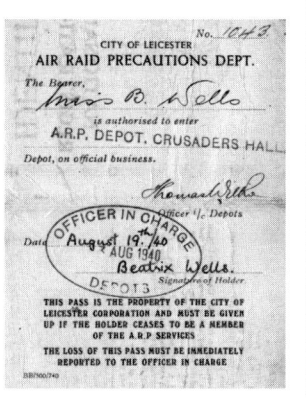

Depot identity pass that enabled Leicester ARP Ambulance Attendant Beatrix Wells, of Landseer Road, to enter Crusaders' Hall Depot, on Clarendon Park Road. [Author]

ARP Casualty Services

Due to the nature of heavy bombing, it was likely mass casualties would ensue. Regular hospital and emergency services would be unlikely to cope with any mass influx of casualties, so were bolstered by the addition of the ARP Casualty Services, under Leicester's Medical Officer of Health (MOH), Dr Ernest K. MacDonald.

In readiness for mass casualties, all hospitals became part of the MoH's Emergency Medical Service and the Emergency Hospital Scheme. The LRI and General Hospital became Leicester's main ARP casualty clearing hospitals, reserving some wards purely for raid casualties. Roecliffe Manor, in Woodhouse Eaves, was reserved as an auxiliary hospital.

By early 1942, there were 1,958 men and women in the Leicester CD Casualty Service. On June 11, 1942, MOH Dr MacDonald received the OBE in the King's Birthday Honours list: 'Dr MacDonald was concerned with ARP from the beginning and saw the Service in which he is specially interested grow from a few enthusiastic ambulance classes to an organisation with a strength of 1,500 at posts and 800 at depots.'

First Aid Parties

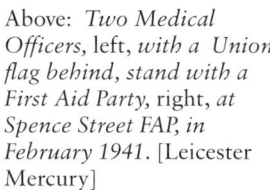

FAPys worked closely with Rescue parties, giving immediate aid to those rescued, and transferring casualties to ambulances, from where they would be sent to FAPs or hospital. FAPys were mainly teams of five men, including a party leader. The FAPy rushed from its depot to the incident in cars, with FA kits, blankets and metal HO-pattern stretchers carried on the roof. In early 1942, there were 467 personnel in Leicester's FAPys. However, manpower reductions led, in spring 1943, to FAPys being amalgamated into the Rescue Service as Light Rescue parties.

Above: *Two Medical Officers*, left, *with a Union flag behind, stand with a First Aid Party*, right, *at Spence Street FAP, in February 1941.* [Leicester Mercury]

Left: *FAPy party personnel, believed to be from Trinity Methodist depot, Narborough Road, with their ambulance in 1942. By this date, they have received their new CD uniforms, but not their area titles yet.* [Leicester Mercury]

Ambulance Service

With the mass expansion of the casualty services, it was clear the peacetime ambulance service was insufficient. With the motor industry concentrating on producing fighting vehicles, supplies of new ambulances were limited, so alternatives had to be found.

In October 1939, Leicester ARP Emergency Committee put before the HO a scheme for the use of ARP ambulance trailers, which could be towed by civilian cars. This was approved and the Eccles Caravan Company was contracted to make the ambulance trailers for £30 [£1,500] each. The ARP Committee also made an urgent request to the owners of private cars: at least 180 were needed for ARP Ambulances and FAPys. However, they did not receive enough. By the Blitz, Leicester had 44 f/t trailer ambulances and f/t cars, plus volunteer

Despite their flimsy appearance, Leicester's canvas-topped ARP ambulance trailers, towed by civilian cars, 'proved quite adaptable to air raid conditions, being very mobile in cases where streets were blocked.' [Leicester Mercury]

vehicles. Despite their flimsy appearance, the 'trailers proved quite adaptable to air raid conditions, being very mobile in cases where streets were blocked.'

In Leicester, the ARP ambulances were staffed by a driver and an attendant, often young women. Joyce Chapman recalled: 'In 1939, I lived at Hillcrest Road with my parents. I wanted to help the war effort so joined first aid. We had lectures and had to pass exams at the College of Arts depot. The Depot Supervisor was Mr Riley. We used to go to Granby Halls for practice. The instructor was Rosa Lord and she used girls with fake blood on. It didn't bother me: It was a big adventure. You were never really scared. The depot had a mess and we played table tennis while we waited. The ambulances and trailers were parked at the back of the College. I didn't really have a uniform, just a blue overall with an ARP badge on it. I had a tin hat and service respirator.'

By 1942, there were 422 personnel in the CD Ambulance Service, with the main CD Ambulance depot at Prebend House, London Road. However, following a MoH circular, on February 16, 1942, the regular Leicester City Ambulance Service separated from city FB control and were taken over by the CD Ambulance Service. Two new ambulances were acquired in 1944, bringing the total to six, with one sitting case car.

In 1944, 15 converted ambulances and four military ambulances were added to the Leicester Ambulance fleet, bringing the total to 69 ambulances, with 408 personnel. Ambulance Officer for Leicester and Leicestershire was Mr F. Cave

First Aid Posts

Based on the British Army's First World War system of casualty clearance, FAPs were for the treatment of lightly wounded casualties or those that needed immediate diagnosis by a doctor. They were also to prevent hospitals from becoming congested with less serious cases. FAPs were permanently staffed under a doctor, the Medical Officer. In September 1940, there were 46 MOs attached to Leicester's FAPs. FA Superintendents relieved the MO of administrative matters. The MO was assisted by qualified nursing and FA staff, mainly SJAB personnel. FAPs were stationed in church halls or swimming baths.

In late 1940, a HO ruling stipulated FAPys should take casualties who appeared seriously injured straight to hospital, instead of the FAP. But Leicester's MOH, Dr E.K. MacDonald, argued 'The value of the FAP as a sorting post is considerable,' and MOs were the skilled professionals to make the diagnosis, not FAPy personnel. Leicester's Blitz Night vindicated this.

There were also the Bond Street and General Hospital Mobile FA Units, which could be sent to major incidents.

By 1942, there were 1,169 personnel in Leicester's FAP Service. As an added reserve, from 1942, there were also p/t FA Points in the suburbs, where small teams could treat minor casualties. At the heart of communities, FAPs also treated domestic injuries and provided other medical services. Leicester FAPs provided nursing assistance during the influenza crisis of 1943-44; childbirth assistance on 106 occasions; the MFAU was used for a diptheria immunisation drive, and in 13 sessions, 430 children received their first injection and 330 children were fully immunised, whilst 3,400 blood donors attended Granby Halls FAP in 1944.

By 1944, Leicester's FAP Service stood at 1,356 personnel. After CD Stand Down in September 1944, FAP personnel were cut to 788, with 10 out of 13 FAPs and FA Points placed on a care-and-maintenance basis. After November 15, 1944, all city FAPs were disbanded, with the exception of Holy Apostles, St Margaret's, Spence Street FAPs and the MFAU: as the *LM* noted: 'it is still wise to be prepared and efficient.'

First Aid Posts (1940):
Bond Street FAP, Public Medical Service - MO: I.G. Tollemache (closed by June 1941)

Bond Street MFAU – MO: Dr E.B. Garrett
Broughton Road FAP, Marriott Road Clinic (closed by June 1941)
Cort Crescent FAP, School Clinic – MO: G. Smart
Cossington Street FAP, Cossington Street Baths – MO: Supt B. Bailey
Granby Halls FAP, Granby Halls – MO: Dr E.L. Lentin
Holy Apostles FAP, Church Rooms, Fosse Road South/Imperial Avenue – MO: Supt E. Kershaw
St John's FAP, Knighton Church Rooms, 70 Clarendon Park Road, Knighton – MO: Dr W.E. Howell
St Margaret's FAP, St Margaret's Works, Thames Street/Archdeacon Lane (from May 1941)
St Philip's FAP, St Philip's Church Rooms, Evington Road, Evington – MO: Dr F.G. MacNaughton
Spence Street FAP, Spence Street Baths – MO: Dr M.S. Bryce
Southfields Drive FAP, Methodist Church Hall, Aylestone – (from May 1941)
Swain Street FAP, Public Assistance Institution – MO: P.E. Grills (Transferred to Telephone House, 66 London Road, after December 1942. Swain Street FAP finally closed on June 6, 1943)

FA Points
Evington Village Hall (from July 1941, upgraded to FAP)
Main Street, Humberstone
Public Medical Services Building, Chester Street (from June 1943, only on alerts)

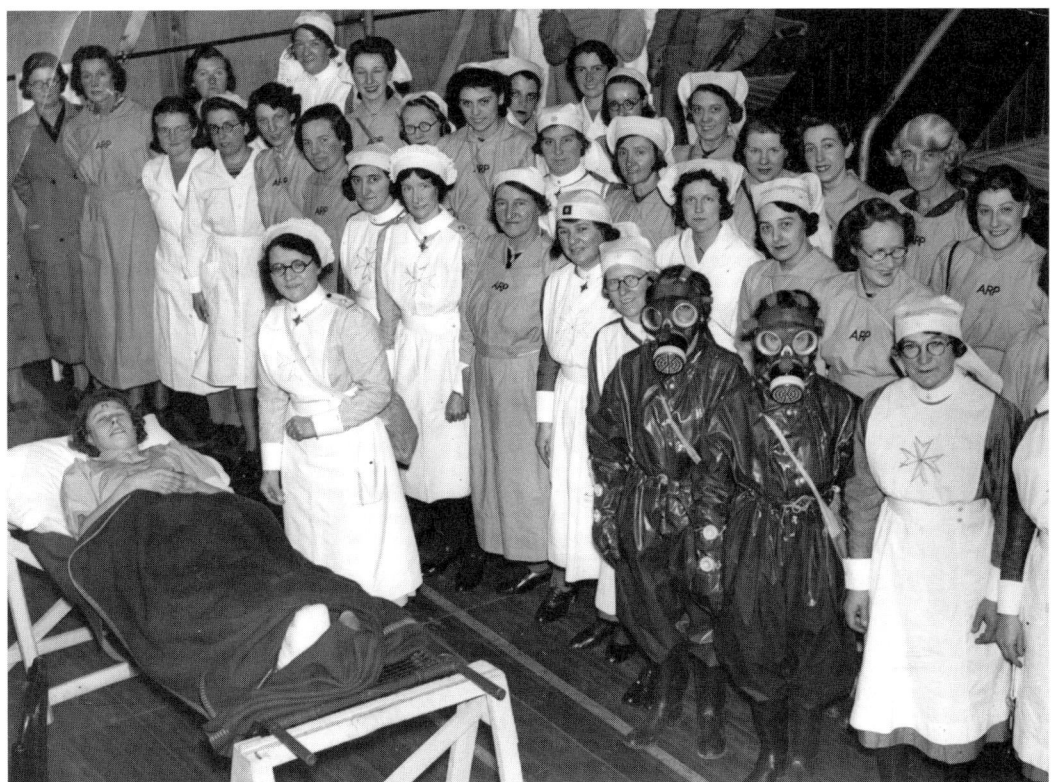

Smiling St John and ARP nurses at Spence Street FAP in February 1941. A mock casualty lies on a metal ARP stretcher with the letter 'M' marked on her forehead, indicating a FAPy had treated her with morphine before her arrival at the FAP. Meanwhile, two stretcher bearers wear anti-gas clothing. [Leicester Mercury]

WAR ORGANISATION OF THE BRITISH RED CROSS SOCIETY AND ORDER OF ST JOHN

The two uniformed voluntary aid bodies, the British Red Cross Society and the St John Ambulance Association and Brigade, though non-governmental, played a major role in the ARP casualty services. As in the First World War, rather than working separately, the two organisations co-operated to form a Joint Organisation in 1939. Their personnel had years of first aid experience: indeed before the war, instructors from both organisations trained ARP recruits. It made perfect sense, therefore, that both organisations should provide staff for the ARP casualty services. Thus, the BRCS and SJAB provided many personnel for the FAP, FAPy and Ambulance Services.

St John Ambulance Brigade

Leicester's St John personnel had been preparing for war since 1936, when they had started training in the treatment of gas casualties. A new Brigade appointment was made in 1938, of Mr Leonard Lee, Corps ARP Commander for Leicestershire, responsible for organising all ARP training of both brigade personnel and public.

Leicester's MOH, Dr E.K. MacDonald, set up a small committee consisting of the County Commissioner, the County Superintendent, the Corps Surgeon and the Corps ARP Officer for the purpose of advising him on staffing FAPs and depots with St John personnel.

The County President of Leicestershire SJAB was Lady Zia Wernher and the County Commissioner George F. Browne. Five Leicester SJAB staff, Medical Officer Dr E.B. Garrett, commander of the Bond Street MFAU; Ambulance Nurse Mrs Hilda Hefford; Ambulance Officer Leonard Lee; Ambulance Nurse Miss Ivy Marsh and Ambulance Nurse Miss Carrie Wells, were awarded SJAB Certificates of Merit and MoHS Letters of Commendation For Bravery, following extraordinary conduct on Leicester's Blitz Night.

In June 1941, Nursing Sister Miss Rosa Lord, of Evington Drive, was awarded the British Empire Medal. MOH Dr E.K. MacDonald wrote: 'Miss Lord, who was a nursing sister of the Order of St John prior to the war, has been in charge of St Philip's FAP, subject to the general direction of the MO in charge, for the whole period of hostilities. She has organised the post in what can only be described as an extraordinarily efficient manner.'

British Red Cross Society

BRCS personnel also served in FAPs. The County Director of Leicestershire BRCS was Mrs Alba Paynter MBE. Miss Dora Greaves and Miss Esme Folwell were the Red Cross and St John's FAP Nursing Officers at the St John's Church Rooms FAP, Clarendon Park. Miss Greaves recalled future actor, director and producer Lord Richard Attenborough, then a 17-year-old stretcher bearer at the post: 'When we did our first aid exercises, it was often Richard who was made up as the corpse!' At the start of 1941, one of two ambulances given by the Canadian Red Cross to the BRCS, were loaned to the Leicester and Leicestershire Joint County Red Cross Committee.

Civil Nursing Reserve

In April 1939, the Civil Nursing Reserve (CNR) was formed to provide additional staff at hospitals and FAPs. The CNR was composed of trained nurses, assistant nurses and nursing auxiliaries. The CNR had a limited presence in Leicester.

ARP Emergency Mortuaries

Pre-war statisticians predicted that for every ton of bombs dropped, 17 people would be killed. They also predicted the Luftwaffe would drop up to 600 tons of bombs per day, indicating additional mortuary facilities would be needed. In response, the Emergency Mortuary Service was created and personnel recruited from local undertakers.

Leicester's main ARP mortuary was under the Crumbie Stand at the Tigers' rugby ground, Welford Road. Two mortuary vans and an Emergency Mortuary Squad were permanently on standby. Ironically, Leicester's Crumbie Stand mortuary was hit by bombs almost at the start of the Blitz Night and over 100 fatalities had to be sent to the reserve emergency mortuary, at Aylestone Baths, Knighton Fields Road West.

Local mortuary procedure followed MoH guidelines. A temporary information label was affixed to the body by ARP Rescue or FAPy personnel at the incident. A mortuary van then took the corpse to the mortuary, where on receipt, the body would be given a reference number. The body would then be stripped and the clothing and personal belongings itemised. A Form CWD (Civilian War Death) would be completed and signed by the Mortuary Superintendent. The body would then be prepared ('tidied'), put in a shroud and placed on a metal ARP stretcher awaiting official identification, by relative, friend or acquaintance. It was stipulated that where practical, photographs should be taken of unidentified bodies to aid the identification process.

Anecdotal evidence suggests after the Blitz Night, there were 'overflow mortuaries' in, of all places, pubs. A former staff member of the Princess Charlotte pub, Oxford Street, states that RAPC fatalities who had been killed in Highfields were temporarily laid out in the bar. This is plausible, as a major RAPC office was nearby on The Newarke. It has also been said Highfields fatalities were temporarily laid out at the Old Horse pub, London Road.

A young girl, whose father worked at Aylestone Baths reserve mortuary, remembers visiting him after the Blitz Night. She was told not to look under the wooden boards covering the foot bath, as that was where 'the bits' were being stored.

The number of fatalities on the Blitz Night appear to have tested the organisation. A month later, the MOH requisitioned 12 open lorries, belonging to local firms, if needed, for transporting fatalities. Some 250 fibre coffins, at 11/5d [£25] each, were also purchased and arrangements made for mass trench burials. In January 1941, Leicester's EMS consisted of a mortuary van with five f/t men. A grim reminder, if one were needed, of the horror of war was recorded in November 1942, when the CD Committee ordered 160 children's shrouds at a cost of £25.5.0d [£920].

Mortuary staff are the most forgotten of the CD services, yet they had the most harrowing role of all. A thought should be spared for them, particularly the Aylestone Baths Mortuary staff, including Superintendent Officers H.W. Cox, F.G. McHugh, plus Deputy Mortuary Superintendent F.W. Murray. On Blitz Night, they had to register, photograph and record scores of bodies brought to them – in all states. The ARP mortuary forms make disturbing reading: 'Burnt to a cinder'. 'Face and nose crushed, eyes missing'. 'Complexion: unidentifiable'. 'Clothing soiled and worthless'. Their most harrowing task must surely have been dealing with child fatalities.

National ARP for Animals Committee

An ILC article from December 1940 reveals: 'Special arrangements have been made at the RSPCA clinic in Wellington Street for the treatment of animals which become air raid casualties. The clinic is constantly prepared for the reception of hundreds of animal raid casualties. Painless destruction is prescribed in severe cases. The clinic exhibits the same atmosphere and equipment as a doctor's surgery. There are the same whiteness, cleanliness, examination table, waiting room and patients' card index. An animal ambulance is constantly ready. The NARPAC organisation is in the hands of Miss Twyman, 3 Elmfield Avenue. NARPAC has arranged for the registration of all pet animals, to which the committee's identity disc can be attached. NARPACs workers are called "Animal Guards" and each is issued with an armlet and 100 identity discs. Leicester's branch of NARPAC is well-supported, and scores of dogs and cats in the city are wearing the blue and white identity disc. Horses, ponies, and donkeys are similarly labelled. Leicester's pet population is in good hands.'

The Fire Services

Auxiliary Fire Service

    Chief Fire Officer: Francis Winteringham (February 1938-December 1940)
                                  Errington McKinnell (January 1941-August 1941)
    Commandant of Leicester AFS: Philip E. Ashwell
    HQ: Central Fire Station, Lancaster Road

The red embroidered 'AFS Leicester' chest badge worn on overalls by Leicester AFS firemen. [Roger Miles]

The main pre-war ARP concern was poison gas, followed closely by HE bombing. However, a post-Blitz survey revealed that for each ton of HE bombs dropped, roughly 1¾ acres was destroyed, but for each ton of IBs dropped, at least 3¼ acres was destroyed.

The authorities were relatively slow to act. They realised small, local fire brigades would be unable to tackle mass fire-bombing, yet it was not until January 1938, the government ordered local authorities to set up an Emergency Fire Brigades organisation, bolstering existing local FBs with a new Auxiliary Fire Service.

Although Leicester was ahead in its ARP preparations, by May 1938, it still had no AFS. Records reveal 1,250 volunteers were needed, but none were in training. It seems Leicester's hand was finally forced two months later, when the Fire Brigades Act became compulsory.

AFS cap badge (top) and 'A.F.S. Leicester 2637' metal identity tag. [Author]

Such a task was huge, and only months before war, Leicester AFS were still desperately preparing. By July 1939, 18 trailer pumps, 36 hydraulic jacks plus 1,000 respirators had been delivered to Brigade HQ, in Lancaster Place. Chief Fire Officer Winteringham requested 500 AFS uniforms, but by October 1939, only had 400 out of 1,300 needed.

As with the ARP Ambulance Service, there was a shortfall of operational vehicles. To make up for the deficit of fire engines (appliances) tough decisions had to be made. On September 18, 1939, Chief Fire Officer Winteringham wrote to 12 medium-sized Leicester companies demanding their firm's trucks: 'In the event of an air raid alarm, the vehicles in your possession shall immediately be taken to the pre-arranged AFS station. If you cannot guarantee the vehicles under these conditions, I shall have no alternative than to take them over entirely.'

Portable fire pumps could be transported on these requisitioned trucks or towed by appropriated cars. The pumps would then be connected into the mains or a static supply. Leicester AFS were supplied with 87 light and 16 medium trailer pumps, plus one heavy and two self-propelled pumps. This rose to 139 trailer pumps, three heavy pumps and an escape unit. Also in 1939, the FB received a Leyland appliance with a powerful 900-gpm heavy pump, which was to prove invaluable during the raids.

Originally comprising volunteers aged over 25, by November 1939, Leicester AFS comprised 435 men, based at 17 sub-stations. Within three months, this figure had increased to 1,859 personnel, augmenting the 53 pre-war Regular firemen.

Leicester AFS Sub-Stations, August 1940:

Sub Station:	Personnel:	Sub Station:	Personnel:
Granby Halls	100	MacDonald Road	80
Dover Street	43	Factory, 15 Freehold Street	40
Queens Road	40	36 Andover Street	60
Stoneygate Tram Depot	57	Gwendolen Road	65
543 Saffron Lane	80	Humberstone	70
(previously at Grace Road till July 1940)		Great Holme Street	84
36 Glenfield Road	40	Asfordby Street Constit'l Club	90
Winstanley Drive	47	Victoria Road East	?
Castles Garage, Church Gate	100	BUSM factory unit	?

Danes Hill House ARP Depot, Hinckley Road, transferred to the AFS in June 1941.
There was an alternative FB Control Room at Hinckley Road Corporation School.

Some of Leicester's larger works, such as Corah's and British United Shoe Machinery Co, as part of the **Leicester Private Fire Brigades' Association**, also had their own work's unit. In September 1941, Divisional Officer Arthur Cramp was elected Chairman of the Leicester and Leicestershire Private FBs' Association Council. He stated: 'The city was fortunate

Taken in early 1941, here are senior officers of Leicester Fire Brigade at the rear of Lancaster Road's Central Fire Station. Included in the group are: seated fifth from left Padre Rev. Herbert A. Jones (Provost of Leicester), then Philip E. Ashwell (Commandant of AFS); Second Officer Arthur Cramp; Chief Fire Officer Errington McKinnell; Third Officer (and Brigade Secretary) A. Farmer; Station Officer Douglas Sargent BEM (AFS Chief Training Officer); T. Bruce Roberts (AFS Deputy Commandant); Divisional Officer Roy Kemp. The appliances are AFS Heavy Pumping Units No. 1 and 2: On the left, a Bedford Heavy Unit, with a Leyland-Gwynne pump, capable of pumping up to 900 gallons per minute. No.2 is a Morris Commercial chassis, with the same pumping arrangement. [Robert Kemp]

having such a splendid second line of defence, which consisted of 500-600 trained firemen with trailer pumps and appliances for the protection of the various works.'

Firewomen also served in the AFS as control room telephonists, staff officers, office personnel, dispatch riders and mechanics, but did not fight fires. Margaret Hatton joined Leicester AFS as a control room telephonist: 'Aged 18, I lived on Vaughan Street. Just after Paris fell in summer 1940, my friend and I went to a service at the Cathedral where they appealed for volunteers. My father refused me permission to join the Forces, so we both went and joined the Fire Service. My friend went to the sub-station on the corner of Glenfield Road and Henton Road, whilst I went to Great Holme Street. My father didn't mind that. We received heavy cotton overalls with "AFS" on them and we served one evening a week. I was at the HQ of Sub-Division 2, a 'bomb-proof' concrete control room inside an extension behind Campions Garage showroom, off Great Holme Street. It was quite big, but not very pleasant in there. At first, the AFS just had commandeered cars towing trailer pumps at the garage. Some were left on Glenfield Road, as there was no room in the sub-station.'

Leicester Private Fire Brigades' Association enamel lapel badge. [Author]

Sadly, not everyone could withstand the apprehension caused by the Phoney War's hiatus. In August 1940, the *LM* reported: 'Tragedy of Leicester AFS Man: At the inquest of Leonard Martin, aged 35, of 2 Camville Road, City Coroner, Mr F.G.B. Fowler, returned a verdict that Martin committed suicide while the balance of his mind was disturbed. Mrs Annie Martin said her husband had good health until two months ago, when his nerves became bad. He was frightened he would not be able to work as a fireman if the real test came in an air raid. A neighbour found Martin had hanged himself.'

AFS control room telephonist Margaret Hatton stands with Leicester AFS firemen in front of their towing car and Standard-Gwynne light trailer pump, capable of pumping up to 180 gallons per minute, behind the AFS sub-station at 36 Glenfield Road, just after the 1940 Leicester Blitz. [Margaret Hatton]

But when the test came, the fire service gallantly faced the Blitz. Not only did Leicester's AFS fight fires in the county, but they also assisted other stretched FBs, travelling to fight fires in London, Coventry, Rugby, Nottingham, Bristol, Stockport, Warrington, Liverpool, even Belfast. Several Leicester AFS personnel were awarded for brave conduct at these places.

On the first day of the London Blitz, September 7, 1940, Leicester Divisional Fire Officer Roy Kemp led a fire column to the burning oil storage plants at Thameshaven and Purfleet. AFS Fireman Henry Neale, of 46 Ivy Road, was awarded the George Medal for bravery. The *London Gazette* reported: 'It became necessary to stop a large leak in an oil tank which had been on fire. The whole operation was very risky. Apart from unexploded bombs, fires and the likelihood of gases being given off from the tank, one slip on the top would have been fatal. While he was proceeding to plug the second tank, two cross jets had to be played on the flames. If these jets had failed, Neale would certainly have been burned. The tank was saved.'

During a severe raid on Manchester on December 22, 1940, Third Officer D. Sargent led a contingent from Leicester fighting flames for many hours in Manchester's docks. He personally dealt with many IBs and was twice caught by bomb blast. He rose from the rank of ordinary fireman during 14 years service in the Leicester Brigade and was instrumental in organising Leicester's AFS.' In September 1941, Sargent attended an investiture held by the King at Buckingham Palace and received the BEM for gallantry and exemplary conduct. Two months later, he was appointed Regional Fire Staff Officer, based at the HQ of the Chief Regional Fire Officer, at the North Midlands Regional Offices, Nottingham.

On May 4, 1941, a column of North Midlands AFS appliances, including over 25 Leicestershire AFS personnel, went to help fight fires in Liverpool. On the way there, the convoy was bombed, but escaped injury. Mrs Eva Mary Hyde, of Knighton Park Road, drove the Leicester AFS mobile canteen to Liverpool. When the convoy arrived, bombs were falling and fires raging. Mrs Hyde drove through them and supplied food and drink. In November 1941, Mrs Hyde received a Letter of Commendation from the MoHS, stating: 'I am directed by the Minister of HS to inform you that the Chief Officer of the Leicester FB, A. Cramp, drew attention to your gallant conduct in May last. Mr Morrison felt your devotion to duty was deserving of the highest praise, and he took steps to bring the matter to the notice of His Majesty the King, who was graciously pleased to give orders for the publication of your name in the *London Gazette* as having received the expression of commendation for your brave services.' Divisional Officer A. Cramp described Mrs Hyde as 'The bravest woman I have ever seen.'

Previously Chief of Bristol's FB, Francis Winteringham, Leicester's ARP Controller was appointed Chief Fire Officer in February 1938. However, much to Leicester FB and ARP

Committee's chagrin, on December 7, 1940, without any consultation and in the middle of the Blitz, Winteringham was suddenly transferred to become Chief of Birmingham's FB. In the 1941 New Year's Honours, Winteringham was awarded the MBE. He later went on to forge a successful career, as NFS Fire Force Commander for West Midlands, and in August 1942, was appointed to the staff of the Chief of Fire Staff, in London. Winteringham was replaced on the January 2, 1941 by Errington McKinnell, a 36-year-old Northumbrian who had served in the fire service since 1923. He had previously been Chief Fire Officer of the Swansea FB and HO FB Inspector for No.1 Region at Newcastle-upon-Tyne.

On April 10, 1941, Chief Fire Officer McKinnell addressed Leicester FB Sub-Committee: 'I have to bring to your notice the very prevalent danger of a shortage of water for fire fighting which may arise as a result of enemy action. In addition to surface steel tanks, the HO decided in December last to allow the construction of a number of large water basins, each holding 500,000 gallons, in certain towns in this region, one of which is Leicester, with a scheme to impound 1,300,000 gallons. Three sites were selected, at St Peter's Lane, Abbey Street and Gower Street. After a quick survey, I decided that, regarding the proximity of the canal and river, the sites selected were not particularly advantageous, particularly in view of the extreme lack of surface water in the north-easterly part of the City. I requested the City Surveyor only proceed with the basin in St Peter's Lane. I decided that to effectively protect the City, it would be necessary to impound a much larger quantity of water, 4,000,000 gallons. This will require the excavation of 10 to 15 basins. The cost will amount to £10,000 [£386,000] and approval has been received from the HO.' In May 1941, there were static water tanks at:

St Peter's Lane	400,000 gallons
Ethel Road	500,000 gallons
Spinney Hill Park	400,000 gallons
Victoria Road East	500,000 gallons
Ulverscroft Road	375,000 gallons
Temple Road	227,000 gallons
Green Lane Road	500,000 gallons
Abbey Street	180,000 gallons

By July 1941, there were three further static water tanks at BP Chemicals, Ulverscroft Road; LNER, Ulverscroft Road and LNER, Graham Street. Later still, static water tanks were placed on bombsites at Queen Street, Frank Street, Grove Road, Conduit Street, Sparkenhoe Street, London Road/Waterloo Street.

As a further supply, dams were constructed in the Evington, Bushby and Willow brooks. By June 1941, 12 had been constructed, eventually rising to 32 dams.

The largest and most obvious natural water supply in Leicester was the River Soar and Grand Union Canal. From summer 1941, a surface six-inch steel pipeline was laid along street gutters, feeding water from the Grand Union to the north-eastern part of the city, which McKinnell had described as having an 'extreme lack of surface water.'

Large base pumps at Mill Lane bridge drew water from the canal along Eastern Boulevard, via Filbert Street, across Aylestone Road, through Granby Hall car park, across Welford Road, to the Recreation Ground, where a large circular static water tank was situated at the corner of Lancaster Road. From here, the water was pumped up Lancaster Road to a 250,000-gallon concrete static water tank on Victoria Park, in the foundations of the bomb-demolished Pavilion. Another six-inch pipeline was laid from here, via Mayfield Road to Evington Road, then to Evington Valley Road, on to St Saviour's Road, finishing in this vulnerable industrial area.

The bolted sectional steel piping was stronger than the regular cast-iron mains, and if fractured by bombs, damaged sections could quickly be replaced. The pipeline was buried where it had to cross roads. Along the route were a number of delivery head valves, from where fire pumps could be fed or further pumps attached to boost water pressure. The pipeline was finally removed in July 1945.

In May 1941, Chief Fire Officer McKinnell reported that 'a survey of the fire risk on and near the banks of the canal, recommended a vessel suitable for conversion into a fireboat be obtained.' In June 1941, 'Alderman W.E. Wilford informed the Corporation a large passenger boat, suitable for conversion, had been found at Nottingham and was being altered. Its cost was £200 [£7,725], plus £75 [£2,900] for the conversion. When completed, it would pump 750 gallons of water a minute – half as much again as their best fire pump.'

The fireboat, officially titled Fireboat No.1, but also named *Lancaster* or *Lorraine*, was moored at the River Soar/Grand Union Canal basin, Eastern Boulevard, near Filbert Street. AFS Company Officer James C. Thornton, who was in charge of the fireboat, recalled that unfortunately, it sank en route to a domestic factory fire near West Bridge: 'The boat started out not far from Leicester Power Station, on an extremely cold, bleak night, where, in places, the canal had a three-quarter-inch covering of ice. While the fireboat was ploughing through the ice, water was seen coming into the engine room. Investigations revealed a 10ft-long slit, caused by ice cutting into the timber bow. This resulted in the fireboat sinking and settling on the muddy canal bottom. However, a resourceful crew member jumped into the freezing water and using hammer and nails, managed to implement a temporary repair by sacrificing a length of canvas hose to patch up the slit – quite an operation hammering nails underwater! Next, we bailed out water from both flooded engine rooms. Soon, we were afloat again, but the main engine wouldn't start. The vessel was equipped with a radial branch at the stern and by turning this to direct the water downwards at 45 degrees, we had propulsion and steering, by swinging the branch from side to side. We managed to propel the boat through the city and beached her, just before dawn, at Abbey Park. Unfortunately, the float was in no state to tackle the factory fire, which its crew passed en route to the park! It was the only time I attempted to reach a fire by boat.'

It appears the fireboat saw little action. Finally, in June 1947, the Watch Committee reported: 'Fireboat *Lorraine*: Correspondence with Customs and Excise and NFS Regional Transport Officer reveals vessel found by Ministry of War Transport unfit for fire-fighting and therefore disposed of.'

The NFS crew of the fireboat Lorraine *manoeuvre her on the River Soar, near Upperton Road bridge, in July 1943. Note the suction hose drawing water from the river to the covered fire pump, which fed the front and rear branches.* [Leicester Mercury]

NATIONAL FIRE SERVICE

Chief Regional Fire Officer for No. 3 Region: T.H. Patrick
Fire Force Commander of No.9 Region: Arthur Netherwood (August 1941-February 1943)
       W. Thomas (February 1943-April 1948)
Chief Fire Officer: Arthur Cramp (August 1941-1945)

The AFS's trial by fire in 1940-1941 revealed shortcomings of an organisation hurriedly created and based on pre-war local FBs, each with their own confusing structures, operating methods and equipment. So, on August 18, 1941, under the direction of the Minister of HS, the AFS and local FBs were nationalised into the National Fire Service.

The NFS was more organised, with new standardised orders, ranks, uniforms, training and quasi-military discipline. Britain was divided into 39 Fire Force Regions. Leicestershire was part of No. 9 Fire Force, together with Rutland, Northamptonshire and the Soke of Peterborough. The Fire Force Region was further divided into Divisions, with Leicester in 'A' Division.

But, according to Police Inspector Fred Shelvey, 'there was almost an insurrection in Leicester when reorganisation was attempted.' The wresting of control from local authority to central government led to acrimony between Leicester's Watch Committee and central government. The *LM* reported: 'Leicester Watch Committee last night passed a resolution vigorously protesting against the 'dictatorial methods adopted by the Government in the reorganisation of the fire services.' As Deputy Regional Commissioner, it was Cllr Keene's job to implement this modernisation. Keene 'stamped his authority on the Region's administration, reorganising the Fire Service into an effective body. By diplomacy and persuasion he knocked the fire service into touch.'

That wasn't Leicester's only dissatisfaction with central authority. Just prior to nationalisation, in July 1941, it was announced that Leicester's Fire Chief, Errington McKinnell, had been appointed Fire Force Commander of No.9 Fire Area. However, just 13 days later, after serving only eight months in Leicester, without notice, McKinnell was transferred to become Fire Force Commander of No.3 (Rotherham) Region. The first the Chairman of Leicester's Watch Committee, Alderman Wilford, knew about it, was when he received a telephone call from the *LM*, who reported: 'Mr A. Netherwood, Chief Fire Officer of Beckenham, Kent, is appointed by the Home Secretary in Mr McKinnell's place. Leicester's ARP Controller C.E. Worthington said: "It is a great nuisance to us to lose Mr McKinnell at the present time." Alderman W.E. Wilford said "Mr McKinnell was very popular with the men and introduced many new ideas. He had only been appointed commander for this area, so you can imagine our surprise."'

NFS cap badge, issued from 1941-1948. [Author]

No.9 Fire Force HQ was based in a large, requisitioned Victorian house, Invergarry, at 23 Knighton Grange Road, Stoneygate, as it was outside the city's main target area and had plentiful rooms for offices. Margaret Hatton, who served in Leicester's AFS/NFS, was stationed there: 'We had 48 hours on, 24 hours off. We went to Lancaster Hall for training and exams: I got 100% and was made a Leading Firewoman and posted to the purpose-built Lancaster Place control room. Then, we were moved to Invergarry, where I was put in charge of a watch, manning the control room in the large concrete bunker in the garden. The house was used for sleeping quarters, had a kitchen with two very good cooks and a dining room. Another house was also commandeered on Princess Road. Although the Blitz died out, there was still plenty to do. Invergarry was in control of Leicestershire and neighbouring counties and there were plenty of exercises and civilian fires.'

In the 1943 New Year's Honours, the King's Fire Service Medal for Distinguished Service was awarded to Arthur Netherwood, Fire Force Commander of No.9 Area. However, within a month, on February 15, 1943, it was announced that Mr W. Thomas, Fire Force Commander for Lincolnshire, was to replace Netherwood, who moved to London.

With Leicester's war factories working 24 hours a day, industrial machinery was permanently driven. Much war produce was stored in local warehouses, creating a greater fire risk. The NFS played an important role saving this industrial output from accidental fires.

In autumn 1943, a large joint Army/NFS operation, Exercise Harlequin, was held in Kent. This was to test local defences in the event of a German counterattack against the build up of forces and material along the south coast for the coming Allied invasion of Europe. Following this exercise, between January and October 1944, an operation called the Colour Scheme was mobilised. This involved the transference of large numbers of NFS personnel and their equipment from less threatened areas to reinforce the vulnerable southern and eastern D-Day launching areas. For the purpose of the scheme, Britain was divided into three colours: Brown, Green and Blue. Fire cover in the Brown Zone, north of the Severn-Wash line, which included Leicestershire, was halved, providing reinforcement to the Blue Zone in southern England. It is known that one Leicester NFS fireman, Ernest Hurst, was killed by enemy action on March 2, 1944, at Lewes, Sussex, whilst serving the Colour Scheme.

NFS Assistant Group Officer Margaret Hatton, née Hall, stands in the front garden of No.9 Fire Force HQ, Invergarry, Knighton Grange Road, c. 1942. [Margaret Hatton]

An instructor stands before a model of Leicester during a fire training exercise at Granby Halls NFS sub-station in 1943. Although no bombs had fallen on Leicester for two years, NFS training remained intensive. [Leicester Mercury]

Men and women NFS personnel at Saffron Lane sub-station, next to the City Arms pub, in summer 1944. On the left is a Coventry Climax large trailer pump and on the right, a Dennis large trailer pump: both were capable of pumping up to 500 gallons per minute. [Leicester Mercury]

Margaret Hatton, a Leicester NFS Group Officer, recalls: 'In 1944, I went down to the NFS Staff College at Saltdean, Brighton. I went as a Junior Officer and then a second time as a Senior Officer, when the doodlebugs were coming over. It was really awful. Looking back the NFS was very professional. I enjoyed it and I enjoyed having the authority. The companionship with all the men and women was great, even with Fire Force Commander Netherwood. He was a jolly chap who would sit down for dinner with you in the canteen.'

In October 1944, it was announced that 'part-demobilisation of the NFS has begun'. Leicester's extensive static water preparations became a hindrance. The open tanks attracted children – sadly, with fatal results. The first fatality occurred on August 14, 1943, when 12-year-old Leslie Smith, of 12 Maynard Road, drowned in a static water basin. The *LM* reported 'his life was lost, despite heroic attempts at rescue. The difficulties of recovery were so great, consequent on the steepness of the sides of the tank, that the boy was in the water half an hour before his body was secured by means of drags. The tank is of the 15,000-gallon type, built into wasteground on Kent Street. It is enclosed with a chain link wire 6ft high, and the wasteground also has a 7ft fence. Afterwards, some earth was found burrowed under the wire.'

In late 1944, Leicester NFS started to dismantle static water tanks. In January 1944, the *LM* reported 'from 16 smaller static water tanks cleared by the NFS in the past fortnight, has been taken 90 tons of rubbish. This hooliganism is not all the work of children. From one tank, was taken a block of concrete, weighing 5¼ cwts. There were bricks and stones in barrowfuls, bedsteads, cycle wheels, two perambulators, a motor engine, chassis and mudguards, 98 milk bottles, 10 dogs, mostly in sacks, 14 cats, seven rabbits and four fowls, a baby's respirator, still in working order after its immersion and a pair of policeman's handcuffs.'

With the NFS's gradual demobilisation, local sub-stations began to close from August 1944, including Bulwer Road; Clarendon Park; Gwendolen Road; Braunstone and Granby Halls. In November 1944, Church Gate; Humberstone; Conduit Street; Melton Road and Saffron Lane closed. From March 1945, Stoneygate sub-station was closed, leaving only Lancaster Place, Abbey Lane and Asfordby Street: Abbey Lane closing on May 7, 1945 – the day before VE Day.

After the war finished, the NFS continued at a reduced rate. As had been promised at the NFS's formation, Britain's fire service was denationalised and returned to local authority control on April 1, 1948. But this was not a return to pre-war local fire services of old and the modernised elements remained. Errington McKinnell also returned to resume command of the re-formed Leicester City Brigade.

Neighbours Leagues

Chief Organiser: Mr Walter Thacker
HQ [to November 1941]: City ARP Department, 24 Halford Street

One of the greatest local symbols of community spirit to emerge during the war were Leicester's Neighbours Leagues. The ILC described its origins: 'Before the war, in August 1939, a group of Leicester housewives formed what they called a Neighbours' Club. That was the start of the NLs which have captured Leicester's imagination: a vast "help one another" movement, which started spontaneously, without any instigation from authorities and is now doing good work in every quarter of the city.'

With the growing threat of air raids, these Neighbours' Clubs took a more ARP direction. As most men were away in the forces, initially, NLs were largely driven by women. The *LM* announced in June 1940: 'Neighbours' Leagues for women are being formed in Leicester. The idea is women should familiarise themselves with every other woman in their street. As soon as the sirens sound, neighbours may join each other in a safe spot. Others will go to the aid of old people, those unwell, expectant mothers and homes with large families. Members will also club together to buy stirrup pumps for dealing with IBs, plus first aid kit.' Cllr C.R. Keene said the ARP Committee gave the scheme a special blessing: 'The idea is a splendid one, which we would like to encourage for the whole city.'

NLs varied from 30 to 300 in strength. They were largely autonomous: each NL had its own funds and organised its welfare and social activities. Every NL member displayed a card in their window bearing the letters 'NL'. This led to an unfortunate misunderstanding: when evacuees fleeing from bombed cities arrived in Leicester, 'they saw the 'NL' signs everywhere – they thought it stood for "No Lodgers"!'

By early 1941, the NLs had really taken off. The *LM* reported: 'There are now 900 NLs in Leicester and about 27,000 people have some experience of ARP work through these organ-isations. One of the busiest men in Leicester is Mr Walter Thacker, Chief Organiser. The appeal made by Mr Herbert Morrison, Minister of HS, about the new national scheme for fire watchers, has stimulated interest in the NL. Since then, Mr Thacker has had 300 appli-cations for stirrup pumps. Leicester people have the satisfaction knowing the NL is stronger in this city than anywhere in the country. Applications for particulars of the Leicester scheme have even come from Australia. Mr Thacker pointed out it was essentially a people's movement and all classes of the community belonged to it. The Bishop of Leicester recently became a member of a group formed in Springfield Road, where he lives.'

In February 1941, the ARP Committee approved the spending of £250 [£9,650] on specially-designed NL enamel badges, to be sold to members for 1/- [£2] each. On March 15, the *LM* reported: 'NLs in Leicester are to have their own badges – and very nice they are, too.

In February 1941, the LM *reported 'the idea of armlets for fire watchers is so those on patrol can readily contact each other on dark nights. Here is Miss Joan Buckler, Neighbours League Organiser for 'C' Division, wearing one designed by her father, Mr H.A. Buckler, for fire watchers in the St John's Road, Holmfield Road and London Road triangle.* [Leicester Mercury]

Through Mr Walter Thacker's ingenuity and enterprise, the badge has progressed from an idea to actuality. The symbolism of the design is subtle, but easily comprehensible. Two circles are interlaced – the League has interlaced many circles. In the centre, on a field red with the blood of sacrifice, is the pierced cinquefoil of the City arms. The colours are the national red, white and blue and the legend "City of Leicester Neighbours League". Five thousand badges are available and I anticipate they will be quickly taken up.' Six months later, it was announced 'Leicester NL has, through Chief Organiser Mr Walter Thacker, forwarded to Russian Ambassador M. Maisky, 1,000 badges similar to those worn by its members, requesting him to send them to Moscow "as a symbol of our fellowship with Russia in these mementous days. If a thousand of your indomitable people will wear one of these badges, it would be extremely gratifying to us and the unity of spirit between our two nations would be increased."' Within a week, 'Mr Thacker received a letter from M. Maisky thanking him and stating the 1,000 badges will be forwarded to the Soviet Union as soon as opportunity occurs.'

'City of Leicester Neighbours League' badge. [Author]

Although the NL was an aid to the official CD organisation, the NL organisation was now large and quite unwieldy in its independence. Following the Leicester Blitz, the city greatly expanded its post-raid CD welfare organisation, overlapping much of the NLs work. Then, in August 1941, the government launched the Fire Guard Service, which performed the main role of the NLs – street fire-fighting. In September 1941, NL Organiser Walter Thacker wrote a candid, private report for Leicester CD Committee acknowledging this: 'The number of NL groups in the city is now over 1,400. There appears to be an obvious need for the co-ordination of the local authority's welfare services and the NL's welfare activities. The NL are now so numerous and widespread, it is impossible to centralise their activities. Their affiliation with the City's Welfare Services would not only assist the NL, but also the City's Welfare Services.'

However, if this sounds like Thacker was secretly selling out the NLs, far from it: he listed several 'recommendations' – more like demands – including: 'The NL shall be free to continue and develop their activities within the framework of the City Welfare Service; Mr Thacker be invited to become a co-opted member of the CD Welfare Sub-Committee, representing the interests of the NL; in view of the Government FG scheme and its effect upon NL street fire parties, Divisional Wardens should help avoid the disintegration of NL fire parties and maintain their enthusiasm under the new scheme.'

The affiliation was publicly announced on October 24, 1941. Rather than the disintegration of the NL organisation, Thacker extended its life, making it more official, whilst, on paper at least, maintaining its independence. For the CD authorities, they could now count on the NL's weight of numbers.

At the end of October 1941, in a final bulletin to NLs before affiliation, Chief Organiser Thacker noted: 'It is natural that the League should now be closely associated with the City Welfare information offices. The offices for the seven Divisions and their NL Divisional Organisers are:

> A: Melbourne Hall: Mr G.H. Godrich
> B: Public Library, Narborough Road: Mrs D. Russell
> C: Public Library, Woodgate: Miss J. Buckler
> D: Public Library, Cossington Street: Mrs Jacques
> E: Public Library, St Barnabas Road: Mr S. Spencer
> F: Public Library, Clarendon Park: Mr G.H. Bent
> G: 11 Glenfield Road: Mr D.G. Woolfenden.
> Central NL Office will close from November 1941.'

However, not all NLs were convinced. On November 28, 1941, the *LM* reported: 'Quickly following their decision to turn down the suggestion of fusion with the City Welfare Services, 'F' Division NL issued a statement affirming determination to stand firm. After being told of 'F' Division's decision, Mr F.M. Drewery, Leicester's Welfare Administrative Officer, emphasised the welfare scheme aimed at encouraging NL's to develop their activities. There was absolutely no thought of destroying them. The CD authorities hoped that once the nervousness was got over, it would be appreciated no interference whatsoever was contemplated.' Whether through the dogged persistence of some NLs or the genuine wish of the authorities not to interfere – or both – some NLs remained independent to the war's end.

In 1964, *LM* reporter William Kidd lamented the NLs' passing: 'They were responsible for thousands of deeds of kindness and courage. How much we have lost by the ending of the Neighbours League movement.'

Fire Watchers and Fire Guards

> FG Officer: Edwin Robins (August 1943-November 1944)
> Deputy FG Officer: Inspector Bernard Ecob (August 1943-November 1944)
> FG HQ: Vestry Hall, Vestry Street

Britain reacted relatively slowly to the firebomb menace and it was some months before civilian fire-fighting parties were organised. In April 1940, the *LM* announced: '1,200 Leicester people will be required to enrol as "incendiary squads" or fire parties, as an auxiliary to the AFS. Parties of three will be given a stirrup pump and trained.'

However, it took the invasion of France and the formation of the NLs for any widespread civilian fire-fighting organisation to appear in Leicester. As a result, the supply of stirrup pumps began to increase, with 400 reaching Leicester in June 1940. Nationally, in September 1940, the Fire Watchers' Order was introduced. This placed an onus on owners of business premises to have a single, designated Fire Watcher. Compliance was mixed.

During the Blitz months, NL fire parties tackled many IBs, relieving the burden on the AFS, allowing them to tackle more serious fires. Three weeks later, it was announced 'Leicester shopkeepers and small factory owners have been asked by North Midland Regional HQ to formulate a voluntary firewatching scheme. It has been suggested that unless a workable voluntary plan is agreed, compulsion under the Firewatchers' Order may be extended to smaller premises. At present, all factories and warehouses employing over 30 hands and buildings over 50,000 cubic feet, must have firewatchers.'

However, it was a national event that caused a revolution in civilian fire-fighting, when on December 29, 1940, the Luftwaffe almost completely burnt out the City of London, with St Paul's Cathedral narrowly escaping destruction. On December 31, 1940, Minister of HS, Herbert Morrison made his famous 'Britain Shall Not Burn' broadcast, berating the public: 'some of you have failed your country. This must never happen again. You cannot stop a HE bomb from bursting, but you can stop a firebomb from starting a fire – fall in the firebomb fighters!'

Morrison also warned that compulsion would be introduced to the civilian fire-fighting organisation, but in the interim, employers should organise voluntary schemes. Two days later, it was announced 'Leicester is pushing ahead with plans to organise a fire-watching and fire-fighting service for everybody. 60,000 copies of Mr Morrison's appeal are to be distributed by the city's 4,000 wardens. However, in many areas, NLs have already formed fire parties. The idea is that houses should be grouped in sevens as a unit for fighting fire-bombs. Last night, for the first time, a Police fire patrol of 50 police and special constables operated in central Leicester until business people can get their own systems working.'

As a further measure, on January 14, 1941, Leicester Emergency Committee decided to deliver a partly-filled sandbag to every house. By February 3, 75,000 had been distributed. Two weeks later, this had risen to 110,000 sandbags. Eventually, the Committee organised supplies of sand on every tram and bus, plus 20,000 sandbags and 320 shovels along main streets within two miles of the Clock Tower.

On January 18, 1941, the Government issued the first Fire Prevention (Business Premises) Order, 1941, making it statutory for all business premises to make adequate fire prevention arrangements. All male employees, 16 to 60, had to perform 48 hours fire watching a month at their work. Two weeks later, it was announced 'approximately 40,000 have enrolled in residential fire parties in Leicester. Through wardens' efforts, 6,411 parties have come into existence, in addition to the NLs. The scheme for businesses is being organised by the AFS and is in progress.' As further encouragement, in February 1941, 323 'Fall in the Firebomb Fighters!' posters were posted around the city. Leicester College of Art also designed Fire Watcher armlets and other posters.

Not all firewatchers did their 'bit': In June 1941: 'A 53-year-old fire watcher, of Heathcote Road, was fined £10 [£384] at Leicester Police Court, after he pleaded guilty to stealing a woman's dress, valued 30s [£58], from Bernard & Lakin Ltd where he was fire-watching.

He asked for a charge of stealing eight other dresses to be taken into account.'

By July 1941, the Chief Constable said 19,000 steel helmets had been issued for street fire watchers. The FB also placed 500 50-gallon water barrels, labelled 'Fire Services', in streets with the biggest fire risk for fire-watchers, in case water mains were cut. A month later, there were over 48,000 volunteers watchers.

By August 1941, 57,000 men had registered for the fire watching pool. However, around 90% had applied for exemption because they were in ARP or war work. This meant there was still not enough manpower to protect the city. It was the same elsewhere, so the Minister of HS announced further compulsion from September 1941. Under the CD Duties (Compulsory Enrolment) Order, all males between 18-60 had to register for compulsory fire watching duties anywhere directed by the local authorities. However, Leicester was ahead of the game: "The new compulsory fire-watching order already applies to Leicester. Registration took place in June. We have the advantage of being two months ahead of other cities," said Cllr C.R. Worthington, ARP Controller.' This order also saw the birth of the more formal Fire Guard organisation.

First pattern Fire Guard armlet, with yellow print writing, issued from late 1941. [Author]

Although Luftwaffe raids had faded, the new FG organisation played a valuable role, such as in September 1941, when FGs were instrumental in saving considerable stocks of food at the burning premises of S. Patey, Son and Co, wholesale grocers, 31 High Street.

A better organised system of fire-watching was introduced under the new FG order: 'A block system, starting on December 1, 1941, will first embrace the area bounded by Halford Street and Gallowtree Gate and will be extended to the Clock Tower. By group control, reserves can be switched to any block pressed in an air raid. It will gradually extend to the whole city.' The plan was to take 'island' sites, of 50,000 or 90,000 square feet, and make a FG team responsible for it.

By the end of 1941, Leicester had 48,276 FGs enrolled, operating in 4,388 parties, sharing 27,000 steel helmets and 1,100 stirrup pumps. Apart from senior officers, FGs had no uniform, except an armlet and helmet. Their 'weapons' were stirrup pumps, buckets of water, sandbags and ladders. FGs manned posts in the heart of the target areas, such as on the roof of Corah's works and the Cathedral. Lewis's tower, Humberstone Gate, was used as a look-out post, known as 'Lewis's watch'. When the FG organisation was at its peak, every 150 yards of Leicester streets, or every 30 houses, had their own FG party, whose members operated on a street rota. Most duty consisted of conversation, boredom, sleep, games, reading or darts.

This rare fire watchers' post survives atop the old Corah's St Margaret's Works, on Watling Street. [Author]

Nationally, it was clear there were not enough men available to complete the FG pool, so in August 1942, it was announced women would be compulsorily enrollable for fire-fighting duties. On September 14, 1942, the order came into force: 'Residential fire-watching will also apply to women between 20-45, who are soon to register.' By November 1942, 65,000 women had registered. CD Controller Worthington said: 'The whole organisation of residential fire-watching is now on the point of large-scale revision. Divisional Wardens, Head FGs and Senior FGs in each Division have been appointed and given specific responsibilities. There are 75 Head and 250 Senior FGs and 25 instructors trained for residential Area FGs. Exemptions will be given to women with children.'

At the start of 1943, the government made a futher attempt to improve the FG organisation. Under the FG Plan, the FG would be separated from the Wardens' Service and have closer ties with the NFS. It became necessary to make f/t appointments costing £17,200 [£600,000]. On August 17, 1943, Mr Edwin Robins, Deputy Town Clerk, was appointed FG Officer for Leicester, to supervise the administration of the new FG Plan.

In February 1941, 323 'Fall in the Firebomb Fighters!' posters were posted around Leicester. [Author]

A private CD report explained: 'In September 1943, the Fire Guard Plan became operative in Leicester. Much of the work had already been carried out in the preceding two years by the formation of Block Schemes of business premises. Leicester was one of the first cities in the country to arrange these voluntary schemes which, by the Orders, became compulsory. The city was divided into 270 FG Sectors, conforming to the wardens' districts. 41 Sectors comprised solely of government or special premises, such as the Telephone Exchange and railway premises. A Sector Captain (replacing Street Captains) was appointed for each Sector, mainly wardens who were previously Senior FGs. Area Captains (in charge of up to five Sectors) were appointed from wardens who were previously Head FGs. All these new officers had to be retrained in the new FG Plan by Deputy FG Officer Inspector Ecob and Training Officer Sergeant Waugh of the Police, under the supervision of the FG Officer.

Both training officers undertook a FG Instructional Course (FGIC) at Falfield, Gloucestershire and became Instructors. It was decided to train as many Sector Captains as possible to qualify as LFGI (Local FG Instructors), so they could train Party and Block Leaders. Weekend classes were held at the four large CD Depots and Mill Hill Lane Training Centre until Easter 1944, when 133 instructors had been trained to LFGI level – a record number for any district in the North Midland Region. As soon as they qualified, they commenced training the Block and Party Leaders in their Sectors, of which there were 16 in each Sector. These Leaders then trained their parties. As there were 56,000 FGs to train, it will be appreciated what a tremendous task was undertaken.'

The FG Plan tried to prevent the NFS from being flooded by multiple calls about single incidents, by making it the sole responsibility of the FG to report fires. Each Sector Captain was linked to an NFS station. Sectors were sub-divided into party areas, each with an Assembly Point. When a fire was discovered, a member of the FG team ran to report the incident to the party leader at the Assembly Point. From here, another FG was dispatched with a written request from the party leader to the Sector Captain to summon the NFS. Having scrutinised the request, the Sector Captain then dispatched a third FG from his own team, on bicycle, to the NFS station, at which point, an appliance was sent. This system attempted less reliance on the vulnerable telephone network – but telephone communications were much faster than messengers: FG communications became more complicated, with more points of potential failure.

Prompted by renewed air raids on London, it would be over a year before the first major test of Leicester's FG Plan: 'The Regional Commissioner held a test exercise of Leicester's FG Plan. One of his officers selected 50 Sectors, 25 of which were tested on the nights of 4 and 5 April 1944. The Emergency Committee invited Nottingham's FG Officer to act as Chief Umpire, Leicester's FG Officer having umpired Nottingham's exercise a few months previously. Leicester's test was a "complete success". The Regional Commissioner therefore ordered the FG Plan to operate in Leicester on May 8, 1944.'

With the gradual relaxation of CD duties, the Regional Commissioner ordered a 50% relaxation in FG duty from August 1, 1944. Soon afterwards, the MoHS ordered a complete relaxation of FG duty in certain districts of Britain, including Leicester. The success of D-Day led to a stand down of Britain's CD services, with the announcement: 'Next Monday [September 11, 1944] is the last night Leicester FGs will have to go to their business premises to sleep'. CD Controller Worthington said: 'Although the stand easy will break up quite a few friendly parties it will remove a serious strain on the health of thousands of FGs, who have so loyally performed this wearisome duty during the past years.' Officially, FG duties in Leicester came to an end the following day.

By the time the FG organisation was fully developed, due to compulsory registration, it became the largest branch of the CD services. As it was overwhelmingly conscripted, it was composed of all members of society and several FGs appeared in court for various misdemeanours. But the vast majority did their duty, saving millions of pounds of war materials by fighting domestic fires. Eight FGs died in the course of their duties – the highest amount of any single Leicester CD service.

Fire Guard message form for summoning NFS assistance. Leicester's Fire Guard Plan of late 1943 attempted to rely less on vulnerable telephone communications, but as the multiple parts on this form show, just made emergency calls more complicated and protracted. [Author]

POLICE

Chief Constable: Oswald J.B. Cole (1939-1945)
Police HQ: Charles Street

Due to the police's main law enforcement role, it is now largely forgotten how integral to the ARP services they were. Leicester's Chief Constable was head of the city's Wardens' Service and was responsible for raising it. Wardens' Divisions were based on police Divisions. Police took charge at major incidents, with one police Inspector, Jesse Weston, awarded the OBE, whilst DS Leonard Norman, DC Brian Hawkes and DC Edwin Trump, were killed on ARP duties.

As early as May 1936, Inspector Harold Poole and Sergeant Walter Broadhurst were sent on an instructors' course at the HO Anti-Gas Training School at Falfield, Gloucestershire, after which, they trained both Leicester's Regular and Special Constabulary in anti-gas precautions. From April 1938, Inspector Poole worked hard training wardens and helping to form the organisation. His duties were taken over by Inspector Fred Shelvey, an ARP Instructor, assisted by Sergeant Broadhurst, PC 79 Cato and Sergeant Bernard Ecob. Under Chief Constable Cole, their work during the 1938 Munich Crisis was invaluable. Some 1,000 wardens at 30 schools distributed respirators to over 120,000 residents.

In 1939, the Watch Committee fingerprinted every member of Leicester Police, to help identify officers if they were killed in an air raid. During August 1939, Central police station was blacked-out, strengthened with baulks of timber and 40,000 sandbags. For six days, every sergeant and constable, all volunteers, filled and placed sandbags in their off-duty time. The amount of sandbags was later doubled, up to first-floor level. Unfortunately, their 800-ton weight caused the pavement to subside. The windows were also protected by £2,000 [£85,000] of steel shuttering and decontamination facilities were installed. An auxiliary police control room was installed in the Town Hall basement, with a reserve 50-line telephone switchboard at Newarke Girls School, Imperial Avenue.

However, by December 1939, the force had been depleted by 31 PCs due to military call-up. Police were working 12 hours a day. Inspector Shelvey, Liaison Officer to the ARP Controller and M/C, recalled: 'I was called out every time the yellow, purple and red warning lights flashed. For the first three years of the war, I averaged five hours on my bed – not sleep – at night.'

The police's role was even more complicated in wartime. A new raft of legislation was added to existing laws. In an age before CCTV, the blackout led to criminal opportunity. Despite wartime propaganda that the nation pulled together and crime rates were low, we now know law-breaking was rife, with widespread black market activities. The local press were full of crime stories: youth anti-social behaviour, theft, vandalism, muggings, gang fights, shopbreaking, occasional high-profile murders – even prostitutes touting around Leicester Clock Tower.

To aid the regular police in their increased duties, there were several bolstered Police Reserves, plus new branches:

A **First Police Reserve** of retired police officers was mobilised. By 1938, Leicester's unit comprised 28 men. By the war's end, only two remained.

A **Second Police Reserve: The Special Constabulary**, p/t and unpaid. During the interwar years, Leicester's SC had been allowed to deteriorate. Following a recruiting drive by Deputy Chief Constable Gabbitas, by April 1939, 314 new officers were recruited. Early in 1939, Inspector William Meese, later Chief Inspector, was appointed liaison officer to the SC and in June 1940, Special Inspector R. Moore was appointed Commandant. The SC averaged a strength of 520, of men from all walks of life. Divided into six sections, 100 War Reserve officers were called upon weekly for two hours of duty, 7pm-10pm and 10pm-1am.

SCs did good work during the raids, especially the Blitz Night, when 450 were on duty. During the war, 14 Specials were commended for good work.

During the first half of 1945, the Specials' average strength was 465, but following stand down in July 1945, over 260 resigned, leaving 204. To mark cessation of their wartime duties, the Lord Mayor took the salute at a special parade in June 1947. Leicester's SC force did not escape the war without casualties: SC William Levers, 56, of Fosse Road South, collapsed and died whilst on duty on March 29, 1943.

Finally, there was a **Third Police Reserve: The War Reserve** of f/t constables, employed for war service only. In 1940, there were 187 in Leicester. This Reserve was kept a small unit, with a maximum of 122 officers by 1941. The Police WR stood down in January 1946.

There were also two new branches. The **Women's Auxiliary Police Corps** was formed in 1939 for administrative duties, freeing male officers for front line work. Although tasked for useful work such as clerical/administration and driving/maintaining motor vehicles, unlike other counties, Leicester Constabulary did not make much use of the WAPC, with only 14 employed as telephonists in 1940, dwindling to two in 1945. The WAPC stood down in January 1946.

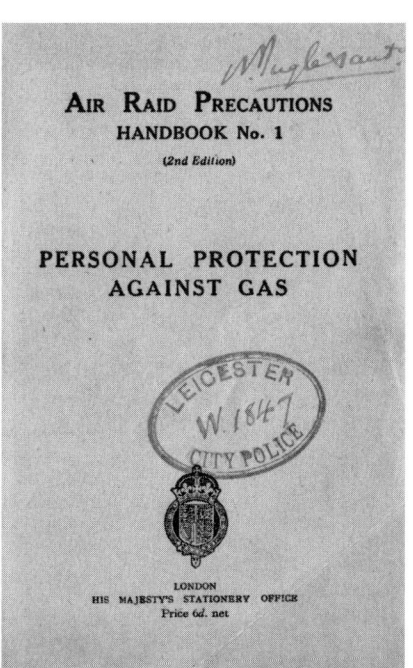

A copy of ARP Handbook No.1: Personal Protection Against Gas, dated 1936, with the stamp of 'Leicester City Police'. Leicester's police force were a key part of the city's ARP, integral from the organisation's inception. [Author]

Kenneth Rayson in his PAMS uniform. [Kenneth Rayson]

Police Auxiliary Messengers parade past Charles Street police station c.1941. They wear their 'dress suit', plus helmets and armlets marked 'Police Messenger'. [Leicester Mercury]

Leicester-pattern PAMS armlet. [Author]

The other new branch was the **Police Auxiliary Messenger Service**. In Leicester, its formation was announced on December 10, 1940: 'To help Police at air raid incidents, it is desired to form a Corps of Messengers, composed of youths between 16 and 18, in a voluntary capacity, who would turn out on an air raid warning.' Like the ARP Messengers, PAMS provided 'an alternative means of communication in the event of a breakdown in the telephone service.' Leicester PAMS was run by Inspector Ecob and Sgt Jackson, and by January 1942, 95 PAMS operated in the city. Kenneth Rayson recalls: 'I lived on Syston Street. Because of the raids, at 13, I decided to become a Police Auxiliary Messenger – helping the force in wartime. I was only the second to join and had "2" on my collar – when we received uniforms. Due to our role of delivering messages during an air raid, we became known as the "Bomb Dodgers."' Mr C.W. Robinson, PAM number 4, recalls a 'dress suit' was the name given to the boilersuits and white lanyards the boys initially wore, until they eventually received proper uniforms. On July 19, 1945, the PAMS were stood down, with a parade, led by their own band, under Bandmaster C.A. Rogers. Watch Committee Chairman, Alderman Wilford, accompanied by Chief Constable Cole and Inspector Shelvey, took the salute.

In the 1945 New Year's Honours, Chief Constable Cole was awarded the King's Police Medal for Distinguished Service, as was Deputy Chief Constable John Gabbitas in the 1944 Birthday Honours. In the 1946 New Year's Honours, Inspector Shelvey was awarded the BEM for services to CD.

Shelter Wardens

Chief Shelter Warden: Mr C.H. Harris
Chief Liaison Officer: Mr T.A. Chapman

It was essential order was kept in public shelters during raids. Not an easy task, shelter wardens acted as carers, mediators and advisers, whilst also maintaining shelter regulations and hygiene.

In March 1940, Cllr C.H. Harris, Chief Shelter Warden, appealed for 500 shelter wardens. Some 626 volunteered, comprising 295 basement shelter wardens and 331 trench shelter wardens. By the Leicester Blitz, there was wardened shelter accommodation for 53,000 residents.

By March 1942, there were 4,051 shelter wardens. By September 1944, it had fallen to 3,626, though still enough to warden all the public shelters. By then, 52,912 shelter passes had been issued to Leicester's public. There were 49 shelter canteens and eight shelter sick bays. In the year to September 1944, 39,440 shelters had been cleaned, 2,120 inspected and 98 supplied with fresh chemicals.

Mutual Aid

Though local ARP services were planned proportionately to the size of the population they served, it was clear a heavy, concentrated raid could still swamp them. At first, local authorities operated a form of ARP reinforcement, known as mutual aid, on a county or inter-county level.

Civil Defence Reserve

As a further precaution, in October 1941, the MoHS instructed Regions to form mobile CD reserves that could operate within each Region or further afield. Units making up this CD Reserve were known as the Regional Column.

Initially, No. 3 Region's CDR appears to have been low-key. It did not have an HQ until almost two years after its formation. Widow Isabella Wright died in July 1942, leaving her home, Willingham House (1790-1976), near Gainsborough, Lincolnshire, empty. A year later, the house, with its large grounds, became No.3 Region's CDR HQ and a Regional Training School. Despite its remote location, it was ideal, as it was unlikely to be bombed, yet accessible to potential targets of Lincoln, Grimsby and the North Midlands.

This proved fortuitous, as on July 15, 1943, CDR personnel were requested to report to Willingham House to help in the aftermath of a major raid on Grimsby. Likewise, two Leicester rescue parties were sent to Cleethorpes on August 25, 1943, to help demolish dangerous buildings.

In 1944, between 28-49 Leicester Rescue Service personnel were transferred to the Regional Mobile Column for reinforcement operations. Some remained with the Column, directed indefinitely. Two Leicester CD ambulances were also transferred in April 1944, until October 1944.

In March 1944, No.1 Unit of No.3 Regional Column were sent to Chingford, Essex, to aid hard-pressed CD units. The local authority reported the Column 'proved a most valuable addition'. During summer 1944, they also attended serious V-1 incidents in Lewisham, Leyton and Walthamstow. On September 22, 1944, the Column returned to its base.

In addition, though not with the CDR, 137 Leicester wardens relieved over-worked London wardens in Woolwich and Greenwich for 14 weeks, two Leicester wardens being injured by V-1 flying bombs. Leicester Rescue Service and City Engineer's staff also helped Crayford, Kent.

Industrial ARP

Leicester's factories were vital to the war effort, making them prime targets. Some of the larger industrial complexes had their own ARP organisations. A good example can be seen at Corah's St Margaret's Works, Watling Street:

'The directors appointed Charles Mackie, Chief Commissionaire, in charge of the works' ARP. The St Margaret's Works Private FB, affiliated to Leicester Private Fire Brigades' Association, was augmented, reaching 39 members in 1941. An Ambulance brigade and a decontamination squad was formed. Several basements were equipped as shelters, one being a central ARP control room in communication with Leicester's M/C. Extensive shelters were constructed on Archdeacon Lane and St John Street, for 180-200 persons in 22 shelters. To relieve the monotony, walls were painted with colourful murals by students from the Art School and music provided relaxation. At Leicester's first air raid, all 3,600 employees moved to the shelters in perfect order. On 19/20 November 1940, the works' FB rendered assistance to the neighbourhood. Following this Blitz, some shelters were converted into a FAP with operating theatre, resuscitation ward and treatment rooms. Fire watching commenced at the works on January 29, 1941. Specially-reinforced look-out shelters were built on top floors. In fire watching, the directors took their part with the humblest employee.'

Black and cream enamel pinback badge made by Thomas Fattorini, of Birmingham, for ARP personnel at Fielding and Johnson Ltd, worsted spinners, of West Bond Street, Leicester. [Author]

Post- Raid Welfare Services

Welfare Officer: Cllr Charles E. Worthington
Deputy Welfare Officer: Mr Harold S. Magnay
Welfare Sub-Committee (1944): Chairman Cllr F.T. Watson; Cllrs: H. Bowerman, Miss E.C. Fortey, Miss E.R. Frisby, C.E. Gillot, C.H. Harris, J. Minto, G.H. Round,

A.N. Vesty.
Cyril Osborne (City Welfare Council); Rev. H.A. Jones (CAB), Mrs D.M. Bates JP (WVS), T.P. Blackham (Welfare Transport Section), A.H. Headley (Divisional Welfare Officers), Mrs A. Paynter (BRCS)

The post-raid services were set up for the billeting and welfare of persons rendered homeless owing to air raids. They were as vital as the main ARP services, yet are largely overlooked today. More astonishingly, records reveal these post-raid services were only really formed as an afterthought, after the main Blitz.

Whilst ARP preparations had been planned for up to four years before the war, little consideration had been given to post-raid planning. The Corporation's Public Assistance Board could only provide limited aid for those bombed out.

With the Luftwaffe increasingly turning its attention to British cities, in September 1940, Leicester ARP Committee printed 50,000 leaflets with information for bombed-out persons. The city's post-raid services were just being formed when Leicester's Blitz Night occurred. Fortunately, the infant organisation was not tested too heavily and was able to cope.

Nonetheless, the raid had been a wake-up call and in the ensuing months and years, the focus of CD tipped towards post-raid planning. A month after Leicester's Blitz Night, ARP Controller Keene wrote a restricted report, laying out the Corporation's first main post-raid provisions: 'Private & Confidential: Summary of Arrangements Made to Meet Intensive Air Attacks: Experience has shown that considerable assistance is required after a heavy attack. Cllr Worthington has been appointed City Welfare Officer. 15 RCs are now fully-manned whenever the alert is given. In addition, 19 buildings are earmarked Reserve Centres. The RCs are largely in school buildings and staffs organised by the Director of Education, the WVS and MOH. Divisional Welfare Offices in branch libraries, will be information centres. [These were based in the suburban libraries, to draw civilians away from the city centre after a raid]. School Attendance Officers will be seconded as Divisional Billeting Officers. With the generous cooperation of the County Authorities, all County Emergency Rest Centres will be available.'

The ARP Controller released a redacted version of his report to the press on January 28, 1941: 'Leicester has re-modelled its plans to cope with air attack. The system of assisting people who might be bombed out of their houses, through 16 welfare centres, has been scrapped. The new system will be based on Divisional air raid sectors. Each Division will have a welfare officer. The new plans will decentralise services as much as possible. Each Division will contain within it all assistance bombed out families require.' The Divisional Welfare Centres and the Divisional Welfare Officers were:

'A' Division: Melbourne Hall	A. Chapman
'B' Division: Narborough Road Library	A.H. Kimberlin
'C' Division: Woodgate Library	G. Odom
'D' Division: Cossington Street Library	Dr E.R. Trotman
'E' Division: St Barnabas Road Library	A. Salt
'F' Division: Clarendon Park Library	A.H. Headley
'G' Division: 11 Glenfield Road (temporary)	L.L. Green

Post-raid problems were thoroughly explored. On May 8, 1941, Leicester ARP Committee visited Sheffield to see how the post-raid services had coped with their heavy Blitz.

The post-raid services eventually became one of the biggest CD organisations, with several thousand members in Leicester. Fortunately, because there were no further mass raids on Leicester, these services were never fully tested. However, in summer 1944, when 30,000 London evacuees fled the V-1 attacks to Leicester, these services swung into action, billeting thousands of evacuees around the city.

Rest Centres

Rest Centre Officer: A. Shilton (Public Assistance Officer)

In the Corporation's *Air Raid Precautions in Leicester* booklet, distributed at the war's outbreak, the only advice offered was: 'If you are homeless after an Air Raid, apply to Relief Offices, Rupert Street.' As an interim measure, it was suggested the city's parks be kept open during raids, so those bombed-out could congregate there. Leicester Emergency Committee did not resolve the problem for over a week after war was declared, announcing the city's clubs would offer temporary shelter to the homeless:

Club:	Relieving Officer:
Liberal Club, Melton Road	Mr G. Adnitt
WMC, Gipsy Lane	Mr F. Fisher
Railwaymen's Club, East Park Road	Mr C. Nutting
Knighton Conservative Club, Queens Road	Mr A. Murray
WMC, Beatrice Road	Mr C. Walker
WMC, Bond Street	Mr W. Cooke
Manchester Club, Humberstone Gate	Mr H. Smith
Aylestone & District WMC, Saffron Lane	Mr A. Murray
Community Centre, Braunstone Estate	Mr C. Burdett

On September 9, 1940, two days after the Luftwaffe's first heavy raid on London, Leicester ARP Committee noted 'Relieving Centres [Rest Centres] must be formed.' Eleven Relieving Centres, based in schools and clubs, were just being organised when Leicester's Blitz Night occurred. Lessons were learned and in December 1940, Leicester CD Committee publicly announced: 'A very considerable extension of Leicester's scheme of RC's is to be undertaken. RCs, on a permanent basis, will accommodate 3,000 with others, on stand-by, capable of dealing with 6,000-7,000 more. They will be stocked with iron rations.'

By February 1941, 'Cllr Worthington said there were 15 first-line RCs. In addition, five centres were operated by the Salvation Army, and the committee had a further 19 second-line centres to replace any rendered useless through attack.'

In March 1942, Leicester CD Committee issued a new leaflet called *After the Raid*, detailing the city's 15 first line RCs, which were no longer housed in clubs, but schools:

1. City Boys' School
2. Willow Street School
3. Melbourne Road School
4. Hazel Street School
5. Narborough Road School
6. Mantle Road School
7. Blackbird Road Pavilion
8. Ellis Avenue School
9. Harrison Road School
10. Moat Road School
11. Green Lane School
12. Mundella School
13. Avenue Road School
14. Linwood Lane School
15. Caldecote Road School.

By 1944, provision had increased slightly, with 17 first line RCs, plus a further 16 Reserve Centres, only staffed in emergencies, providing accommodation for 9,182.

During the 1944 reception of London evacuees, RC accommodation was used overnight on two occasions for those who remained unbilleted. RCs were staffed by WVS.

Emergency Feeding

Feeding Officer: H.S. Magnay

Food supplies would be disrupted after heavy air raids, yet, again, local records show little evidence any substantial emergency feeding preparations had been made before the war.

As it was, the bombed-out were adequately fed during Leicester's Blitz Night at local RCs. But there was a massive expansion of emergency feeding arrangements afterwards.

A CD report noted: 'By 1944, Leicester had 51 Emergency Feeding Centres in schools and chapel halls, each equipped with hard fuel cooking apparatus and staffed by Emergency Feeding Teams. There were also emergency feeding arrangements at the 17 first-line Rest Centres and 14 British Restaurants. There were also arrangements for assistance by 56 commercial catering facilities, plus the main bakeries and 27 fish and chip shops. In total, there were facilities for providing over 50,000 meals at any one preparation. This could be trebled or quadrupled in a day. Also available were the Education Committee's Central Kitchen in Milton Street and the Humberstone Cooking Depot, each capable of producing 3,000 meals. A semi-mobile kitchen could produce 1,000 meals in one preparation. This was

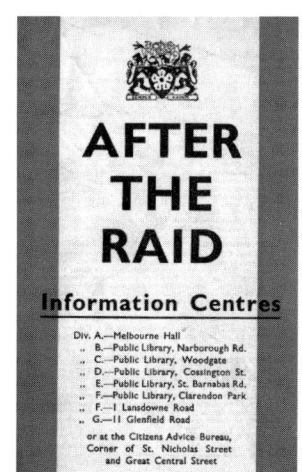

In March 1942, Leicester CD Committee issued a new leaflet called After the Raid, *informing householders about the city's 15 first line Rest Centres. [Author]*

staffed by Education Committee employees, as well as WVS and GTC. The Authority could call upon assistance from the Mutual Aid Scheme, and in the last resort, the Military.'

British Restaurants

Superintendent of British Restaurants: Miss M.G. Gibbs (April 1941-March 1944)
Miss E.D. Bott (April 1944+)

The nationwide MoF British Restaurants scheme enabled workers to have wholesome, ration coupon-free meals for a shilling [£2]. These restaurants could also be used in a post-raid emergency mass-feeding role. Leicester's first two British Restaurants were opened by the Corporation in March 1941 and by June, served 678 meals daily. By March 1944, Leicester's 15 British Restaurants served 7,369 meals daily and had served 1.7 million meals over the previous year, with an annual turnover of £80,000 [£2.7 million]. The oldest and smallest, Ivanhoe British Restaurant, was serving 900 meals a week and the newest, on Lee Street (now Lee Circle car park), opened by Lord Woolton, Minister of Food, on March 24, 1944, provided 6,000 meals weekly.

No.		Meals served daily	Date opened
1.	St Faith's, Brandon Street	370	28.1.1942
2.	Ivanhoe Mission	160	1.3.1941
3.	Clarendon Park Baptist church	380	1.3.1941
4.	St Margaret's, Canning Place	570	14.8.1941
5.	Aylestone Park Men's Adult School	250	9.10.1941
6.	Girls' Social Guild, Colton Street	520	16.10.1941
7.	St Barnabas Church Room	128	4.12.1941
8.	St Andrew's Church Rooms	156	11.12.1941
9.	St Stephen's Church Room	100	22.1.1942
10.	King Richard's Road	120	12.2.1942
11.	St Peter's Church Institute	96	26.3.1942
	Milton Street		30.4.1942
12.	Great Meeting Schoolroom, East Bond Street	150	7.5.1942
13.	Westcotes	100	24.9.1942
14.	Central (Lee Circle)	500	20.3.1944

Mobile Canteens

One of the greatest morale-boosters for hard-working ARP personnel and traumatised air-raid victims was a good cup of tea! This was delivered and served at the incident by open-sided vans. Nearly all Leicester's mobile canteens were donated by charity and staffed by WVS. They also saw service in Leicester, Coventry, Liverpool and Birmingham.

Leicester's first privately-donated vehicle was the Leicester ARP Mobile Canteen, given to the city by Frears and Blacks Ltd, on July 12, 1940. On December 13, 1940, 'Mrs H.S. Jacques presented a cheque for £150 [£6,350], subscribed by 'D' Division Neighbours' League, to CD Committee Chairman C.R. Keene, for a mobile canteen for the defence services.' By January 1941, there was also a mobile canteen called 'YWCA No.3: Leicester'.

On January 13, 1941, Lord Mayor W.J. Cort inspected a new Salvation Army mobile canteen for use by HM Forces and in case of emergency, the city services, in Leicester Town Hall Square, with Cllr C.R. Keene, Mr Cyril Osborne, Chairman, Leicester Welfare Council and Brigadier H.R. Pennick, SA Divisional Commander.' Within months, this vehicle was doing sterling work: 'One of the first supplies of hot drinks and food to reach Coventry after their recent ordeal on April 8/9, 1941, came from Leicester. Within a short time of receiving a message, Brigadier Pennick and Mrs Pennick set out with a mobile SA Canteen and for four days, gave invaluable help to bombed people and rescue workers.' Also that month, another mobile canteen was presented to Leicester CD Services, by Leicester Shoe Trade Managers and Foremen.

On February 3, 1942, Mr J. Stonehewer, of the Ford Emergency Food Vans Trust, presented Lord Mayor Cllr Miss Frisby two emergency food vans, which Mr Henry Ford gifted to Leicester. They were 'part of a national service of 350.' The drivers were WVS. Each van could transport 800 soups or 350 meals.

By 1944, Leicester had four Emergency Food Vans – three Ford and one YWCA. They were used daily to transport meals to schools.

Experience showed mobile canteens would be unable to feed large numbers of homeless, so from April 1941, the **Queen's Messenger Convoy Service** was formed. In May 1941, the Regional Commissioner stated he would 'send to [Leicester] following a serious air raid, the Queen's Messengers convoy, of three mobile canteens, three mobile kitchen vans, one water carrier van and two food supply vans. The convoy was capable of feeding 1,000 persons an hour. Convoy staff would remain on duty for the first 24 hours, then staffing would be provided by local WVS. The convoy would set up at rendezvous around the city e.g. Belgrave Gate car park.'

Cheers! From front left: *Emergency Committee Chairman Cllr C.E. Keene, Mayoress and Lord Mayor William Cort, with Post-Raid Welfare Officer Cllr C.E. Worthington promote the Ministry of Food's Queen's Messenger Convoy Service, with a cup of tea from a mobile canteen in front of the Town Hall in May 1941.* [Leicester Mercury]

SALVAGE AND REMOVAL

Officer-in-Charge: G.H. Garside (Parks Superintendent)
Deputy Officer: Mr J.W. Watson (Parks Dept)

Although other counties provided a salvage service for bombed-out residents, the personnel were usually drawn from the Rescue Services or private contractors. It appears Leicester was one of the few, if not the only authority, to have a specific CD Salvage and Removals Service, with specially-tasked personnel. Another post-raid service formed late, it was only created on August 19, 1940, just two days before Leicester's first bombing. The personnel for this new service were drawn directly from the City's Parks Department staff. Parks Superintendent G.H. Garside explained: 'Sixty men are standing to, with three lorries and eight horse-drawn vehicles.' By September 27, 1940, the service consisted: three incident clerks; two night clerks; four checkers; two transport foremen; three motor transport squads, each consisting of a vehicle driver and four men; six horse drawn vehicles; six foremen stackers and nine stackers, plus a reserve of 10 men. Checkers compiled inventories as items were salvaged from bombed homes. Each item was then labelled.

The service's biggest challenge happened after the Leicester's Blitz Night, as Garside reported on November 25, 1940: 'The magnitude of the raid severely tested the organisation, but it did not break down. Over 200 loads were moved. Premises were requisitioned for storage: St Patrick's church and rooms on Royal East Street; the Spiritualist Church rooms on Causeway Lane; 27½ New Walk; 8 Sparkenhoe Street; 81 Highcross Street; 13 Great Central Street and 10 Vestry Street.'

Post-raid salvage continued for months afterwards. On December 12, 1940, Garside reported: '70 members of the Parks Dept staff had been engaged since the 19th on salvage work. The problem of finding storage for all these belongings was multiplying.' By January 2, 1941, the service had removed 1,672 loads.

As the Salvage and Removal Service was so new, there was no existing insignia for the service, so the WVS made 'ARP SALVAGE' badges for 30 sets of overalls. But in just four months, Garside reported: 'The first set of overalls are now badly worn and torn, due to the heavy nature of the work.'

When insignia for CD battledress was introduced in late 1941, similarly, there was no official shoulder title for the Salvage and Removals Service, as it was a local initiative, so on March 30, 1942, the CD Committee resolved that cloth shoulder titles be made locally for the service. It was decided on April 27, 1942, two gross [288 – enough for 144 personnel] titles be purchased from Messrs Lewis Falk, at the price of 37/6d per gross [£136 total].

Garside produced a private report for the CD Committee in January 1941, describing the problems the service faced: 'Storage: There is insufficient storage to give one confidence for the future. This weakness has destroyed the organisation in other cities. Should large-scale operations be directed against Leicester, the service would break down. Lack of transport: 31 vans were enrolled, but only two responded.' In response, by 1944, the Corporation had built four storage huts in Victoria, Rushey Fields, Spinney Hill and Braunstone parks.

Surprisingly, in July 1945, the Salvage Officer submitted a list of unclaimed salvaged property recovered following the November 1940 Blitz. None of the articles exceeded £5 [£167] value and were disposed of, the proceeds going to rates relief. By October 1945, there were still unclaimed personal effects in storage from the Leicester Blitz five years earlier.

A rare 1941-dated surviving battledress of Leicester's unique 'Salvage and Removal' service. [Author]

Women's Voluntary Services

WVS County Organiser:	Mrs Isabella B. B. Noel (December 1938-1945)
WVS Borough Organiser:	Mrs Maurice Simpson (1938-June 1940)
	Mrs Dorothy Maud Bates JP (June 1940-1945)
WVS HQ: (1940-mid 1942):	31 Rutland Street
(1942-1945):	33 Horsefair Street
WVS Clothing Dept:	Grey Friars
WVS Clothing Store:	Queen Street and 23/25 Rawson Street

The WVS, or Women's Voluntary Services, were a key part of the CD services, performing often mundane, but essential wartime work.

Pre-war, most ARP publicity had been aimed at the male population, so in May 1938, the Home Secretary asked Stella Issacs, Marchioness of Reading, to form an organisation to encourage women into ARP work. On June 18, 1938, the Women's Voluntary Services for ARP was launched with much publicity. Lady Reading made a promotional tour of Britain's major cities, visiting Leicester in October, just one month after the Munich Crisis. She appealed to a meeting of 3,000 women to make 'a payment for the privilege of living in the best country in the world.'

WVS metal pin-back badge, issued from 1939. [Author]

Yet, there was some opposition – and from an ultimately, ironic source. Dorothy Bates, who attended this inaugural rally, afterwards wrote to the *LM* on October 29, 1938, challenging the WVS and ARP by 'deploring the fact that women's energies should be diverted from preventing war, into coping with its effects… I refuse to accept this.' As Hinton points out, ironically, 'Two years later, having finally accepted disaster could not be avoided, Mrs Bates was leading Leicester's WVS.' Pre-war, Mrs Bates, was a leading figure in the middle-class women's movement, a Labour Party member and chairman of the National Council of Women. Police Inspector Shelvey admired her: 'Sometimes I was in her good books, sometimes not. But she did an excellent and efficient job throughout the war.'

In February 1939, the organisation's name changed slightly to WVS for Civil Defence, though it generally became known simply as the WVS.

Before the war's outbreak, the WVS helped with billeting evacuees and gasmask fitting.

Once war came, their tasks multiplied. Very often, their work was tiresome and repetitive, such as canteen work, making hundreds of sandwiches or cups of tea, then washing all the crockery afterwards, often late at night.

On Blitz Night, 1,500 bomb evacuees passed through WVS-staffed Rest Centres. One Leicester WVS volunteer, 42-year-old Janet Wates, had just returned from serving food in blitzed Coventry, when her Shirley Road home was bombed, killing her as she slept.

The WVS's roles continued to grow. By the war's end, WVS staffed Information Bureaux, British Restaurants, CD and servicemen's canteens, mobile canteens, including the Queen's Messenger Convoys, post-raid emergency feeding, even organising school meals. Their welfare role was also wide-ranging, from salvage work and National Savings drives, to staffing children's clothing centres.

On April 22, 1942, Lady Reading again visited Leicester, paying tribute to the city's WVS: 'Lady Reading addressed Leicester WVS in De Montfort Hall. The Lord Mayor, Miss Cllr E.R. Frisby, presided. The WVS in Leicester had now a membership of 10,000 and only one person was paid. Many had given their best.'

In July 1942, the basic petrol ration for civilians was abolished. So sufficent cars would be available for official transport duties, the government established the Voluntary Car Pool. It was adminstered by the WVS, in Leicester, under Mr T.P. Blackham and Mrs Tomlinson. In May 1943, the *LM* explained: 'In the yard of the former County Police HQ, in Horsefair Street, half a dozen or so motor cars wait ready to go almost anywhere, provided the journey is of national importance. They are the front line of the Voluntary Car Pool, operated by the County WVS. Those attached to the pool do not just hang around awaiting an emergency. Work is done for Government departments, local authorities, hospitals and Police. The pool also collects the money from British Restaurants. A mileage rate is allowed: the owners pay for petrol, insurance and all running costs.'

WVS woollen armlet, with crimson writing, issued from 1943. [Author]

The WVS realised many women would like to play their part in the WVS but were restricted by other responsibilities. As a result, a p/t form of WVS work was introduced, named the Housewives Service, mainly assisting local ARP wardens and welfare work. In June 1942, the organisation was renamed the Housewives Section. As the air raids diminished, more CD personnel were called up into the armed forces, so, in July 1942, Leicester WVS undertook a course of five lectures, providing concise CD training. The WVS decentralised its organisation to follow more closely the Wardens' Service. In December 1942, the *LM* reported: 'Under a new national scheme, each street is to have its WVS representative. Mrs Dorothy Bates, Leicester's WVS Organiser, said it did not involve recruitment, for they had 7,500 active WVS workers in Leicester, and there were 1,700 streets. Their house would be marked with a card in the window.' Within a year, at least 60% of Leicester's streets had a WVS representative.

By 1944, a Corporation report noted that although Leicester's WVS membership had more than halved due to war work, 'in September 1944, membership stood at 4,312, an annual increase of 500, mainly due to recruitment of Street Representatives as Incident Inquiry Point Officers'. Almost 400 WVS were serving in Leicester's British Restaurants. In summer 1944, over 4,000 evacuee children were attended to by Leicester WVS, and over 2,000 families were dealt with at Clothing Stores. The WVS also collected 458 tons of aid for V-bombed Londoners.

With large numbers of troops serving overseas, there was an increased demand for welfare workers to run clubs for the Expeditionary Forces Institutes. In November 1944, a request was made for WVS volunteers to serve overseas at these clubs. Mrs Dorothy Bates, County Borough Organiser, said: 'The WVS are responsible for all welfare work in such clubs e.g. recreation and library facilities, all of which promote homely, happy surroundings in which the men can spend their leave. The minimum service is 12 months and volunteers must be over 25 years.' A month later, 'Miss Daisy Painter, of 59 Belvoir Drive, Aylestone, is the first member of Leicester WVS to volunteer and be accepted for service abroad. WVS personnel will run clubs under the aegis of NAAFI for overseas troops. Miss Painter is currently in charge of the City Ambulance Service Canteen.' In April 1945, the *LM* announced: 'Two Leicester friends, Miss Betty Aston and Mrs Betty Lester, have volunteered and been accepted for service in India. They are expecting to go abroad after three months' training with Leicester WVS.'

In the 1945 New Year's Honours List, Mrs Ella Noel, of Blaby Hill, head of Leicestershire's WVS since December 1938, was awarded an MBE. Finally, near the war's end, on

April 17, 1945, Lady Reading, national head of the WVS, visited Leicester and, after a tour, paid tribute to Leicester's WVS: 'I am thrilled to be here again to see you all. In the day of her darkest need, you served your country with every ounce of energy. You have done your job, well and truly.'

The WVS's important work was finally recognised in 1966, when the Queen bestowed 'Royal' to their title, making them the WRVS.

Public Assistance Board

15 Rutland Street

The Public Assistance Board was a pre-war Corporation department that provided social service advice and financial benefits. The scale of the PAB's work grew massively during the Blitz. The PAB became a vital support to bombed-out citizens, providing limited financial support, replacing lost ration books, identity cards, furniture etc after an air raid. They also helped rehome those who had lost everything.

Information Bureau

Horsefair Street

The Information Bureau, a pre-war Leicester Corporation public information organisation, publicly disseminated official Corporation ARP advice generated by the Information Committee, in a series of posters and leaflets. In July 1941, Chairman of Leicester's Information Committee Cllr C.R. Keene resigned his position and became Deputy Regional Commissioner, to be replaced by Cllr C.E. Worthington.

Citizens Advice Bureaux

CAB Hon. Secretary: J.E. Quain
CAB, 29 Horsefair Street (before June 1940)
  1 St Nicholas Street

Formed the day after Britain declared war, CAB volunteers provided free helpful advice to the public on wartime matters, from legal advice to post-raid aid. In 1941, the Chairman of the CD Committee, Cllr F.T. Watson, paid tribute, stating 'the CAB had become an integral part of the CD scheme.' The influx of evacuees and war workers greatly increased the CABs work, so from July 1942, the MoH paid half Leicester CAB's expenditure. In February 1943, the Region set up Mobile CAB Squads, which could attend areas following air raids. In 1944, the Corporation stated: 'Whatever happens to the CD Services, it is apparent the CAB must continue.'

Emergency Information

Emergency Information Officer: Kenneth Holmes (Principal, College of Arts)

The Emergency Information department prepared advice in the form of posters, official noticeboards and leaflets for public distribution if regular channels of communication broke down after a heavy raid. As such, it was never really used. Although run by the Corporation, the department was directed by the Regional Information Service.

Benevolent Organisations

Several volunteer benevolent organisations also provided additional help to the CD Services, including the **YMCA, YWCA** and the **Salvation Army**. Both the YWCA and SA operated mobile canteens. Several youth organisations also aided the CD services, notably the **Boy Scouts**, who acted as messengers at the start of the war before the official CD Messenger service had been raised, and **Girl Guides**, who practiced first aid.

CD Comforts Committee

Chairman: Mrs Cllr E. Swainston
CD Comforts Fund shop: 23 Rutland Street (May 1941-November 1942)

In March 1941, the *LEM* claimed Leicester CD Comforts Committee were the first to produce warm clothing for local ARP services: 'Two months ago, the Committee made their initial appeal for knitters to provide woollen garments for the men protecting our city. Leicester was first off the mark in the country. This was largely because Cllr Mrs Swainston got a committee of hard workers together very quickly. The WVS lent them part of their HQ, and the British War Relief Society in America sent wool. In January, 80lb was made into 400 garments. Mrs Swainston announced 2,188 articles had already been distributed.'

By September 1942, the CD Comforts Committee received official appreciation: 'Workers for the Leicester CD Woollen Comforts Fund had the satisfaction of hearing at first hand from NFS Divisional Officer Cramp how the cosy garments they had knitted had been appreciated by the city's fire-fighters while serving in different parts of the country. Mr O.J.B. Cole, Chief Warden, also expressed the appreciation of wardens, who received 4,200 knitted garments through the fund. Nearly 12,000 garments have been knitted for Leicester's CD workers in its 19 months existence. For the present, the fund will close.' The CD Comforts Committee finally vacated their Rutland Street shop on November 19, 1942 – two years to the day since the Blitz Night.

ARP Training

ARP Training Officer: Mr A.S. Turner

It was recognised that the ARP services would only be as efficient as they were trained. Millions of citizens would need to be trained to create an effective force. A pyramid system of instruction was used. In January 1937, several Corporation officials were sent for training at the national Civilian Anti-Gas School at Falfield, Gloucestershire. On return, they passed on their knowledge and by this trickle down effect, ARP personnel were trained.

ARP staff also attended other national training schools. In June 1938, Leicester ARP officials were sent to an ARP School, at 6 Whitehall Gardens, London, SW1. In April 1942, the National MoHS CD Staff College opened at Stoke D'Abernon, Cobham, Surrey.

Local and Regional training schools also opened. In October 1941, it was noted Leicester's Milton Street School Rescue Service Training Centre had temporarily moved to the Friday Street depot. In June 1942, No. 3 Regional Training School for team leaders opened at Chesterfield, Derbyshire. There was another regional training school at Lenton Hurst, Nottingham, for staff officers. CD personnel were also sent on a physical training course at the Grammar School, Louth, Lincolnshire, in August 1943.

Leicester C.D. Inter Depot Competition 1944 Winners Aylestone L.B. Harris' silver award medallion. [Author]

But most CD training was carried out at local level, in the form of lectures, exams, training films and exercises. Proficiency tests were intensive, particularly for first aid staff. As the war continued, to keep CD personnel on their toes, a Regional team competition was introduced.

The MoHS also issued a plethora of ARP and CD training handbooks, manuals, memoranda, pamphlets, circulars, films and slides. Also, unofficial commercially-produced booklets could be purchased. One, *First Aid At the Incident*, was written by Leicester's MOH. Dr E. K. MacDonald, in 1943. The CD Committee purchased 7,010 copies of the manual for £566.11.3 [£17,300] and sold 4,190 copies for £375.9.1 [£11,500], 1,319 remaining unsold.

First Aid At The Incident by Leicester MOH, Dr E.K. MacDonald, published in 1943. [Author]

THE AIR RAID WARNING SYSTEM

The more time civilians had to take cover, the more lives would be saved. In 1939, there were four warning states:

Yellow: A preliminary warning, telephoned to ARP Controls and Report Centres, giving 22 minutes' warning enemy aircraft would be overhead.
Red: The 'action' or 'alert' warning, 'Raiders Approaching/Imminent': a two-minute, fluctuating siren, supposedly giving 12 minutes' warning of the enemy's arrival.
Green: 'Raiders Passed/All Clear': a slightly calmer, single, continuous siren, also lasting two minutes.
White: A message to the ARP organisation indicating all precautions could be relaxed.

For Leicester, RAF Fighter Command warned ARP M/C, who notified Central police station, who controlled the city's sirens. In 1939, there were 16 air raid sirens in Leicester. The most prominent and central siren was on top of Lewis's tower, Humberstone Gate. John Banner recalls 'Its spine-chilling warning could be heard over a wide area.' Two different types of siren were tested on top of Lewis's. One, an elaborate but powerful rotating beam siren, made by Parmeko Ltd, of Percy Road, Aylestone, was first heard on September 14, 1938, audible for up to eight miles. Ray Elgood recalls installing the siren:

'I joined Parmeko Ltd in 1937. Work was being undertaken to design and build a giant air-raid warning siren to cover the bulk of Leicestershire. The design was for a large motor with a shaft at both ends, each carrying a fan of about 3ft in diameter blowing into two horns, also 3ft, and with a bell mouth of 2ft. In the horns were perforated spinning discs to interrupt air flow and produce sound. Each horn produced a different note to generate the warbling effect required. It all then rotated on a base, so it covered a full 360 degrees. The whole lot weighed a ton-and-a-half but split into three pieces. With that, we could have blown the raiders out the sky! This huge construction had to be mounted on top of Lewis's tower. It was impossible to get it inside and there were no hoist points. I was given four ex-sailors, used to knots and spars, to build staging to pull the siren up outside the tower. We had three days to install it and do tests. Many times it nearly fell, but it was up and tested successfully: health and safety – what's that? However, the Ministry said "we've changed our minds and are having dozens of smaller units supplied by Gents Ltd."'

This other siren, a Tangent model, made by Gents of Leicester, was also tested and remained on top of Lewis' for several decades after the war. Gent and Co. Ltd, of Faraday Works, St Saviour's Road, Evington, had been producing electrical products since 1872, specialising in clocks and alarms. Gents developed their Tangent Electro-Motor Syren during the First World War and with this experience, applied in 1938 and won the sole HO grant contract to manufacture air raid sirens. A new block had to be built at the factory to enable the increased manufacture. Gents' sirens provided warning for all parts of Britain, plus Cyprus, Egypt, Gibraltar, Malta and South Africa, and following D-Day, France and Belgium.

The siren was designed by Mr J. George Evatt, of Stoughton Drive North. Born in 1898, he started work at Gents in 1915. Gents' standard siren, often seen in wartime newsreels, was advertised in their May 1939 trade catalogue as a Tangent 4hp, double-ended siren, audible for four miles. Weighing 348lb/158kg, they cost (AC) £50.0.0 [£2,420] and (DC) £70.0.0 [£3,380] each. Gents also produced a number of other warning sirens, from 1/10 to 8hp. By the war's end, 4,500 4hp sirens had been produced, plus 1,000 smaller and 6,000 hand-operated sirens.

When the bombing came, the sirens – or as some called them, 'si-reens' – had the desired effect. The two-minute, fluctuating banshee wail was disturbing enough to make the popu-

Left: *The initial model of air raid siren was tested on the roof of Lewis's, on Humberstone Gate, on September 14, 1938. It was a powerful rotating beam siren, made by Parmeko Ltd, of Percy Road, Aylestone, audible for up to eight miles* [Leicester Mercury].
Right: *A gentleman – in a fetching suit with plus fours and jazzy socks – inspects a Gents' Tangent 4hp double-ended siren on the roof of Lewis's Tower, Humberstone Gate, in September 1938. The wooden structure is a sound reflector to distribute the siren's warning horizontally. In the background is Hannam Court on Charles Street.* [Leicester Mercury]

lation run to shelter – indeed, sometimes too disturbing: on August 28, 1940, one elderly Leicester man collapsed and died during the warning.

After the retreat from France, Britain did its best to re-equip. But many manhours of production were lost by blanket alerts sounded over wide areas, when bombers were either nowhere near or only passing. On July 25, 1940, the green and white warnings were combined and a new purple warning was introduced. This was a night precautionary warning to local authorities and factories on the raiders' predicted course, to extinguish lights but not sound the red alert, until factory roof watchers saw raiders approaching. This meant production could be maximised and continue until the last moment.

However, when the raids started, there numerous complaints that the sirens had only sounded after bombs had fallen. Out of the seven raids on Leicester, in the first two and on Blitz Night, bombs fell before the siren sounded. This led to rumours the sirens were deliberately not being sounded until bombs were falling. But this was not the case. Britain's coastal radar only looked outwards, so once enemy bombers crossed inland, unless they were spotted by the Observer Corps, which was difficult at night, the bombers' movements were practically unknown. This was not secret. As early as August 1940, the authorities warned in the *LM*: 'It is impossible for Fighter Command to know what course enemy raiders may take and where they may drop bombs. There are bound to be some bombings without warnings. Everyone must be prepared, as a civic duty, to take some risk.' Nonetheless, despite the air raid warning system's deficiencies, it saved thousands of lives.

As the war continued and raids diminished, the sirens were heard less. To keep them functional, they were tested the first Monday each month. By 1943, there were 17 sirens around Leicester, 12 large and five small.

On May 2, 1945, the national and industrial alarm system was discontinued. Although Leicester had only been raided seven times, its sirens sounded 223 times:

	Day	Night	Total
1940	14	81	95
1941	22	68	90
1942	2	18	20
1943	0	7	7
1944	0	8	8
1945	0	3	3
Totals:	38	185	223

By February 1947, 13 sirens remained in Leicester. Seven months later, the remaining sirens were sold for scrap to the Universal Motor Repair Co. Ltd for £12.10.0 [£381] each and Lewis's large 25hp siren for £24 [£732].

Following Leicester's Cavendish Road bombing in August 1940, when the sirens had not provided warning, the SRO suggested establishment of **Wardens' Observation Posts** to inform M/C of any unexpected fall of bombs. On September 11, 1940, it was suggested a Wardens' Observation Post be built on the roof of the Municipal Offices in Charles Street, with a telephone link to the M/C below. After the West End bombing on November 15, 1940, this post was abandoned, to be replaced by posts on the Imperial Hotel, Spinney Hills; Mellor Bromleys Ltd, St Saviour's Road and Corah's, St Margaret's Works, manned by factory personnel. By July 1941, this had changed to posts at FB HQ, Lancaster Road; the Imperial Hotel and one on St Margaret's church tower, the first two manned by AFS personnel to 'spot the dropping of flares or first bombs.' By May 1942, however, due to the lack of raids and manpower problems, they were 'manned only on receipt of siren warnings or special instruction from the ROC.' Fortunately, they were never needed again.

EVACUATION

One of the greatest air raid precautions, directly responsible for saving millions of lives, was evacuation. Realising cities would be major targets, plans had been drawn up in 1938 to remove those most vulnerable. Britain was divided into three zones: 'evacuation' or 'danger' zones, mainly larger cities where bombing was expected and evacuation of children and mothers was highly recommended; 'neutral' zones, urban areas such as Leicester, which were under some threat but where children could remain and 'reception areas,' such as rural Leicestershire, where the threat was thought least. With its central inland location and good rail links, officially, Leicestershire was earmarked to receive 30,000 evacuees, mainly from London, Sheffield and Birmingham.

Today, the evacuation is generally believed to have been a mass exodus, leaving the cities childless. However, the scheme was not as widely utilised as imagined, as many parents suffered last minute cold feet. In September 1939, under the official scheme, 8,000 children were billeted in Leicester, with another 9,000 arriving independently: Leicestershire had planned to receive 30,000.

Generally, though not exclusively, children from working-class families took up the government's scheme, to be billeted with strangers, whereas middle and upper classes organised their children's evacuation independently, to stay with friends and relatives. The exact number who arrived independently is not known, but Professor Titmuss states in Leicestershire, the ratio was lower than the official evacuation.

Of more concern, in coming months, due to lack of bombing, homesickness or incompatability, evacuees drifted back to danger areas. By the end of 1939, of 9,865 children billeted in Leicestershire, 4,453 had returned home. But by summer 1940, with the threat of invasion, a second influx of evacuees arrived, many from East Coast towns.

Evacuees weren't just inward bound: in July 1940, 'Nearly a thousand parents attended a meeting in Wyggeston Girls' School. Alderman R. Hallam, chairman of the Education Committee, said over 1,100 parents had completed forms for their children's evacuation to the Dominions. Education office staff had been busy collating the forms, which had been forwarded to the Overseas Reception Board, London.' There were delays due to shipping space: This proved fortunate. On September 18, 1940, evacuation ship SS *City of Benares* was sunk by a U-boat, killing 77 out of 90 child evacuees. Evacuation overseas lost its parental appeal.

Nonetheless, some city children were evacuated abroad. On November 29, 1941, the *LM* reported: 'Leicester parents recorded messages at Birmingham today for broadcast to their children overseas in the BBC's "Hello, Children" broadcast. They were: Mr and Mrs L. East, 84 Romway Road, broadcasting a message to their daughters, Marguerite and Rosemary East, c/o Mr F.E. Parkhurst, 170 North Franklin Street, Wilkes Barre, Pennsylvania, USA and Mr and Mrs A. Seville, 8 Egerton Avenue, whose children, Hilda and Puddy Seville are at 3 Dally Street, Queenscliffe, Sydney, New South Wales, Australia.'

By autumn 1940, evacuees were now no longer fleeing the *possibility* of air raids, but actual bombing. On October 10, 1940, 700 evacuees from London's East End, including Belgian refugees, arrived at De Montfort Hall: 'Though tired after the long journey, they showed splendid courage. They were served with hot-pot, sandwiches and biscuits by a host of willing helpers. An ARP concert party provided a little musical diversion. The guests were then accommodated with mattresses and blankets and slept the night at the receiving centre. Today, they are being billeted in ten city wards.' A week later, it was reported 'Leicester has in seven days received and billeted over 2,000 evacuees, and to date, the number officially received is 7,000. Hundreds more have arrived privately.' Also, in January 1941: 'Leicester Channel Islands Committee, of which Cllr Percy Russell is chairman, arranged a party for children of the Channel Islanders evacuated to Leicester.'

The evacuation experience proved to be mixed. Many generous residents opened their doors, whilst other doors were only opened by the threat of compulsory billeting orders. Some evacuees were welcomed into warm, caring homes, others entered into cold, resentful households. In turn, evacuees also varied: some were polite and grateful, others, opposite. One Leicester resident recalled: 'The evacuees were strange, wild creatures, with a different tongue and were invariably very tough – as we found to our cost.' Either way, the evacuation experience, for evacuees and their hosts, would never be forgotten.

A final, largely forgotten evacuation – as great as the 1939 evacuation, if not greater – occurred in summer 1944, when the Germans launched their V-weapon attacks against London. The *LM* reported:

'Leicester took 30,000 evacuees, 9,200 arriving in 13 organised trainloads. Leicester was already bulging at the seams with war workers and military units. But between July 7 and 16, all evacuees were found homes. The CD welfare organisation had done its homework well. When the evacuees arrived, many had little more than what they stood up in. The first trainload of 800 arrived on July 7. The children were taken to schools, where they were sorted into groups attached to billeting officers and taken from house to house. By July 10, 4,000 children had arrived. On July 12, a trainload arrived two hours late, because of engine trouble, and gave the organisation its biggest test. It was 9.15pm, Central station was full of mothers, babies and toddlers. The welfare officers decided it was too much to pull 800 mothers and kids into rest centres overnight, so welfare people, police, wardens, WVS cut all red tape and by 11pm, found homes for 650. However, Londoners continued to pour in and voluntary billeting began to meet with resistance, so limited compulsory billeting powers were invoked. In the main though, Leicester had opened its warm heart to the people of London.'

On August 18, 1944, 'CD Controller Worthington revealed the city had accommodated more evacuees from the danger area than any other city or town in the country.' On September 2, 1944, Chairman of London County Council, Dr Somerville Hastings, visited Leicester. 'He not only expressed his satisfaction with all that been done for London's evacuees, but also his admiration of the organisation.' Soon after, the *LM* published this letter: 'I can never express in words my gratitude to the men and women of Leicester who have opened their houses to the children. I have three children there, so know what I'm talking about. Although I miss them terribly, they are so care-free, they had almost forgotten what a buzz-bomb was; in fact, the boy said he doesn't want to come home after the war. When I tried to thank people, they only laugh and say they don't need thanking. This is the only way I know how to thank "The City of Kindness" – A. Rickwood.'

By February 1945, the *LM* reported 'Leicester still houses 8,798 evacuees, compared with between 15,000 and 20,000 last summer.' This seemed to be a hardcore of evacuees who, wisely, whilst V-weapon attacks continued, remained in Leicestershire.

While there had been a steady trickle of mothers and children leaving Leicester for some months, the official all-clear for evacuees to return was from the end of May. Special trains were laid on. The first parties assembled for departure from Leicester LMS station on June 4; the last, with 467 children aboard, left on June 20, 1945.

It has been stated 'Leicester housed more evacuees than anywhere else in Britain.' As records are so hazy, it's almost impossible to verify such a statement. However, on October

Tired and digruntled London evacuees fleeing Hitler's V-1 flying bombs arrive at London Road LMS station in July 1944. The woman's face on the right says it all. Leicester provided sanctuary to around 30,000 evacuees. [Leicester Mercury]

13, 1946, during a Royal visit to Leicester, King George VI stated: 'Leicester might well be proud of its citizens. I thank them all for what they did and would like to express my sincere appreciation to the households who welcomed refugees and evacuees. This was a work of practical sympathy.' The Queen added: 'We couldn't have succeeded without you.' Lord Mayor Worthington replied, 'Although we were subjected to attacks of the air forces of Your Majesties' enemies and over 100 of our citizens lost their lives, we were able to welcome refugees and evacuees from severe bombing attacks. Leicester householders opened their doors willingly to facilitate this great work of mercy.'

The Blackout

In January 1938, the ARP Act compelled local authorities to enact initial ARP measures. But by this date, Leicester's ARP preparations were well under way. On January 28, 1938, the Lighting Experiments Committee of the Air Defence Research Council used Leicester for an experimental blackout. Leicester was chosen as it was one of the few cities with a central lighting control and became one of the first big cities to undertake a large-scale blackout. The blackout was the compulsory obscuring of lights to hinder enemy bombing. A car headlamp mask was tested and became the standard HO pattern. On the night of August 6/7, 1938, Leicester held another trial blackout, calling it a 'Home Defence Exercise.'

As an advanced precaution, the blackout was introduced across Britain two nights before Britain declared war. Immediately, there was a noticeable rise in traffic accidents, clearly attributable to the blackout. The weekend following the declaration, the *LM* reported: 'One man was killed and 16 injured in Leicester during the black-out. So dark were the streets and so many people about, there was a state of almost chaos in parts of the city. Saturday night saw the worst scenes. The cinemas and public houses emptied at the same time, adding to the crowds already groping about in the dark. Ambulance bells seemed to be ringing almost continually. People had been knocked down by buses, trams and cars. The fatality was Henry Malpas, age 54, of Loughborough Road, knocked down by a Corporation bus near Checketts Road.'

Sadly, Malpas was to be the first of many blackout fatalities. Although his death made local front page news, blackout fatalities in Leicester would become so common, they eventually just filled a few paragraphs. Individual accidents were reported, but probably for morale, blackout fatality totals never seem to have been published.

On September 11, 1939, 'The first cases against Leicester people for offences under the light restriction regulations were heard at Leicester Police Court. A constable stated a hostile crowd gathered around a brilliantly lighted window at an office at 24 King Street and threatened to smash the window. Also, a 23-year-old shop assistant was fined £1 [£50] for permitting light to be displayed at a shop at 54 Granby Street. Future offenders would be more severely dealt with.' In November, an ARP Section Leader was fined 10s [£25] for an unobscured light at Cort Crescent FAP. A policeman said it 'must have been seen a mile away.'

Criminals took advantage of the darkness. Blackout gangs robbed pedestrians and smash and grab raids occurred in the city centre. In his annual crime report, Leicester's Chief Constable attributed a dramatic increase in crime to the first three months of blackout, with 2,172 reported crimes, as opposed to 1,679 in 1938, including 123 burglaries, opposed to 76 the previous year.

In an attempt to counter the negative attributes of the blackout, Leicester's Lighting Department developed and installed a system of dimmed street lighting, called 'star lighting', announced in February 1940: 'All Leicester's street lamps are to be lighted again. Experiments have been carried out in Rutland Street and Charles Street with the approved mask and 25-watt bulb. In an air raid, these lights would not be switched off. It is considered they would not be visible from the air. They throw a dim light downwards, just sufficient to show the kerb and other objects.'

By May 1940, public consternation had delayed the installation of the starlights, the public worrying over the financial cost and that Leicester would be lit up for the Luftwaffe. However, eventually, 10,000 starlights were installed, lighting half the city's streets.

A corporation official displays a 'starlight' fitting, to be fitted to 10,000 Leicester lampposts, which provided minimal lighting to the city streets during the blackout. [Leicester Mercury]

The black-out was rigorously enforced: 'An ARP Warden was summoned at Leicester Police Court for a black-out infringement at ARP HQ, on Halford Street. Police stated on June 9, 1940, a light from the top storey was seen. The warden was fined £1 [£45]. Chairman Alderman W.E. Wilford told him that at these premises, the best example should have been shown.'

It was not always easy to enforce the black-out: 'A voluntary air raid warden who went to a house to complain about a light in the black-out, was pulled into the house, assaulted and threatened. In Leicester Police Court today, a moulder of Birstall Street, was fined £2 [£90] and £2 7s [£100] costs for permitting the light to show, and £5 [£215], or two months prison, for assaulting Warden William Lillyman. Warden Lillyman said on November 23, 1940 [just three days after Leicester's Blitz Night], he saw a light from a bedroom window in Birstall Street. He shouted "Put that light out." Defendant got Lillyman by the throat, threatened him, then tried to hit his head on the ground.'

By mid-1944, Luftwaffe raids had all but stopped. As a boost to morale, the government announced from September 17, instead of a blackout, there would be a 'dim-out'. CD Controller Worthington said: 'This is the most cheerful war morning since September 1939! I am delighted with the Minister's prompt action in raising the black-out, which has undoubtedly been one of the greatest hardships citizens of Leicester have been called upon to endure. As each winter came, the sense of Stygian gloom became more tiresome.' When the dim-out was introduced, 'between 2,000-3,000 people gathered at the Clock Tower to see the first of Leicester's new lighting. It was a young and joyful crowd. Trams and buses were full to see the memorable event.'

The blackout was finally lifted on April 23, 1945, just two weeks before VE Day.

Gas Masks

The horrors of chemical warfare in the First World War caused lasting fear. As a result, 'ARP started on the footing that we pushed gas down everyone's throats,' recalled Edward Doughty, Leicester anti-gas officer.

As well as instructional booklets, films and lectures, arguably the greatest anti-gas precaution was the supply to every citizen of a respirator or 'gas mask'. By 1939, 38 million gas masks had been distributed to Britons. The most common type was the civilian respirator, but there were also the 'Mickey Mouse' infant respirator, the baby's respirator helmet, a helmet respirator for hospital patients and another for those with head deformities. The ARP services were equipped with specialist civilian duty respirators or the standard military service respirator.

In the event of a gas attack, oilskin-covered wardens would alert the neighbourhood with rattles to warn residents to don their respirators. Fortunately, these rattles would only ever be heard during ARP exercises and then post-war, by City fans at Filbert Street! To signal the attack was over and the gas had dissipated, wardens would toll handbells.

Respirators were first publicly distributed from respirator assembly points, usually schools, during the Munich Crisis of September 1938. The cardboard boxes they were kept in arrived later. More durable respirator containers were commercially-available.

Around 120,000 respirators were issued in Leicester. Although the adult population were adequately supplied with respirators, there was a nationwide delay in the production of baby and infant respirators: 'In the last weekend of October 1939, 4,900 respirators for babies and infants were issued in Leicester. Twenty schools were staffed by wardens for this purpose, and health visitors demonstrated the apparatus. It was estimated over 6,000 respirators would be needed for Leicester's baby population.'

Spare or replacement respirators were stored at depots, where they were also repaired. There were respirator depots at 115 Granby Street and St George's Hall, Colton Street, plus a Regional reserve respirator store at 99 Melton Road.

Gas masks still survive as poignant reminders of the Home Front. They should never be worn, as their filters contain asbestos.

Shelters

Shelters Sub-Committee (1944): Chairman Cllr C.H. Harris, Cllr H. Bowerman, Cllr C.E. Gillot, Cllr F.J. Jackson, Cllr G.H. Round, Cllr F.T. Watson.

Britain's shelter programme was based on the policy of dispersal: the population sheltering in small groups, in numerous shelters. Probablility factored that although a greater number of shelters may be hit, there would be fewer overall casualties than if larger, more vulnerable shelters were hit. As a result, most shelters were small, accommodating from one family up to around 150 shelterers.

Government directions on the subject had been distributed to local authorities since 1936. But the sheer cost and scale of the shelter building plan meant that by the war's outbreak, Leicester's shelter programme was still hurriedly under way. A HO inspector's report, dated October 24, 1939, was damning: 'The one thing which Leicester City was gravely deficient was public shelters. The position is indeed most unsatisfactory. Nothing seems to have been done before the war at all and the result is that they are very likely to get difficulties with materials. I proposed very strongly to the Chairman of the Emergency Committee that they were very much behind other cities and must get on quickly. They seem to have paid far more attention to their school shelters than to public shelters, which was rather curious.' The Council's own figures seem to bear this out:

> '20/10/1939: *Public & Private Shelters weekly return from the City Surveyors Office, Town Hall, Leicester:*
> *Anderson Shelters: Number indented for: 28,137; delivered by railway company: 21,771; delivered to houses: 21,771; erected (estimated): 19,300.*
> *Domestic Surface Shelters: estimated number required: 8,000; applied for approval: 231; sanctioned to date: 17; erection completed: 45; erection in hand: 25.*
> *Communal Shelters: Persons: Public shelters: 2,531; trenches: 4,652; basements: will take 2-3 weeks to reach 3,995 spaces; factories and commercial buildings (available to public between 7pm-7am): 4,127; school shelters (after school hours): 15,000.*'

The Corporation reacted to the criticism. By the end of 1939, 82% of Leicester's public shelters had either been completed or were in the course of construction. By spring 1940, Leicester's estimated population, including evacuees, stood at 265,000. It took until July, before the Corporation reached their target of providing shelter for 15% of the population.

Public Shelters

There were several different types of public shelter: surface, basement, underground and railway arch. After Leicester's Blitz Night, people 'shopped around' for the best public shelters and queued at dusk.

Underground shelters were mainly built on parks, playing fields and wasteland. Gordon Wainwright remembers: 'My parents were directed to the big underground air raid shelters in Lee Street, built of concrete slabs with earth piled on top. There were long seats each side. The walls ran with condensation, making it impossible to lean back against the slabs, and everything was bitterly cold. Later, we went more prepared, with blankets, food and hot drinks.' A woman wrote: 'In the shelter on Charles Street, we were all strangers, but every time a bomb came whistling down, we would huddle together in sheer terror.'

Many **basements** in shops, offices, factories and homes were reinforced with beams and made into shelters. Edith Widdowson was in a shelter in Nugent Street, underneath a shoe factory: 'During the Blitz Night, two little girls, aged about five, had been in the Fosse Cinema, when wardens brought them in. Until 6am, they entertained us with dancing and singing. We never knew their names, but when the all-clear sounded, my husband and another fellow walked and found their mother down a shelter in another part of the city.'

Communal street shelters were erected by contracted local builders in streets where housing density prevented installation of Anderson shelters. A setback occurred in May 1940, when 387 communal shelters needed repair due to sub-standard mortar: 62 needed complete demolition and rebuilding. In July, 128 street shelters were built or being built. Following Leicester's first bombing on August 21, this suddenly increased, with 398 street shelters built/being built in September and 430 in October. This programme continued throughout 1940, including the Blitz, only slowing in 1941 due to shortages. Street shelters were erected on the roadway. This proved convenient for access, but dangerous for road users.

On December 10, 1940, 'motor-cyclist Ronald Smith, 25, of 60 Grange Road, Wigston Fields, was killed when he collided with a surface shelter in Beckingham Road, as he rode to work in the black-out.' The Leicester Coroner recommended City authorities remove the shelter to a side street, saying it was 'a danger where it stood on this important road'. A verdict of accidental death was recorded.

Despite the railways being key targets, as an additional measure, from September 16, 1940, brick baffle walls were built in LNER **railway arches** and seating provided for 450 persons. It was also estimated tunnels under platforms at London Road LMS station could provide shelter for 1,120. Sheila Ayres, née Preston, lived in William Street and recalls that, where St George's Retail Park now is, 'there is a bricked-up arch at the top of William Street. The arches provided sanctuary for me and my family during raids. People would play concerts and have fun. Mother would wrap us in blankets and lay us in wicker baskets to sleep. I was only four and still remember the tension, but also the comfort of neighbours providing warmth and support.'

Nonetheless, despite this hurried work to provide the population with shelter, on November 16, 1940 – just three days before Leicester's Blitz Night – Chief Shelter Warden, C. H. Harris wrote a private report for the CD Emergency Committee. It did not make reassuring reading:

'It is now obvious that shelter accommodation in the City is inadequate, by virtue of the following facts:- a) Large influx of evacuees. b) Anderson shelters are not being used, because of people's preference for congregating in public shelters and because a large number of Andersons are waterlogged. The same applies to brick and concrete domestic shelters. If all factory shelters were volunteered, we should still require to build more shelters to accommodate the population. Trench shelters, to the extent of 80%, are extremely wet. Surface shelters and shop basement shelters are generally in good condition. Basements under houses are, in several cases, flooding badly and unusable. Factory shelters are very satisfactory.

'All shelters should be cleaned out more often and disinfected. More sanitary closets are required. I advise all shelter wardens be instructed to open shelters at dusk, because people are now queuing outside to spend the night in them. In some cases, doors have been forced open. This habit was first attributed to London evacuees, but has been quickly followed by Leicester citizens. The stealing of electric lamps, oil lamps, tools and anything portable is pretty general. It is pretty obvious Leicester Police force cannot cope with this. The shelter wardens organisation is working well, but the men suffer a lot of indignity due to people not recognising their authority, and consequently, we are losing some. We require large numbers of additional surface shelters all over the city. This is substantiated by the gross overcrowding taking place in shelters.'

Public surface shelters developed a bad reputation for vulnerability. However, during Blitz Night, despite over 100 HE bombs falling, no surface shelter collapsed, even when bombs exploded only yards away: at worst, a few suffered cracked walls, but the occupants survived. Unfortunately, the same could not be said of basement shelters, where several were killed. Although solidly built, it may seem surprising large factory basements were converted into public shelters, considering factories were prime targets: as we shall see, two city factories were struck – with public fatalities in their basement shelters.

Not all shelters were new: John O'Gaunt's cellar and that of Leicester Castle's Great Hall were used as refuges.

Interestingly, rather than using the standard shelter street signs, Leicester used a black and yellow diamond-shaped sign, designed by students at Leicester College of Art, who also designed all Leicester's ARP street signs.

In December 1940, the *LM* reported: 'A bigger shelter programme is announced.' Basement shelter exits were also strengthened, with brick and concrete porches erected over emergency exits. But it wasn't just the Corporation's initiative. Also that month, Braunstone Tenants' Association sent a petition to the CD Committee pressing for bomb-proof shelters for the estate. The Association's Executive Committee also pressed for the concreting of Anderson shelters to make them waterproof.

The government were aware of shelter problems and under Lord Horder, a national review was undertaken. On January 17, 1941, the *LM* reported: 'Leicester's shelter system was searchingly inspected by Miss Ellen Wilkinson, Parliamentary Under-Secretary to the MoHS. She has toured the country and is well-informed on these problems. Miss Wilkinson was

Leicester Shelterers and the Shelter *leaflet, issued by the city's ARP Department in 1941. [Author]*

Public shelters in Leicester were indicated by yellow/black diamond-shaped signs, designed by Leicester College of Art. [Author]

received at the Town Hall by Lord Mayor and Lady Mayoress Cllr W.J. and Mrs Cort and ARP Controller Keene. The first visit was to the shelter under Town Hall Square. Miss Wilkinson gave careful study, asking questions on ventilation and condensation. Next, she saw basement shelters at the Cripples' Guild, where a bunk system has been installed. From there, she went to the underground shelter at the corner of Charles Street and Halford Street. This afternoon, Miss Wilkinson inspected Anderson shelters on Braunstone estate. She was loud in her praise for that of Mrs E. Trollope, of Gaddesby Avenue. It is concreted, painted and kept reasonably warm by a candle burning in a flower-pot. Miss Wilkinson told the CD Committee she had been very much impressed by the work the city was doing.'

There had been public demands since before the war for deep shelters, but the government steadfastly refused, officially reasoning they could lead to a troglodyte 'deep-shelter mentality': unofficially, they didn't have the money or want to spend it on expensive deep shelters. Local officials also towed this line, as in January 1941, when it was reported: 'The authorities are now in favour of smaller surface shelters. Leicester's shelter scheme had cost £500,000 [£19.3 million]. Shelter was provided for 230,220 persons. It was estimated those entitled to free family shelters numbered 170,000. Altogether, 166,157, or nearly 98%, had been provided free shelter.'

By late 1941, 37,401 city shelters accommodated 276,865 citizens. This comprised 26,000 Andersons, 6,000 brick pillboxes, 2,000 Morrison shelters and 655 communal surface shelters. Works shelters were made available at night and there were a few deeper shelters, such as that under Lee Circle. In residential areas, shelter space was allocated via 50,000 passes. To ensure shelters were accessible, 4,000 shelter wardens were recruited. In 1942, the re-building or repair of 385 unsatisfactory street shelters and the concreting and drainage of 12,554 Anderson shelters was undertaken.

By 1944, 267,603 – about 95% of Leicester's night population – were accommodated in 36,218 shelters.

By 1942, 50,000 shelter passes were allocated to Leicester residents to enable them to use the city's public shelters. [Roger Miles]

One persistent problem was vandalism and inappropriate use of shelters, as reported in September 1942: 'Wilful damage to air raid shelters in Leicester is costing the ratepayers £10 [£365] to £20 [£730] a week. Mr Tolhurst, Assistant City Solicitor, told Juvenile Court magistrates this during a case in which three boys, two aged 12 and the other nine, admitted damaging the door of Southfields Drive shelter. The damage cost £50 [£1,820]. The parents were ordered to pay 10s [£20] and 10s costs.'

By March 1945, many shelters had been stripped of their fittings by the Corporation to prevent vandalism. People also started to dump rubbish and unofficially use them as public conveniences.

Domestic Shelters

In November 1938, Home Secretary Sir John Anderson commissioned engineers William Paterson and Oscar Kerrison to design a simple but sturdy, cost-effective domestic shelter that could be mass-produced. Once installed under two foot of earth, the corrugated-steel arch **Anderson shelter**, was surprisingly very strong, providing shelter for up to six people. By late September 1939, 20,820 Anderson shelters had been delivered to Leicester, of which 18,000 had been erected. The shelter was provided free to families with an annual income under £250 [£12,000], but up to £12 6s [£600] for higher incomes.

A problem soon encountered was that where there was a high water table, Anderson shelters soon flooded. In April 1940, Leicester ARP Committee's decided to spend £24,000 [£1.02 million] on waterproofing the shelters. By August 1940, 33% of Leicester's Anderson's remained flooded. Some 2,900 had been concreted. The Corporation concreted 200 Andersons per week, but when they reached 4,200 shelters, out of 8,050, work was restricted due to lack of materials and on August 25, 1940, the MoHS ordered no new Anderson shelters be erected. By the Blitz, many Andersons continued to flood, proving cold and inhospitable during winter nights. But, although not proof against a direct hit, Andersons saved many lives from blast and shrapnel, even at close range.

After the war, most Anderson shelters were collected by the Corporation and reused in allotments and gardens as sheds, meaning very few Andersons remain extant. However, in 2012, an amazingly preserved Anderson shelter was discovered in Braunstone, complete with its bunk beds – even two pillows still on them!

The second shelter supplied by the government, was the **Morrison shelter**, named after the second Minister of HS, Herbert Morrison. Made of a reinforced metal box frame, they were intended to withstand a falling house. As they were for use indoors, they were more accessible and warmer than Anderson shelters. Costing £7 [£270] to buy, they were issued free to householders earning less than £350 [£13,500] a year.

Unfortunately, Morrison shelters arrived too late for the Blitz of 1940/41 and were not available until summer 1941. Even then, there were supply delays. On August 19, 1941, the *LM* reported: 'The first consignment of 1,000 Morrison 'table' shelters has arrived in Leicester. These shelters, constructed of steel, are for use on the ground floor of a house, and can accommodate two adults and two children. Moreover, it is possible to use the shelter as a table, and some people have used them for table tennis.'

Two weeks later, 'Approximately 1,800 applications have been made in Leicester for Morrison shelters. It was announced a fortnight ago Leicester was to have an allocation of 1,000, arriving at 200 per week.' When a *LM* reporter inquired at the Town Hall as to whether any had been delivered, the reply was: 'We've not received a complete shelter. We have parts, but it is not possible to start distribution until certain other parts arrive. Each shelter consists of 350 parts and they come from four different firms. The biggest problem is labour. It's hoped people will get neighbours to help erect the shelters. Some strong Boy Scouts have offered their services.' It was not until two months later, on October 15, 1941, that: 'Leicester's first batch of 200 Morrison shelters have been delivered to city homes. We are hoping to get another 200 sent out within the week, but transport is our biggest problem,' a *LM* reporter was told at the Town Hall. 'Among the first to get their Morrison assembled were Mr and Mrs G.H. Greasley, of 11 Norwood Road, who fixed it up in a couple of evenings.' However, due to the metal shortage, on December 7, 1942, the supply of Morrison shelters was discontinued in Leicester.

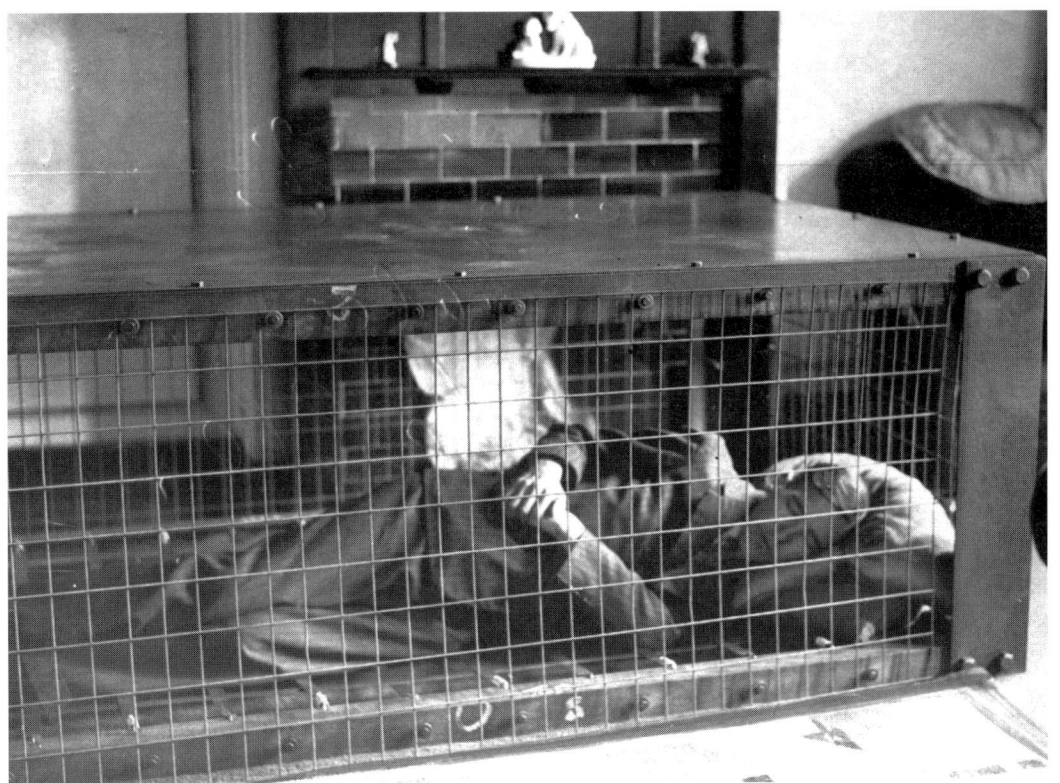

A local publicity photograph showing a Leicester man resting in a new Morrison shelter in his home, in October 1941. [Leicester Mercury]

Local newspapers were also crammed with adverts for building companies offering all types of shelters and ARP materials for sale. For those who could afford them, there was a plethora of different types of **private-purchase garden shelters**, above and below ground. On London Road, there are at least two concrete 'pillbox' type shelters, of a HO-approved design, alongside some of the grander houses. Residents could also apply to the Corporation or pay builders for **domestic surface shelters** in their backyards. These reinforced brick shelters had a thick concrete roof and could accommodate a family. Some survive today.

This domestic surface shelter, in a backyard in Highfields, shows exterior shrapnel damage to its upper side portion, but apart from the wooden door appearing to be blown off, would have protected its occupants. [Via Terence Burford]

School Shelters

Clearly, shelter provision for school children was a priority. Most school shelters were either underground or brick surface shelters, usually in playgrounds or playing fields.

The boys of Mantle Road School, were the first elementary school to build their own shelters, building four, each 43ft long by nine-feet wide and seven-feet high. The brick walls were built by the boys to save adult manpower and were 14-inches thick, on a four-inch bed of concrete, with a reinforced concrete roof nine-inches thick. The pupil builders learned many practical skills. They inscribed their foundation stone: 'A.R.P. Shelter built by the staff and boys, 1939. E Chatwin, headmaster.'

Peter Jackson recalls: 'The shelter at Coleman Road School was constructed from concrete, like an underground bunker. It was just sufficient height for a man to stand up and around 6ft wide. It seemed to be a labyrinth, but that was probably due to the gloominess, as it was sparsely lit. The shelter was L-shaped, with only one entrance. It was dank and smelly, with no heating. During cold nights, condensation ran down the walls. The only attempt at ventilation was a large, manually-cranked paddle-type centrifugal fan, made from plywood. It threw around cold air when any "inmates" operated it. Along the sides were slatted timber benches, where lucky "early" ones would lay their blankets, hoping to get sleep. The rest had to lie or sit on the concrete floor. The shelter was also available for night-time use by local residents.' These shelters were demolished and filled in 2008.

In 2001, a depression in the Humberstone Junior School car park revealed the school's air raid shelter below. Some residents tried to save the shelter for posterity: Sharon Clarke, of Humberstone Community Forum Committee, stated: 'It's a piece of social history.' Unfortunately, the shelter was destroyed.

The pupils of Mantle Road School were the first elementary school to build their own air raid shelters, building four. They even made an inscribed foundation stone, dated 1939. [ROLLR]

Shelter Demolition

With no air raids on Leicestershire since summer 1942, in December 1944, Leicester's new St Margaret's bus station was built on the site of public air raid shelters.

After VE Day in May 1945, workmen removed the blast wall at the entrance to the Municipal Offices, on Charles Street. But this was easy compared to the removal of thousands of air raid shelters. The main delaying factor in demolition was the shortage of labour. Most manpower was still in the services. There was, however, one source of male labour – German POWs and ironically, they were tasked in shelter demolition. Up to November 1945, 42 public surface shelters had been demolished in Leicester. By January 1946, this had risen to 110.

However, in November 1948, coinciding with the resurrection of CD and the growing Cold War, a confidential letter from North Midland Region requested further shelter demolition be discontinued. In March 1950, this became an order – which probably partially explains shelter survival today.

Sadly, often the authorities' answer to our dwindling wartime heritage is instant demolition, even though it is post-war sealing work, rather than the shelters themselves, that have failed. But there does appear to be a spark of hope. In April 2011, the *LM* reported 'an underground shelter network lost for 70 years underneath Braunstone Park and the nearby Grade II-listed hall, has been discovered. Stuart Bailey, of Leicester Civic Society, hopes the tunnels can be restored as part of plans to renovate the hall.'

Uniforms and Insignia of Leicester's ARP/CD

Initially, Leicester's ARP volunteers were simply issued with the national metal 'ARP' badge and a cloth armlet, worn with civilian clothes. Wardens either wore a yellow cloth tie-on armlet, with printed writing, in red capitals, 'AIR RAID WARDEN', with a red border, sometimes called a Birmingham-type armlet. Others were seen with a simpler white cotton armlet, with blue embrioidered capitals, 'AIR RAID WARDEN', believed to be a purely Leicester type. This design was also seen with the wording 'GROUP WARDEN', with a large background outlined letter e.g. 'A', signifying 'A' Division, plus 'CASUALTY INCIDENT OFFICER' and 'DIV RECORDS OFFICER.' Leicester's FAPys wore a simple white cotton tie-on armlet with a red cross.

The Leicester pattern blue embroidered wording on white cotton armlet issued to ARP wardens. This example belonged to warden William Pratt, who was killed at Grove Road on Leicester's Blitz Night. [Andrew Dally]

The 'ARP' uniform badge, of red embroidered writing on bluette material, worn on the left chest. [Author]

Young female ARP wardens parade in Leicester in September 1940. They wear the ARP 42 woman warden's bluette coat with the red ARP cloth badge and the ARP 44 women warden's felt hat. They carry a civilian duty respirator in a white cotton bag slung over their shoulder. There was no standard footwear – as can be seen! [Leicester Mercury]

The silver or white metal 'ARP' badge issued to ARP personnel, designed by sculptor Eric Gill. [Author]

CD Committee records show it was expected that uniforms would not start to be issued until October 1939, costing 11s [£27] each. But by February 1940: 'Leicester's ARP volunteers are to be issued with clothing of uniform type. Part of the cost is borne by the Government, and the actual charge to the rates will be £1,129 [£48,000], the clothing for paid personnel costing £325 [£14,000] and for unpaid workers £804 [£34,000].' This comprised a (ARP 41) bluette boiler suit for male personnel, and for women (ARP 43) driver's coat and (ARP 45) drivers' cap; or (ARP 42) wardens' coat and (ARP 44) wardens' felt hat; FAP staff (ARP 46) nursing overall and FAP nursing cap; or (ARP 47) report centre overalls. This initial order included: 100 (ARP 46) women's overalls for FAPs; 100 nurses' caps and 54 (ARP 47) Report Centre overalls. On March 15, 1940, 864 (ARP 41) bluette overalls for male personnel, costing £453.12.0d [£19,500], arrived.

However, post-Dunkirk, uniform production for the armed services took priority and the supply of ARP uniforms fell, with orders of ARP overalls for p/t volunteers cancelled on July 8, 1940. Not until later in the war, when supplies were more plentiful, did some p/t personnel receive uniforms. Many simply wore their civilian clothes with the official (ARP 54) cotton armlet, issued from July 1940, which carried the words 'CIVIL DEFENCE' with the CD rainbow device, in yellow print. By the Blitz, most f/t ARP services appear to have received uniform.

ARP Uniform Insignia

The official ARP 54 Civil Defence armlet, of yellow print writing on a blue cotton band, issued from July 1940. [Author]

In May 1940, CD Committee records show the first attempt at a system of rank insignia, with the ordering of 900 chevrons for ARP wardens' uniforms.

Interestingly, although Leicester ARP uniforms bore the national red ARP cloth chest badge, no evidence shows they wore standard red area cloth chest titles, identifying 'LEICESTER', as other cities did. This was probably a budgetary constraint and area titles would only come two years later with the arrival of CD uniform. However, a September 1940 photograph shows wardens of Leicester's 'B' Division, wearing white cotton triangle badges on the left arm of their (ARP 41) bluette overalls, with the printed wording: 'W' 'B Division' 'Group ?' 'Sector 41.'

In May 1941, CD Committee records stated: 'For identification during inter-divisional assistance, it has been decided to adopt a system of coloured triangles on the arm of wardens' uniforms.' These cloth triangles were seen on later Leicester CD uniforms, below the shoulder titles. However, as no definitive identifying list has been found and there are only have black and white photographs, it has not been possible to identify which colour triangle each Division wore!

A press photograph, dated March 28, 1942, showing two Leicester CD workers in their new uniform. [Leicester Mercury]

Leicester's ARP services wore helmets with standard initialled identification lettering, e.g. 'W' for Warden, 'R' for Rescue, 'FAP' for First Aid Party etc.

Nationally, in mid-1941, it was announced the ARP services, renamed CD services in September 1941, would be issued with a more durable and warmer military battledress uniform for men and a smart, single-breasted jacket, with skirt or slacks, for women. Again, deliveries of this new uniform were delayed. A press photograph of 'Leicester CD girls in their new uniform' reveals this did not arrive until March 1942.

Following the CD stand down in September 1944, it was announced: 'If they desire, CD volunteers in Leicester may keep their uniforms. Some 9,000 p/t workers are concerned in this decision of the Emergency Committee. It follows the lead given by the MOHS, although the decision was left with local authorities to whom the uniforms belonged. Steel helmet, respirator and eye-shields must be surrendered. The Ministry points out that use could be made for refugee relief in Europe of uniform, particularly greatcoats.'

CD Uniform Insignia

New insignia, comprising golden yellow cotton embroidered on dark blue cloth, was issued with the new CD uniforms, as was a new cloth CD breast badge, surmounted by the Royal crown. Local photographs also show the former ARP cloth badge worn instead on this new uniform as an economy measure.

Leicester CD Committee records show that on July 21, 1941, '800 distinguishing badges for the Rescue service were ordered from Messrs I & I Cash of Coventry, costing £13.6.8

[£515].' This may have been an advance order for the new CD battledress uniform, however, a HO issue of new official shoulder titles, identifying the branch of CD, was also issued from late 1941.

Although photographs occasionally show individual variations, CD regulations were strict about what insignia was to be worn on the new uniform. CD dress regulations forbade former airmen from wearing RAF wings, even though the HG were allowed to. However, Leicester's CD Controller, Cllr Worthington, clearly ignored this, wearing his First World War RFC wings on his chest!

Chest area titles, identifying the local CD authority, had been absent from Leicester's ARP uniforms. But on February 9, 1942, CD Committee records stated 'in accordance with provisions of HSC 189/1941, a local marking will be provided for each new uniform issued, named "Leicester".'

The Post-Raid Services eventually became one of the biggest CD branches. Yet due to clothing restrictions, most members were not entitled to CD uniform. However, at a meeting of Leicester CD Committee on September 16, 1942, it was reported 'regarding the issue of a new type of national badge to Rest Centre volunteers. An initial supply of 600 badges has been requested, which will be issued free, but subject to payment by the volunteer of 1/- [£1.92] in the event of loss. However, issue of the new badge makes no provision for remaining volunteers in the Post-Raid Welfare Services and the adoption of a local badge is recommended. A specimen is submitted, which can be purchased for 1/2d [8p] each.' Initially an order for 800 badges was made, however, about a month later, it was ascertained at least 1,736 badges were needed: 'An amended estimate has been obtained from Messrs. Fattorini Ltd for the larger supplies at the rate of 11d [£1.76] per badge. 3,000 passes for Welfare Service volunteers (including RC personnel) will be required, costing £8.10.0d [£307]. Total cost of badges and passes is £100.3.4d [£3,620].'

From February 1944, CD personnel were entitled to wear red service chevrons on their right sleeve wrist, one for every year of service. There were problems with supply, as highlighted by a letter to the *LM* in July 1944: 'Might I draw attention to the fact that NFS, Messengers, Police and PAMS have received and are wearing their service chevrons, while CD people are still waiting? Many have given their services since CD's inception.'

After the war, stocks of CD equipment remained in store for several years. In August 1947, Leicester CD Committee minutes recorded: 'Messrs A.E. Piggott & Sons scrap merchants paid £15 [£444] to dispose of 10 tons of steel helmets and cloth badges, shoulder flashes, armbands, etc for £2 [£60].'

'Leicester' area title, worn on the CD uniform chest pocket with the 'CD' service badge. [Author]

'The City of Leicester Civil Defence Welfare Services' enamel badge featured the city emblem and writing in brass on a blue background, issued from late 1942 to Leicester's post-raid services. [Author]

Leicester CD Controller Cllr C.E. Worthington, third from right, *wears his new uniform during a parade in 1942. Note, against official CD uniform regulations, he wears his First World War Royal Flying Corps wings on his chest.* [Leicester Mercury]

Leicester's Military Defences Against Air Attack

As most of Leicester's AA defences were located in the county, for a fuller history of these defences, see Beneath Hitler's Highway: Leicestershire Versus Luftwaffe Air Raids, 1939-1945 *by Austin J. Ruddy, forthcoming.*

Heavy Anti-Aircraft

From the start, with the threat greatest in the South, records suggest Leicestershire's anti-aircraft defence cupboard was bare. But even during the Battle of Britain, when Leicester came within Luftwaffe range, the city was left out the equation: Midlands HAA defences were: July 7, 1940: Birmingham 63 guns, Coventry 44, Derby 36, Nottingham 16, Grantham 4, Leicester 0. By the Blitz, Nottingham and Derby GDA had 40 3.7" AA guns, the same level of protection as Manchester, Portsmouth and Coventry. But Leicester still remained without HAA guns.

A few interviewees recall seeing a single AA gun on Victoria Park. It may either have stopped briefly or been a recruitment drive. Another tell-tale sign there were no local HAA defences was that there are no reports of dud AA shells or shrapnel falling on Leicester. This was a common problem – sometimes causing fatalities – in cities with HAA defences.

On Leicester's Blitz Night, eye-witnesses recall: 'You could almost wave at the bomber pilots. There was no ack-ack, so the pilots could come as low as they liked.' Ron Davis, then a schoolboy, wrote: 'I saw a bomber in a searchlight, but there were no guns to fire at it.' This is correct: Leicester had no HAA cover – see The Great Anti-Aircraft Scandal.

Following this scandal, it appears complaints from local officialdom brought results. Six weeks later, 2nd AA Division's 32nd AA Brigade ordered the deployment of HAA guns around Leicester, creating Leicester GDA. By March 1941, Leicester received eight 3.7" mobile HAA guns of 244 and 409 Battery, 78th HAA Regiment. The gun sites were:

March 1941	Renamed August 1941	Location	Map Reference
'A'	H1	Thurnby	SK 645027
'C'	H3	Enderby	SK 552999
'E'	H5	Anstey	SK 563068
'F'	H6	Syston	SK 625103

Leicester's HAA defences saw limited action. By late 1943, due to lack of enemy activity, the sites were only partially-manned and by April 1944, were abandoned, except for the AA Z-Rocket Battery on Victoria Park.

In essence, it is clear Leicester's HAA defences were an after-thought and were not there when they were needed most. Despite the limited number of HAA guns available in 1940, just a handful of HAA guns during Leicester's Blitz Night, may have disrupted the enemy's bombing, preventing the free-range they had over the city. Whether HAA defences would have resulted in fewer citizens killed is a question that can be asked, but not answered.

Again, Derby, Nottingham, Coventry, Birmingham, even Rugby, had barrage balloon defences but no records have been found to suggest Leicester had any such protection. There is a claim in Boynton's book on Victoria Park that a barrage balloon was stationed there. However, no documentary confirmation has been found: indeed, what records there are show the opposite – Balloons in August 1940: Birmingham 168, Coventry 56, Derby 32, Leicester 0. If there was a barrage balloon on Victoria Park, like the HAA gun recalled, it may have been for a limited time or a recruitment exhibit.

'Z' HAA Rocket Battery

From July 1943, by day, servicemen and women (ATS) of the 227 (Mixed) AA Regiment RA, and by night, 101st Battalion Leicestershire Home Guard, manned 'Z1', a 3-inch AA rocket battery on Victoria Park, hence the joint official designation, '227 (101st Leicestershire Home Guard) ('Z') Anti-Aircraft Rocket Battery'.

The battery occupied about a quarter of the main playing field, on the corner nearest Mayfield Road. Nissen huts were situated around the tree-lined edge of the site, with vehicle access via Victoria Park Road. From October 1943, there was also a 40mm Bofors AA gun positioned in the corner nearest the centre of the park, for close defence against low raiders.

The battery became operational on July 22, 1943, with three No.2, Mk.1 Projectors (U2P), which fired two 3-inch unguided AA rockets. In June 1944, the battery's armament was upgraded to new, nine-rocket No.4, Mk.1 Projectors (U9P), making the battery capable of firing 81 rockets in a single salvo. By September 1944, Victoria Park housed 11 rocket projectors.

Leicester's AA rocket site was strangely positioned: its fire was instantly limited by the tall surrounding trees and houses. Leicester Z1 Battery became non-operational from November 1944.

Enemy aircraft were last seen over Leicester in 1942, almost a year and a half before the battery was installed. Although Leicester had 15 siren alerts in 1943 and 1944 as enemy aircraft passed nearby, the battery never fired in anger. Records show that throughout 1944, the battery was Leicester's sole HAA protection.

Home Guard Light Anti-Aircraft

The main LAA weapon of 1940 was the excellent 40mm Bofors gun. However, records reveal that once again, Leicester lost out: as of July 7, 1940, LAA defences were: Derby 12 guns, Nottingham 4, Grantham 2, Leicester 0.

By 1941, several of Leicester's more important factories had light machine-guns mounted against low-flying raiders, manned by works' Home Guards.

As the Luftwaffe lost dominance, they were unable to repeat their mass raids. Nonetheless, they still attempted to maintain their campaign by sending fast, low-flying fighter-bombers against industrial targets. In response, from November 1943, HG LAA units armed with 20mm cannons were formed. In Leicester, 530 'A' (1st North Leicester Battalion) LAA Troop were based at British United Shoe Machinery Co. Ltd, Belgrave Road, then involved in vital war production. Leicester's LAA HG crews had a short service of just five months. As with the HG Z-Rocket Battery on Victoria Park, it appears these LAA defences also never fired in anger.

For a full history of Leicestershire's HG AA Defences, see the author's book: *To The Last Round: The Leicestershire & Rutland Home Guard 1940-1945*.

Searchlights

As Leicestershire was on the bombers' path to the industrial Midlands, from the war's start, searchlights were sited across the county.

Unfortunately, searchlight unit records are sparse: however, we know the main units in Leicestershire were the 58th (Middlesex) and the 38th Searchlight Regiments. Most searchlights were positioned in 'lanes' across the countryside from east to west, to provide constant illumination of enemy aircraft. A handful of searchlights were within the city boundaries.

As Leicestershire had no HAA defences during the 1940 Blitz, searchlights performed an important role tracking enemy bombers, indicating their course and using their beams to dazzle the bomber crews, particularly during bombing runs. Unfortunately, profusions of searchlights helped enemy bombers identify where cities were and there were even accusations that occasionally, searchlights inadvertently aided the enemy when their beams reflected off low clouds and illuminated targets.

Most searchlight sites only had a single Lewis machine-gun for air defence and proved vulnerable to enemy attack. There are several reported incidents on Leicester's Blitz Night of daring Luftwaffe pilots flying down searchlight beams to either strafe or bomb the site.

Mrs Esmeralda Carrick, née Worrall, recalls: 'near the spinney, in Liberty Road, Glenfield, the searchlights were combing the sky. I saw red tracer bullets from the planes as they tried to put out the lights, but thankfully, didn't succeed.' E. Woodcock, may also have witnessed this attack: 'We, in Rotherby Avenue, were on top of our Anderson shelter, watching the flashes and flames lighting the sky, when above us, a German bomber was caught in the searchlights – how we cheered. Then, suddenly a line of lights came from the bomber down the searchlight beam and out it went. We were bundled into the shelter, where we stayed the night.'

Decoy Sites

The RAF's No.80 Wing operated night decoy sites, which mimicked a bombed city and diverted German bombs away from their intended target. The main decoy sites for cities were known as SF, Special Fires or Starfish sites, each manned by 24 crewmen. As with the other HAA defences, these decoys were another delayed response to Leicester's bombing. Starfish-defended cities were numbered chronologically: Leicester was 28, introduced in March 1941, the same date as its HAA sites. Four Starfish sites were located around Leicester, from the north-east to the south, about four miles from the city centre, in the expected direction of bomber attack:

Decoy Area K3: Starfish No. 28: Leicester

Site 28a) Gaulby: (Map ref: SK 694020): Decoy for: 'A certain factory in Leicester.'
Site 28b) Beeby: (Map ref: SK 656076): Decoy for: London Road station and goods yard.
Site 28c) Newton Harcourt: (Map ref: SP 635982): Decoy for: Railway junction at Knighton.
Site 28d) Willoughby Waterleys: (Map ref: SP 577939): Decoy for: Wigston railway junction.

All Leicester's decoys sites were closed by September 1944. No records indicate these decoy sites ever saw action.

Other Defences

The Germans widely-employed smoke generators to mask their cities from Allied bombing but the British used this defence sparsely. In May 1940, 'smoke screens from coal consuming furnaces in Leicester were tested on advice of the HO, but were never put into operation.' Nonetheless, this defence was used in Derby, Nottingham and Coventry.

However, camouflage, comprising painting and netting, was used in Leicester. Important works, such as BUSM, BTH and Lockheed, were liberally painted with camouflage. The Akiens, well-known Belgrave steeplejacks, were employed installing camouflage netting over some of Leicester's larger factories and in 1939, painted large trees on the cooling towers at Leicester Power Station, which were still visible when they were demolished in 1983.

CD Committee minutes also record that 'in September 1941, the City Surveyor reported it was proposed to camouflage:

Would this camouflage have fooled the Luftwaffe? Giant 'trees' were painted on the sides of the cooling towers at Leicester power station. [ROLLR]

a) *The War Memorial at Victoria Park, with 24 nets at 31/- each [£1,500] and 13,000 yards of scrim, at 5/6d per roll of 100 yds [£1,430].*
b) *Municipal Car Park, Bedford Street, by painting the roadway and some adjoining roadways, an area of approx. 8,000 sq. yds, at 6d per sq. yd [£7,720].*
c) *Concrete roads, New Parks Estate, by painting roadway surface, comprising approx. 60,000 sq. yds [£58,000].*

Bomb Disposal

Despite Germany's pre-war use of sophisticated bomb fuzes, astonishingly, practically no preparations were made in Britain for dealing with UXBs. Initially, it was thought the ARP services could just pick up UXBs and stack them up for collection by the military.

Fortunately, albeit at the last moment, Army Royal Engineer Bomb Disposal Sections were formed in May 1940. BD personnel had some of the most intense and stressful experiences of the war. Each RE BD Section composed an officer, who defuzed the bomb, a sergeant, a lance sergeant, four corporals and 14-25 other ranks who dug down to the bomb and removed it after defusal.

Initially, BD equipment was very basic: a spanner, hammer and stethoscope – plus a lot of luck. But as the war developed, BD Sections were better equipped, from the simple Crabtree Discharger, through to BD discharger fluid, which disabled the fuze's condensers, through to the electro-magnet Clock-Stopper and later, Stevens Stopper sugar solution, for use on the No.17 time fuze. Nonetheless, even with this equipment, bombs were highly dangerous, the Germans occasionally planting Zus 40 booby traps beneath fuzes to deliberately target BD officers.

From summer 1940, one RE BD Company was assigned to each of Britain's CD Regions and were similarly numbered: so No. 3 BD Company became responsible for No. 3 (North Midland) CD Region, of which Leicester was part. No. 3 Company was formed on September 1, 1940. Its Commanding Officer was Major John R F McCartney, with its HQ at 293 Mansfield Road, Nottingham. The Company composed of 12 Sections.

No.42 BD Section was the main BD section that disposed of UXBs in Leicester and Leicestershire during the Blitz of 1940/1941, though the exact date of its arrival in 1940 is unknown. Captain R. Shaw RE remained Section Officer until November 17, 1940, when he was replaced by Lieutenant R.C.A. Lee, who disposed most of the UXBs in Leicestershire during the Blitz.

Thirty UXBs were reported following the Leicester's Blitz Night and by November 24, 1940, 15 had been dealt with or exploded spontaneously. It was only on that day, several days after they had been dealing with UXBs, that 'HQ No. 3 BD Coy RE supplied the Section with excavation tools, earth auger, rope ladder, rubber knee boots, a stethoscope and a drum of carbide'! The unit's war diary also records:

> *December 11, 1940:* the Section moved into 1 and 4 Cross Road, Stoneygate. 'Accommodation for men quite good, but no room for transport or stores. CO visited Section and ordered it to return to barracks of Leicestershire Regiment, Brentwood Road.' The Section started work on UXBs in Northamptonshire and Stamford.
>
> *February 5, 1941:* party from the Section commenced cleaning fatigues at Old Hall, Cossington. Two weeks later, the Section started to move stores and equipment into Old Hall. 'Stables being utilised as sleeping quarters, pending such time as house has been properly fitted out.'
>
> *February 19, 1941:* No. 42 BD Section moved from Brentwood Road to new billet at Cossington, owned by Mrs Clair Symonds.

Throughout the first half of 1941, No. 42 BD Section operated in Leicestershire. On June 13, Lt Lee was posted elsewhere, handing over to Lt Ross F. Britain RE. On June 20, Lt Eric Wakeling moved to Cossington, becoming Section Officer. Lt Wakeling's stay was also short, with Lt Gordon M. Jensen RE taking over on July 7.

No. 42 BD Section may have defuzed other UXBs in Leicestershire, but unfortunately records do not always identify which unit defuzed each bomb. However, we do know they defuzed the vast majority of UXBs in Leicestershire.

No. 3 Company's bomb cemetery, where defuzed bombs were stored, was in the marsh area of Leash Fen, Derbyshire.

From August 1944, No. 3 BD Company moved to Withernsea, East Yorkshire, on dangerous beach mine clearance.

Today, it is not known how many UXBs may still be buried in Leicester. 10% of all German bombs failed to explode and there have been suggestions a UXB might still lie in the River Soar, off Upperton Road.

Home Guard Auxiliary BD Squads

Due to the importance of Ministry of Aircraft Production sites, in 1940, as an auxiliary to hard-pressed army BD Units, squads of volunteer workers, named Auxiliary BD Squads, were raised to locate, report and clear sites in preparation for BDUs. The ABDS scheme was extended to all factories with a workforce over 1,000. From September 1942, it was decided all ABDSs would become sub-units of their local Home Guard battalion. Due to Leicester's large industrial base, by November 1943, five ABDS units existed:

Home Guard ABDS Sub-Section:	No.of Men
• British Thomson-Houston Co. Ltd, Melton Road	20
• Jones & Shipman Ltd, East Park Road	18
• Imperial Typewriter Co. Ltd, East Park Road	?
• Partridge, Wilson & Co. Ltd, Evington Valley Road	?
• GPO, Campbell Street	?

By March 1944, all of Leicester's ABDS's were Category B: 'units able to work on bombs and remove some fuzes, but only under RE supervision'. All ABDS units were trained by No. 3 Bomb Disposal Company, RE. It is not believed Leicester's ABDS units ever saw action on their own premises. For a full history of Leicestershire's ABDS, see the author's book *To The Last Round: The Leicestershire & Rutland Home Guard 1940-1945*.

The RAF

From 1936, Britain was divided into RAF Fighter Command Groups. These were further divided into Sectors, each based on an RAF fighter station. In 1940, Leicester lay within No. 12 Group, which stretched from the Wash to the Mersey and from York to Birmingham. No. 12 Group's HQ was at Watnall, Nottinghamshire. More specifically, within No. 12 Group, Leicester was part of the RAF Wittering Sector. There were no RAF fighter or nightfighter bases in Leicestershire, so RAF Wittering, in Cambridgeshire, provided the main aerial defence for Leicester.

The Luftwaffe

Outlawed by the Treaty of Versailles, following the First World War, Germany surreptitiously rebuilt its air force, until, in open defiance, the Luftwaffe was revealed to the world in 1935, under its Commander, Herman Göring. Hitler suddenly had 1,888 aircraft at his call.

An opportunity to blood the Luftwaffe arose after 1936 with the outbreak of the Spanish Civil War, when Hitler's political bedfellow, General Franco, led a coup against the government. The Luftwaffe aided Nationalist forces, most notably in the bombing of Guernica. The world suddenly saw the power and callousness of the Luftwaffe.

By summer 1940, the Luftwaffe bomber force facing Britain was divided amongst three main Air Fleets (Luftflotten), each divided into several Bomber Groups (Kampfgeschwaders or KG) of about 90 bombers, each consisting of three or four operational units (Gruppen) of 30 bombers, further sub-divided into three Squadrons (Staffeln) of 12 bombers.

Air Fleets that operated against Leicestershire included: Luftflotte 2, commanded by Generalfeldmarschall Albert Kesselring in Brussels, operating from airfields in France and Belgium. Its main bomber units were KG2, KG3, and KG53. Luftflotte 3, commanded by General Hugo Sperrle in Paris, operated from airfields in north-west France. Its main bomber units were KG27, KG51, KG54 and KG55, assisted by an operational training unit, LG1.

Between 1939 and 1941, the Luftwaffe employed three main types of bomber, all twin-engined medium aircraft. The most numerous, the Heinkel He 111, was able to carry 2,500kg of bombs, whilst the other main type, the formidable Junkers Ju 88, could carry 2,000kg. The nearly obsolescent Dornier Do 17Z, used in small numbers, could only carry 1,000 kg.

In 1940, the Luftwaffe had the most advanced bomber force in the world, possessing the most advanced tactics, ordnance and electronic navigation equipment. But ultimately, the

Blitz against Britain failed because the Luftwaffe did not have sufficient firepower: they had no viable heavy four-engine bombers capable of delivering a devastating bombing campaign.

Targeting Leicester

Germany had started aerial reconnaissance of Britain in 1936, three years before the war, using German civil aircraft, photographing military and urban centres. Several such spy flights overflew Leicestershire. Just three months before the war's outbreak, a German aircraft photographed Aylestone gasworks on June 8, 1939 – photography which would prove portentous the following year.

Analysing, identifying and annotating these photographs, the Luftwaffe's 5 Abteilung 95th Branch (Foreign Powers Section), compiled target files. Additional information about the targets was freely available from British company trade brochures. During the war years, despite strict censorship avoiding naming bombed factories, large adverts appeared in the local press, such as 'Wadkin Ltd, urgently require women over 31 for highly important work. Apply to Green Lane Works, Green Lane Road, Leicester' – indentifying the factory was on war work!

The 5 Abteilung allocated each target a number, prefixed by GB, for Grossbritannen [Great Britain]. The first part of the number included the particular target group, such as gas works: GB 52, and the second number identified the specific target: so Aylestone gas works was target GB 52 5. Other known Leicester targets included:

Multiple targets in a target area ('zielräume'):
 LMS Station, London Road
 LMS Goods Yard and Warehouse, Leicester
 LMS Sidings, Leicester
 LNER Station and LNER Warehouse, Belgrave Road
 GCR Station, Great Central Street
 Three GCR Warehouses and sidings, Western Boulevard
 West Bridge Station and LMS sidings, Tudor Road

Key Targets ('zielgebiete'):
 GB   50:   John Richardson & Co. chemical works, Evington Valley Road
 GB   51:   John Bull Rubber, Evington Valley Road
 GB   52:   Partridge Wilson & Co. Ltd/Standard Engineering Co. Ltd/Pochin Bros, Evington Valley Road
 GB   53:   Steel and Busks machine factory, Temple Road
 GB 6 55:   Co-op Flour Mill, LMS
 GB 50 9:   Leicester power station
            Wadkins Engineering, Green Lane Road
            Jowers Holland & Co Ltd shoe factory/Dallow, Lambert & Co. Ltd/Bent & Sons hosiery, Green Lane Road/Spalding Street
            J. Timson & Son, Lancaster Street/Green Lane Road
            B B Chemical Co (Bostik) ('factory of unknown type'), Ulverscroft Works, Ulverscroft Road
            Lee Healey & Co rubber works ('Hosiery works'), Marlow Road
            Belgrave gas works
            Leicester University

Smaller targets:
 Belgrave gas works wharfs
 John Rawson & Sons Ltd boot manufacturers, Evington Valley Road
 Cleco Engineering ('Saw Mill'), Hastings Road
 English Bros Timber Merchants ('saw mill'), Welford Road
 Underground reservoir, Coleman Road
 Freemans Common abattoir
 J H Jones & Sons Ltd brewers ('grain mill'), Danvers Road
 Frears biscuit factory, Woodgate

During the war, aerial reconnaissance photography was assigned to specialist Luftwaffe Aufklärer units. On December 15, 1940, a high-flying aircraft took a photograph of Leicester, once again paying attention to the gas works and power station. The aircraft was detected by radar and although RAF fighters were scrambled, it escaped – hence the photo's existence today.

Maps of Britain's cities were also compiled, identifying important features such as railway stations and factories. Today, sometimes erroneously called 'bombing target maps' or 'invasion maps': they were actually military geographical survey maps, that could be used for any purpose – target acquisition included. Basically they were simply copies of pre-war British Ordnance Survey maps overprinted in German. Often the maps were out of date, missing new roads, even whole housing estates.

Leicester was covered by two maps, GB 6 BB 17 f and g, which appear to have been compiled in 1940, with a second edition in January 1942. What is immediately apparent is not only what they identify, but what they don't. Though railway facilities, bridges, even hospitals, are well-marked, only a handful of factories appear, even though Leicester was bustling with works on vital war production. Such glaring omissions, as Corah's giant St Margaret's Works, riverside industries such as Donisthorpe or HTH Peck and others such as Bentley Engineering, on New Bridge Street, never received a single bomb.

This German booklet, published for military use only, in March 1942, by the Department for War Maps and Surveying, identified targets and locations of interest in the North Midlands. [Author]

The Luftwaffe's thin intelligence on Leicester perhaps explains why the city was not bombed more heavily. However, it is also significant, and more than coincidental, that marked target areas did receive bombs.

BOMBING TACTICS

Although the Luftwaffe is now mainly remembered for its night raids, from 1940 until 1942, single bombers made day and night raids on Leicestershire in störangriffe (nuisance raids) or or piratenangriffen (pirate attacks) raids, based on stealth, perhaps the most famous local example being the attempted attack on Leicester gas works in August 1940.

In Luftwaffe night raids, unlike popular pre- and post-war misconceptions, the sky did not suddenly go black with bombers. The raids were organised, methodical and controlled, often drawn out over six hours.

First to arrive, were pathfinder beleuchtergruppen ('firelighter units'), expert crews who either used advanced navigational skills or electronic equipment to arrive at the target. They dropped powerful parachute flares to identify the target area or schwerpunkt ('bombing concentration point'), on to which they poured 'fire-ribbons' of IBs that coalesced into a brandbombfeld ('fire-bomb field') for the following bomber force to drop their HE loads.

Left: *Illustration GB 6 BB 17 66 showed a Luftwaffe aerial view of Leicester power station and gas works – which were targeted, but not hit. [Author]*
Right: *Illustration GB 6 BB 17 55 shows a view of Leicester Co-operative Society's flour mill adjoining the LMS railway – which was targeted and hit. [Author]*

At night, formation flying was impractical. Bombers took off at four-minute intervals, giving a spacing of 10 miles between aircraft, forming a 'crocodile'. The main bomber force crossed the British coast singly, confined to a belt 15 miles wide. This tactic made it difficult for RAF nightfighters to locate the bombers, as there was only one raider per 180 square miles. It also made RAF nightfighters use more fuel and dragged out the raid's duration, made the ARP services work longer, deprived civilians of sleep and disrupted war production, as workers spent longer in shelters.

Once the main HE bombers were over the target area ('zielräum') they remained for as long as possible, circling, identifying and aligning a bombing run to the target. Bombers released bombs every few minutes, to cause maximum disruption and draw out the raid.

On a typical bombing run, the target was sighted through a gyro-stabilised telescope. Low-level attacks required bombs to be dropped manually, creating a greater margin of error, possibly explaining why the August 1940 bombing of Leicester's gas works was so inaccurate.

Although the Luftwaffe often marked key targets ('zielgebiete'), bombing was still not pinpoint accurate, so often several targets were grouped into a target area ('zielräum'), such as an industrial area containing several factories, or a station and sidings, which could be attacked with a stick of bombs. Other factors, such as target obscuration by cloud and smoke, darkness, together with distractions of searchlights, nightfighters, plus crew anxiety, all affected bombing accuracy.

Once aircrew returned to base, they were debriefed by Luftwaffe intelligence officers who compiled bombing reports. Although some of Luftflotte 3's reports have survived, unfortunately those of Luftflotte 2 did not escape the hurried mass destruction of records at the war's end.

Luftwaffe Ordnance

Parachute Flares (Fallschirmleuchtbombe): Used for nocturnal target identification, parachute flares were dropped in 3ft long aluminium cylinders, either singly or in fours. Their fuzes fired five seconds after leaving the bomber, releasing a 10-foot parachute, allowing the flare to slowly sail down, sometimes for up to 10 minutes, with a bright white incandescent light, illuminating large areas. Witnesses testify 'it became like daylight.'

Incendiary Bombs (Brandbomben) (IB): The basic and most common type of IB was the 13-inch 1kg B1E magnesium/thermite bomb, which burnt with a heat sufficient to melt steel. Although volatile, if tackled early, they could be extinguished with a sandbag or stirrup pump. Despite their small size, for every ton dropped, IBs destroyed twice the acreage of HE bombs. In the 1940-41 Blitz, IBs were mainly released in clusters of 36 from 'Molotov Bread Basket' containers. By 1941, a small explosive charge was fitted in 10% of IBs to deter firefighters.

Oil Bombs (Flammenbomben)(OB): Rarely used, mainly due to their ineffectiveness, two types of OB were employed, the 110kg Flamm C 250 and 200kg Flamm C 500. Both contained a thick, black oil mixture, which if properly ignited, burned furiously. Fortunately,

The German B1E 1kg incendiary bomb. It was 13.5 inches long with a simple impact fuze in the nose. It fired on impact, igniting its thermite filling and magnesium body, sending out a large shower of sparks that set fire to its surroundings. [Author]

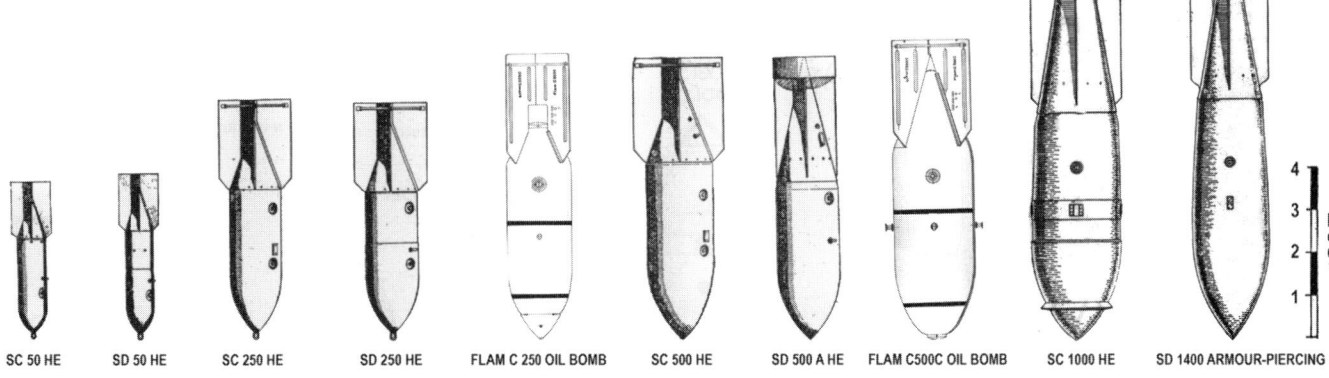

Luftwaffe ordnance known to have been dropped on Leicester 1940-1941. [Ian Franklin]

their igniter mechanism was highly inefficient, often failing to function on landing, the bomb simply breaking apart and disgorging its messy contents.

High Explosive (HE): The Luftwaffe employed two main types of HE:

SC (Sprengbombe-Cylindrisch) bombs were thin-cased, general purpose demolition bombs, with a high charge ratio of up to 55% HE, for maximum blast effect. About 80% of the HE bombs dropped on Britain were of this type. Those known to have been dropped on Leicester included 50kg (most commonly used), 250kg, 500kg and 1,000kg 'Hermann'.

SD (Sprengbombe-Dickwandig) bombs were thick-cased, semi-armour piercing fragmentation bombs, for anti-personnel use or against hardened targets, such as factories. They only had a 35% explosive filling but had greater penetrative qualities. Sizes believed to have fallen on Leicester include 50kg, 250kg, and 500kg.

Ocasionally, PC (Panzer-Cylindrisch) bombs were used. More streamlined, these specialist thick-walled armour-piercing bombs were armed with a slight delay fuze for penetrating large concrete and steel-framed buildings, such as factories. The PC 1400kg 'Fritz' version was used on Leicester.

Occasionally cardboard flutes, called 'Trumpets of Jericho' or 'screamers', were fitted to HE bomb tail units. As the bombs fell, air rushing through these flutes created a screaming whistle, to damage civilian morale.

HE Bomb Fuzes: In the early years of the war, German bomb fuzes were the most advanced in the world. Uniquely, they used an electric current to arm the bomb. The main types of Luftwaffe fuzes included:

Number 15, 25 and 28 fuzes: electrical impact fuzes that could be set for instantaneous operation or a few seconds delay to allow some bomb penetration.

Number 17 fuze: a clockwork long-delay fuze, detonating the bomb between two and 80 hours later. Often fitted with a Zus 40 anti-withdrawal booby trap.

Number 50 fuze: A highly-sensitive anti-handling booby trap fuze, which could detonate the bomb, even if only a pencil was tapped against it. As with the Zus 40, it was designed specifically to kill bomb disposal personnel.

Parachute Mines (Luftminen) (PM): Sometimes mistakenly called 'landmines', PMs were originally designed to be dropped by aircraft against shipping. However, their lack of ground penetration, due to their parachute retardation and shape, combined with their high 70% explosive content, made them ideal blast weapons against urban areas. Two sizes were dropped on Leicester: the smaller, known to the Luftwaffe as Luftmine A (LMA), or to the British, Type D, was 6ft long and weighed 500kg. The larger, known to the Luftwaffe as Luftmine B (LMB), or to the British, Type C, was 9ft long and weighed 1,000kg. Due to their size, they were carried externally, mainly in pairs. Both were dropped on 27ft diameter parachutes. They fell at 40 mph and detonated up to 17 seconds after hitting the ground. Due to their parachutes, they were difficult to aim and were at the mercy of the wind.

Leicester Versus the Luftwaffe War Diary 1939-1945

1939

In 1939, Leicester had a pre-war population of 240,000. Like other industrial cities, Leicester had felt the Depression's bite in the 1930s, yet mainly due to its hosiery industry, the city was still largely prosperous.

On June 8, a high-flying German aircraft flew freely over over Leicester taking reconnaissance photographs, paying particular attention to Aylestone Road gas works and power station.

On August 23, Germany signed a non-aggression pact with Russia. This was taken to signify Germany had avoided war in the east, so was free to fight a war in the west. ARP Control received the HO codeword 'Lowin', putting Leicester's ARP scheme into operation.

Now, a last minute scrabble started to ready for war. On August 25, all Police leave was cancelled and the Police War Reserve called up. Leicester's ARP stores were permanently manned and 50 men were sent to the Erskine Street depot to assemble 1,000 respirators. Workmen dug up Town Hall Square, constructing trench shelters.

On the night of Thursday, August 31, Controller F. Winteringham had an emergency meeting with Leicester ARP Committee. Of great concern was the shortage of ARP volunteers in the city centre. The Lord Mayor made an appeal in the local press for volunteers.

On Friday, September 1, Hitler and Stalin invaded Poland in the first major European clash. War seemed inevitable. The blackout was immediately introduced. The *LM* stated: 'People are asked to keep out the city centre after dusk and church Sunday schools will be closed.'

Lord Mayor Alderman T.J. Gooding warned: 'I wish to impress upon all citizens they will be called upon to give the greatest service to others, forgetting self. We must show the greatest degree of fortitude. God will be with us until victory is assured.'

Clarendon Park FAP received its first casualty that Friday. An elderly man, Charles Morris, of Wigston, collapsed on a bus. The bus driver followed the newly-erected ARP signs to the FAP, but the doctor 'could only pronounce life extinct.'

At 1pm, on Saturday, September 2, the day before war, Leicester's ARP authorities received a telegram from Whitehall instructing that 'as far as ARP work was concerned, they must consider themselves now on a war-footing.' ARP and AFS services were mobilised. Posters were put up instructing what to do in an air raid. A series of national ARP leaflets were posted to households. A booklet produced by Leicester ARP Committee, 'Air Raid Precautions in Leicester – Very Important – Read this and keep it carefully', was distributed to 81,000 householders.

The 16-page Air Raid Precautions in Leicester *booklet, issued by the Leicester ARP Committee to householders at the war's outbreak in 1939. [Author]*

The world held its breath as they waited for Hitler to respond to Britain's ultimatum to withdraw German troops from Poland. On Sunday, September 3, at 11.15am, on a quiet, sunny morning, Britons heard a tired Prime Minister Chamberlain announce on the wireless that, despite a final note to the German government to withdraw their troops, 'no such undertaking has been received and consequently, this country is at war with Germany'.

Paul Billings was at home in Milverton Avenue, digging up his garden to install an Anderson shelter: 'It was awful. My friend listening with me dashed off to be with his family. I think we half expected to see the sky black with bombers.'

Leicester's ARP M/C must have thought 'This is it!' when at 02.48am, on Monday, September 4, they received a yellow warning. Fortunately, it did not develop into a red for another 11 months.

However, the lack of air raids left an anti-climax, and some questioned ARP. At the war's start, Controller Winteringham called up only a fifth of wardens and FA personnel. As it would be nine months till the first bombs fell, this saved a lot of taxpayers' money – though

Winteringham was not to know this. For some years before the war, there had been barracking from various parties against the Corporation's ARP expenditure.

ARP Committee Chairman Keene also received criticism over ARP spending. Alderman W.E. Wilford complained ARP could get out of proportion. Thousands were being paid for work which could be done voluntarily. Keene reminded critics there had been no air raids and they had no means of telling how many personnel were needed.

Nonetheless, a further recruiting drive occurred. The public were beginning to face up to the danger, with 400 new wardens volunteering. By November, 8,000 Leicester men and women had enrolled in the ARP services. Just over a quarter, 2,159, were paid f/t.

But, 80 paid ARP messengers' employment was terminated, saving £14,000 [£680,000] a year. The Emergency Committee also approved the suspension of five FAPs and 440 personnel, saving about £1,200 [£60,000] a week. It was also proposed to cut the 668 FAPy personnel to 360.

Leicester and District Trades Council, on December 19, was told 'Leicester is seething with discontent over the ARP dismissals.' Cllr Keene replied: 'Had it been possible, the Committee would have gladly retained the staff.' Lord Mayor Alderman George Parbury said: 'There has been some criticism of cost, some perhaps justified, much perhaps not. One has to regard this service as insurance. I have no doubt that even one bomb dropped in this city would radically change the opinion of many people on ARP expenditure.'

In Leicester ARP Emergency Committee's annual report, it was stated capital expenditure during 1939-40 was estimated to be £269,000 [£13 million]. £195,000 [£9.5 million] would be refunded by Government, leaving £74,000 [£3.6 million] to be met by the Corporation by a loan. 3½d [50p] would be added to the rates. Despite the complaints of autocratic spending, Cllr Keene and his Committee forced through these much-needed ARP measures.

1940

After mass air raids failed to materialise, the conflict went into stagnation, becoming known as the Phoney War. Some, however, started to take their anxieties out on the ARP, calling them 'army dodgers' and dubbing the AFS the 'darts club': in March 1940, a Leicester AFS unit did not particularly help their cause by posing in the *LM* playing darts!

However, on April 9, the Phoney War became real, when German troops invaded Denmark and Norway. The ARP increased exercises: on April 21, the *LM* reported: 'A squad of police captured the crew of a "German bomber" which made a forced-landing during combined ARP exercises all over the city. Mr Winteringham, Controller, stated the exercises could have been more successful given more volunteers.' Although there were now 1,200 city wardens, more were required, so adverts appeared in the local press.

Suddenly, on May 10, Hitler launched a huge Blitzkrieg on the Western Front, rolling back the Allies. It seemed the war was moving closer to Britain and minds focused against invasion. The immediate response was the formation of the Local Defence Volunteers (later Home Guard) on May 14. In 24 hours, 1,300 volunteered for Leicester's LDV, but in six days, when the ARP Committee appealed for 2,000 ARP volunteers, only 139 came forward. In an invasion, bombing would be stepped up, yet the city's ARP services were not even up to their basic complement. Even worse, some ARP personnel left to join the LDV.

In a bid to boost ARP recruitment, Lord Mayor Parbury appealed to the patriotism of Leicester people. He believed with 'a little direction', Leicester can 'close this wide breach in ARP defences.' The 4,133 shortage included 1,806 wardens, 150 stretcher bearers, 332 women ambulance attendants, 381 ambulance drivers and 800 AFS firemen. By June, 1,000 people volunteered, which ARP Chairman Keene said 'was creditable, but not enough.'

Things didn't get any easier for Leicester's ARP chiefs. In mid-May, with the threat of increased air raids, the Committee distributed a map showing all public shelters in the city centre. However, on June 21, North Midland Command ordered all shelter maps be removed from shop windows, as they could aid the Germans in an invasion.

In June 1940, the Luftwaffe began bombing Britain's coastal towns. But there was a local feeling the Germans were only after London and the south, were too afraid to fly this far inland and Leicestershire didn't have enough targets. It was also said the Luftwaffe would never find Leicester, as the city sat in a valley, over which fog descends at night, hiding it from the air...

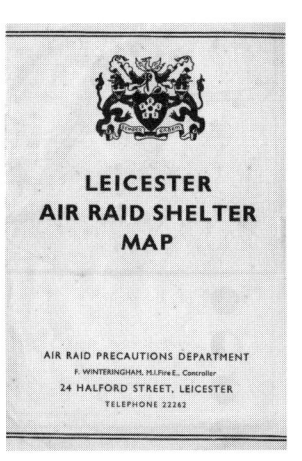

The Leicester Air Raid Shelter Map was distributed across the city from May 1940. [Author]

Leicestershire is attacked

On night of June 18/19, 1940, the Luftwaffe launched its first large scale attacks on inland targets, targeting East Anglian airfields. A week later, Leicester Special Constable George Ingles recalled: 'Busy Leicester, still mainly following its peace-time pursuits, awoke on the moonlit night of June 25, to hear the first eerie wail of the sirens between 12.25am to 03.57am. Though many hurried from their beds to the cold shelters on that Tuesday morning, no bombs were heard, [but] the rumble of hostile aircraft brought the first vivid pangs we were fighting this war on our doorsteps. Many anxious eyes scanned the moonlit sky to see columns of smoke and explosion flashes that seemed to indicate an enemy attack in the direction of Desford.' What they had witnessed were the first German bombs to fall on Leicestershire during the Second World War, causing slight damage and casualties at Dunton Bassett, Ullesthorpe and Lutterworth.

Ingles continued: 'Several times during those next few weeks of summer, the sirens brought that peculiar sensation – rumbling in our stomachs. Yet, that was the only upheaval we suffered, for still no bombs disturbed our ways of life. We began to think, hopefully, Leicester was not on the list of cities to be attacked.'

Leicester's first ARP fatality was reported on July 1, not through enemy action but the blackout. 'A misunderstanding about the use of lights during an air raid cost Raymond Smith (20), an ARP worker, his life. After a preliminary warning, Smith and another ARP worker were cycling to a post without lights, when Smith collided with a car and sustained fatal injuries. It was stated at the inquest, an instruction had been given that no lights should be carried. The Town Clerk said there had been a misunderstanding and all vehicles must carry masked lights. A verdict of accidental death was returned.'

On July 15, the *LM* reported: 'If you were awakened at midnight by your bed rocking and your house vibrating and said to yourself "Hello, Jerry has come" – you were wrong: it was merely a slight earthquake. In Leicester, people dashed to their shelters and ARP workers awakened by the tremor, dressed and hastened to their posts.'

Meanwhile the Battle of Britain was being fought tooth and nail over Southern Britain. Many still think a Luftwaffe Messerschmitt fighter was shot down in Victoria Park. Graham Hall recalls: 'My uncle took us to see a crashed German plane in the park. He had a word with the policeman guarding it and I was lifted into the cockpit. I remember seeing bullet-holes in the side, the aroma of oil and fuel and also the propellers all bent back.'

'The Lord Mayor's Leicester & County Spitfire Fund' numbered enamel pinback badge. [Author]

Roy Bonser explains: 'Lord Beaverbrook, Minister of Aircraft Production, started a campaign where the public could "buy" a Spitfire for the RAF, for £5,000 [£215,000]. Spitfire Funds popped up all over the country. Locally, the initiative appears to have started in Belgrave and on August 13, 1940, Lord Mayor of Leicester, Alderman Parbury, announced the formation of Leicester and County Spitfire Fund. Immediately, two local benefactors, SHB Livingston and David Burrows, owner of British Waste in Saffron Lane, got the fund rolling by each "buying" a Spitfire. The fund's headquarters were at Browett's car dealership, 64 Granby Street.'

A Messerschmitt Bf 109E was erected in Victoria Park. The public were invited to throw change into buckets as they viewed the fighter. Andy Saunders reveals that on August 12, 1940, Unteroffizier Leo Zaunbrecher, of 5/JG52, was shot down over Hastings by Pilot Officer John McClintock in an RAF Hurricane of No. 615 Squadron. His Messerschmitt crash-landed at Selmeston, Sussex. Zaunbrecher suffered a bullet wound. He became a POW and his Messerschmitt became one of the first to go on display around Britain, including at Birmingham, Manchester and Glasgow. The Messerschmitt 'landed' at Victoria Park on August 28, before departing for Leeds on September 8, 1940. Over 50,000 Spitfire Fund badges were sold at sixpence [£1.30] each.

Between August 8 and November 6, 1940, Leicester's Lord Mayor's Spitfire Fund collected £35,343 [£1.51 million]. It was so successful, by its closure in April 1941, it had 'bought' seven Spitfires: the City of Leicester I, II, and III; Brenda: The George Parbury; The Harry Livingston, and St George. Of the seven, only St George fought in the Battle of Britain. All Leicester's Spitfires saw combat and downed further Messerschmitts, bar the George Parbury, which tragically crash-landed at RAF Biggin Hill in June 1941, killing the pilot.

Wednesday, August 21, 1940

The date had no reason to be memorable, yet by the day's end, it would enter into Leicester's long history – for all the wrong reasons.

It was a dull, overcast day. At 10.04am, M/C received Air Raid Message Yellow, indicating raiders could be over the city in 20 minutes.

In Wigston, Duncan Lucas, with 28th Leicester Scouts, spotted a plane flying low over the Star and Garter Inn, towards Leicester: 'We thought it was an RAF Hampden – but then saw crosses on the wings.' Bob Burton, then five, recalls: 'My stepfather and I were walking across Elston Fields, when we saw a large aeroplane with a big black cross on the fuselage. The plane was so low, we could see the pilot in his motorcycle-type helmet.'

Ron Davis, then nine, recalls: 'I was in the garden and heard an aircraft making an unusual sound. The plane came through the cloud about three-quarters of a mile away and flew round in a circle. I thought it was an RAF Hampden in trouble, looking for somewhere to land. The aircraft then went back into the cloud. I could still hear it, when it reappeared, flying in a straight line. I then saw several objects falling from it.' John Chaplin, also nine, was playing on the railway bridge, near Evesham Road. Using a stick, Mr Chaplin recalls: 'I was enjoying myself, pretending to shoot at the plane.' Mr Chaplin was pulled off the bridge by a neighbour who rushed him to his Anderson shelter.

Twelve-year-old Irene Burdett and friend Doris Buswell were walking down New Bridge Street, when they suddenly heard loud engines. They looked up and saw the bomber fly over: 'It started machine-gunning and Doris ran off to the shelter under Bentley's. I was so shocked, I just froze to the spot.'

Mrs P. Wilson was leaving her home on Fayrhurst Road: 'I kept walking, not realising it was a German plane. I remember a little girl pushing a pram and a woman running out of a house to pull her in. I looked up and saw what looked like pieces of silver paper floating down. It all seemed dream-like. A large building, next to the City Arms pub, had been taken over by the AFS. A fireman ran out to grab some children, but he buckled at the knees, as he was so desperate to get the children under shelter. He then fell his full length on the pavement. I ran home.'

Mrs J. Bass was cycling down Aylestone Road, when 'an old man started waving his arms, shouting "Jerry!" I saw a long, thin aircraft flying from Knighton towards Aylestone Road. As we watched, the bombs were released and I was amazed that they didn't fall like a stone, but veered the same direction as the plane was flying, gradually getting lower until out of sight. Then came the explosions. We saw an air raid shelter on Aylestone Road, so ran to it – only to find it locked!'

That evening's *LM* reported: 'A shopkeeper standing in his doorway saw the German raider: "As it came through the clouds, I saw bombs drop from it. I yelled 'Take cover! Lie down!' Some people in the street copied my example and lay down. By doing so we missed the worst of the blast. The plane was on view for only a few seconds. As soon as it released its bombs, it rose into the clouds again."'

In seconds, the bomber fled as quickly as it had come, leaving death and destruction all along **Cavendish Road**. The bombs hit at 10.10am: the moment frozen in time on the bomb-blasted clock in Sturgess' butcher shop.

Mrs Edna Hancox, later Boothby, had popped to the shops with her two children: 'People started screaming and everywhere was chaos and panic. I'm thankful for the lucky escape my children had.'

Rowland Lord was a 16-year-old van-boy collecting laundry from houses in Cavendish Road: 'I saw the black crosses on its side and bombs coming out. I jumped a gate and ran to a nearby house. I was shaking. People were walking about covered in blood.'

The desperate task of rescuing survivors began. Lives hung in the balance. ARP worker Mrs J. Bass, rushed from Aylestone Road: 'People were frantically trying to reach those trapped. Then, the emergency services started to arrive. I went to an ambulance with a badly injured man. Granby Halls FAP had been opened to receive casualties and we delivered our casualty. I never knew what happened to my patient, but often wondered about him.'

The bomber had swooped so low, its eight bombs had fallen close together along a 300yd stretch of the road, east to west:

ARP officials examine the sad remains of 4 Saffron Hill Road, where young mother Ada Machin, 20, was killed when the first HE bomb to fall on Leicester struck her home. Items still stand on the bedroom mantelpiece and the dressing table mirror remains unbroken. The furniture has been blasted out into the street. [Via Terence Burford]

20-year-old Ada Machin, who was killed at her home on 4 Saffron Hill Road. [Beryl Springthorpe]

Incident 1): An HE, probably SC 250kg, fell on 4 Saffron Hill Road, just off Cavendish Road, burying 20-year-old Ada Machin and her two children Sidney, three, and Beryl, two, under rubble. Sidney survived with abrasions, but developed a stutter from shock. Tragically, his mother Ada was dead: the first person to be killed by enemy action in Leicestershire during the Second World War. Beryl also showed no signs of life, so mother and daughter were taken to the ARP mortuary under the Crumbie Stand at the Tigers' ground. Then, things took a macabre turn. As Beryl lay with the fatalities, someone saw her breathing. She was rushed to the LRI where she received treatment for a fractured skull, and was released a month later. The blast also flattened number 8, killing husband and wife, Frederick and Annie Chafer, 52 and 54.

Fate saved several lives that day, as Doris Freer explains: 'Our four-roomed home was demolished. My husband had been on firewatching duty and went to bed, but for some reason, in a different bedroom. He had a rude awakening when the bomb blew away the rear of the house and our bedroom. Afterwards, he managed to slide down the ruins to safety, but his mother, Alice, was badly injured with horrible blast and glass injuries to her face.'

Incident 2): One, possibly two, HEs fell behind two houses, demolishing both. One HE, probably an SC 250kg, caused a crater 30ft x 6ft. The *LM* reported: 'A shopkeeper said:

"When I had recovered from shock, I went into the street but could see nothing for smoke and dust. This cleared and across the road, I saw two houses had been completely demolished. I heard cries from under the bricks. I threw the bricks aside and found a three-year-old boy. With some help, I got him out. He was crying and badly shocked. Then I found another boy, aged 12. I took them to my shop, carrying the smaller boy, who could not walk. I got blankets for them, stopped a passing car and took them to hospital."

Ernest Potterton, then 17, was working at the Leicester Winding Company, on Cavendish Road. He rushed into the street and helped free a boy from the rubble of Deacon's Corner Shop. Another boy was was five-year-old Anthony Smith: 'The blast was so great, it caused our house, number 147, to collapse like a pack of cards. My little sister Irene, aged four, was killed, and mother, Dorothy, aged 32, later died at the LRI. My brother Derek and I survived. I was buried under the rubble, and next day, my sixth birthday, had my right leg amputated below the knee. It was very traumatic, but the nurses were so kind.' Anthony overcame his handicap. Fitted with an artificial leg, later in life, he had a roofing business which, naturally, involved climbing ladders.

Three days after the bombing, a hearse drove Anthony's mother, who had been pregnant, and sister down Cavendish Road. In a moving scene, workmen repairing gas mains in the gutter stopped work and removed their caps as the hearse drove slowly by. The Bishop of Leicester conducted the funeral service of mother and child, plus two other victims at Saffron Hill Cemetery: 'The mourners included a guard of honour, of AFS, ambulance workers, doctors and nurses, the head of the ARP and the Chief Constable. ARP personnel numbered 150. At the graveside, the Bishop said "they gave their lives to the great cause to which the nation was committed, just as much as those who lost their lives in the fighting ranks."' The *LEM* added: 'The woman's husband is a warden, who, at the time of the raid, was on duty elsewhere in the city. Her coffin, covered with wreaths, was borne by six ARP workers, while on the child's coffin were several small sprays of flowers. As the two coffins were lowered into the grave, many women wept.'

In a moving scene, workmen repairing mains in the gutter, stopped work and removed their hats as coffins of Dorothy Smith and her daughter Irene are driven past the bombed remains of 124 Cavendish Road, on August 24, 1940. [Leicester Mercury]

Incident 3): An SC50kg, fell in front of shops, causing a 12ft x 2ft crater and considerable damage.' Brian Bass, then three, was playing near the shops: 'Mam was working in Partridge's butchers at 134, whilst I was riding my bright red and yellow tricycle on the pavement. Next thing, I felt like I was picked up and dropped down a hole, with bricks and paving stones coming on top of me. I felt no pain. Mam said they found me because they saw my arm sticking out the rubble. I can just remember being pulled out – but never saw my tricycle again.' Brian was very lucky: the bomb had exploded just yards from him in the road, rupturing 300yds of gas main. Apart from a broken thumb, Brian escaped the bomb's crushing blast and shards of hot shrapnel.

Incident 4): An SC 50kg HE, partially demolished 124 Cavendish Road, the home of Samuel Reeve, although it's believed no one was injured: 'Crater 14ft diameter. Next door house partially collapsed.'

Incident 5): Another SC 50kg HE fell in the front garden of Storer's Bakery, at 118 Cavendish Road. Eight people in the bakery escaped injury, probably because the garden soil absorbed the blast. 'Crater 14ft x 2ft. Considerable structural damage.' Hazel Jacques recalls: 'My brother Alan was helping Mr Storer the baker. This day, they went a different route on their deliveries or they would have been back at the bakery as the bombs fell.'

Incident 6): Five people, though injured, had a remarkable escape when another SC 50kg HE fell in the road outside 95 Cavendish Road, causing a 12ft crater, demolishing three houses. Butcher Joseph Lord, 52, in his shop at 97, suffered head injuries when his windows were blown in. The *LEM* reported: 'A man said he and other neighbours ran through clouds of dust and flying debris to the butcher's shop, where they heard cries. "We found him pinned under a door and got him out." On the other side was a factory. "Bombs dropped either side of us," said the forewoman. "We ran outside and were able to get an elderly woman from next door. She was quite calm and kept saying, "Wait a minute, I'll help myself."'

A workman repairs mains in the crater left by an SC50kg HE, which fell outside Partridge's butchers, left, *at 134 Cavendish Road. Brian Bass, then three-years-old, had a remarkable escape, riding his tricycle on the pavement when the bomb fell. [Via Terence Burford].*

A dramatic shot showing the crater outside 95 Cavendish Road, made by an SC50kg HE bomb which caused three houses to collapse, injuring five people. Curtains flap above Joseph Lord's butcher's shop. [Via Terence Burford]

Incident 7): It is believed an SC 50kg demolished 73 and 75 Cavendish Road. Ten-year-old Ronald Price's first recollections were of rescuers clearing debris from his eyes and mouth. His home, 75 Cavendish Road, was totally demolished. An elderly neighbour at number 73, widow Sarah Payne, 76, to whom Ronald had just been talking, was killed. Ronald regained consciousness, thinking: 'How did I get here? There was no pain or anything.' Ronald spent months in hospital. As well as head and leg injuries, he suffered amnesia: 'When I got home,

A 50kg HE bomb fell behind homes on Cavendish Road, crushing an Anderson shelter against the back of a house. Fortunately, its owner was not inside it – he was asleep in bed after having been on Home Guard duty overnight. [Via Malc Tovey]

Widow Sarah Payne, 76, was killed, leaving behind her pining dog, Peggy. [Leicester Mercury]

I couldn't remember anybody – but at least I was alive.' Next door, a man who had been on Home Guard duty all night was in bed when the bombs fell. His Anderson shelter was blown 12 feet against the back of his house. The *LM* reported three days later, that whilst the funeral of Mrs Payne was taking place, 'Peggy, a black and tan terrier, her sole companion for many years, was fretting in her new surroundings at the RSPCA kennels. The dog's only injury, a cut over an eye. When the hearse arrived, neighbours, who knew Mrs Payne as 'Auntie', came out into the streets to pay their last respects. They were joined by the ARP men working in the vicinity, some of whom, steel helmets in hands, spontaneously constituted an unofficial guard of honour with the police. Her funeral service was attended by a large congregation, prior to interment at the cemetery.'

Incident 8): The last SC 50kg HE fell at the rear of the Methodist church, at the junction with Richmond Road, damaging the church and making a crater in the yard. One woman, in the stokehold of the church, was blown down and buried beneath cinders, escaping with bruises.

After dropping its bombs, the raider circled and flew back over the railway, apparently firing at a train passing over Knighton Fields Road bridge. It is said bullet holes can still be seen in the bridge's parapet. CD Officer Edward Doughty recalled the bomber's tail disappearing into the clouds over Wigston.

Six people had been killed and 25 injured. An army sergeant, over a mile away, suffered 'neurosis' and was sent to the LRI. Twenty-two properties were either demolished or seriously damaged and 120 needed repairs.

Whilst it would have been little consolation, had the bomb-aimer's aim been true and the gasometers been hit, the death toll could have been far higher. The raid happened so quickly, the sirens only sounded three minutes after the bombs fell and the bomber had fled.

Out of Leicester's 230,000 population, a study revealed 15,484 (only 7%) had taken shelter. Vera Plant remembered: 'When the sirens sounded, I opened the bedroom window and called out to a passing warden passing, "Is it real?" The warden looked up and shouted: "Of course it's bloody real, can't you hear the plane?" My mother and I went to the shelter with neighbours. After a while, the warden looked in on us and said: "What do you think? Some silly bitch just shouted 'Is it real'." Everyone laughed. I felt a right charlie.'

News of the bombing travelled fast. Doris Freer, whose home on Saffron Hill Road had been bombed, was told by her boss at Corah's to 'go home as something had happened'. She rushed to Cavendish Road, only to find soldiers with fixed-bayonets blocking it off. Interestingly, a secret Ministry of Information Home Intelligence report noted: 'In Leicester, the guarding of air-raid damage by troops with fixed bayonets is considered unnecessary and likely to cause resentment.'

Within hours, rumours spread like wildfire. A *LM* reporter noted: 'A rumour quickly spread a German 'plane had crashed near the Gas Works. Six people were killed but in a few hours, this was multiplied four-fold by rumour. I visited this road shortly after. What I shall always remember is the bravery of a mother carrying her bandaged child. She was the fearless spirit of Britain.' Two weeks later, the rumours still spread, so the *LM* wrote an article repudiating them: 'In spite of alarmist rumour, we are able to state the number of fatalities was six.' The casualty list, only posted at the police station for 24 hours, gave rise to the rumour the injured were 'dying like flies.'

Within hours, scientists from the MoHS Intelligence Branch arrived in Leicester. Their once-secret report commented: 'There are no targets of military importance within two miles. Assumed target: Gas works. Bombs dropped from 2,000-3,000ft [sic]. Dive-bombing attack.'

Within three days, Leicester's efficient ARP organisation compiled a more comprehensive report:

10.10hrs: *x8 HE bombs dropped from 400-500ft, 300yds in length. City gasworks 329yds distant.*
10.13hrs: *Air Raid Warning Red.*
10.30hrs: *Air Raid Message White.*
Wardens: *First on scene and reported the dead to DRC at 10.20hrs. Assisted in rescue and FA work. Assisted Police.*
Rescue: *Highway workmen in the district arrived before the sirens sounded and rescued two injured boys. Nine rescue squads arrived at various times. Eight properties demolished, 14 seriously damaged, 78 slightly damaged. Rescue Squads carried on through night and following day. Roads cleared and sewers examined to ascertain damage.*
Police: *Took control immediately and established Incident Post. All houses visited and missing persons checked.*
AFS: *Crews sent from Saffron Lane and stations in Division 1. Gas main fires kept under control. Crews assisted in rescue and FA work.*
Casualty: *Convoys sent from Aylestone Gas, Crusaders' Hall and Granby Halls depots. Casualties taken to Granby Halls, Marriott Road FAPs and LRI.*
Gas: *8" low pressure main fractured and on fire in road. Gas cut off in three hours.*
Electricity: *Supply affected to 23 roads. Restored to all but six roads in three hours.*
Water: *Main burst in road. Repairs completed 17.30hrs.*
Care of homeless: *42 persons provided with tea and biscuits. No billets required.*
Telephones: *57 lines out.*
Housing Department: *120 houses temporarily repaired on day, including 163 windows, 61 roofs. All families in damaged houses visited. Contents of 22 houses removed.*

The dead were taken to Crumbie Stand Mortuary. Granby Halls, Broughton Road and St John's FAP treated around 25 injured.

A few years back, a yellowed file of Dr E.K. MacDonald, Deputy ARP Controller and MOH, was found in a car boot sale in Derby. This remarkable record reveals Leicester's ARP services' first blooding proved to be a baptism of fire.

MacDonald considered that whilst 'the Services performed their duties excellently, there were numerous points to be raised.' The report reveals the Report and Control organisation failed to fully function on its first major test: 'The chief difficulty was the meagre information that came to M/C from Divisional Control,' wrote MacDonald to the Controller Winteringham. 'The bombs dropped at 10.10hrs – I didn't get any information until 10.25hrs and only then from the Police. 'F' DRC only submitted one report, did not give any idea of casualties and didn't say how many parties had been sent. 'B' DRC didn't say if any parties had been sent.'

When they finally functioned, the DRCs seem to have over-reacted, requesting depots 'Send all parties'. This caused congestion at the incident and 'some ambulances had to park 80yds from the casualties, due to traffic/parking problems.'

The All Clear 'came very rapidly' (actually 20 minutes) after the incident and 'the vast majority of ARP personnel didn't report.'

'I have had a rather bitter complaint from Mr Gooseman, head of Rescue Service, that while some of his Highways men were extricating casualties, they were ordered off by the Police. The Police took control well, though it was difficult with sight-seers, but they did not, in my opinion, put up their Incident flags and Incident Post soon enough. I believe it was 17.00hrs.'

'My main criticism of the whole affair is the lack of co-ordination, the lack of one person to take charge of all Services.'

'Casualty Service: The main criticism is that no doctors were available at Granby Halls FAP when casualties arrived and regular doctors didn't turn up until 11.24hrs, long after all casualties had been dealt with.' Long before bleepers or mobile phones, the doctors were engaged on their regular rounds and could not be contacted. 'Owing to the excellent Granby Halls staff, no disadvantage accrued to the casualties. All casualties suffered very severe shock.'

'Rescue: The men worked heroically for very long hours. Rescue Leaders complained their efforts were considerably hampered in the early stages by senior AFS members standing about inspecting damage, although there were no fires. The major criticism made was that demolition work started before a complete search was made for buried persons.'

Thomas Wilkie, Depots Officer, wrote: 'The Rescue lorries attached to Milton Street depot are a constant trouble: both have been repeatedly sent for repairs, and within a day or two, given out when on duty. One lorry gave out on Horsefair Street on siren call. The other lorry was found to be out of order. The first lorry was tried again and left the depot 11 minutes late. At College of Art depot, one Rescue lorry had a flat battery. As a result, we had one Rescue squad unable to function. At Uppingham Road depot, there was a squad of Rescue personnel but no lorry. The volunteers went to the incident in unauthorised cars. Their lorry never arrived, so at 11.07am, Mr H. Payne, master builder, returned in his private car and lashed the Rescue trailer to it, then made his way back to the occurrence.'

'AFS: Too many AFS pumps were sent, but this was not their fault. Despite broken gas mains, there was a considerable amount of smoking on duty and I stopped many and asked the Police to.'

The report also revealed: 'The FA and Rescue Parties report the absence of Iodine, roller bandages and tweezers. These are not supplied with the equipment. Gum-boots were found to be a great handicap: nails and debris pierced the soles and pieces of glass dropped inside, cutting feet, which were also soaking from perspiration. These boots provide no ankle support clambering over debris. A good, heavy, nailed ammunition boot is the solution. Leather gloves are essential for safe-handling of debris: the men's hands were cut and blistered. Neither axes, hammers, chisels or screwdrivers are included in the Rescue kit. The ARP Mobile Canteen wasn't notified early enough and all personnel were charged for everything, causing grumbling. With the dust, copious quantities of tea are required. The Mobile Canteen worked splendidly the whole night.' On August 26, 1940, this report was sent to the Controller.

Since the war, there have been various theories why the raid occurred, the most common being an opportunist attack. Others suggest the crew were testing a new navigation device, even that the pilot had been called a coward and was proving his bravery. But there has been no proof to substantiate these theories.

But, we do know the bomber flew a planned approach to the city, and that it circled the gas works before making an aligned bombing run. That day's German communiqué stated: 'In the course of armed reconnaissance, the Air Force attacked isolated objects of military importance in the Midlands.'

Ramsey states: 'to keep pressure on Britain, the Luftwaffe ordered scattered attacks by one or two aircraft… Poor weather provided ideal cover for frequent scattered raids, which proved difficult for the defences to counter'. Dr Stephen Bungay also explains: 'They ranged all over Britain… in order to show the British they were vulnerable everywhere.'

Gas works were targeted that day, with one bombed by Do17z's at Skegness. They were a major target: if incapacitated, a whole city's domestic supply and, more importantly, industrial war production, could be disrupted. A surviving reconnaissance photograph, interestingly, taken three months before the war by a spyplane, shows the Luftwaffe considered Leicester's gas works a worthy target.

From its defined flightpath and calculated bombing run, together with the surviving reconnaissance photograph, it suggests the raid was not random, but planned.

So, who was this lone raider who brought warfare, death and destruction to Leicester's streets for the first time in 300 years, since the English Civil War in 1645? The aircraft was identified by several witnesses as a Dornier Do17z bomber. This relatively fast, twin-engine aircraft was designed for low-level attack. However, maulings from RAF fighters made it look slow and vulnerable, forcing it to fly low, stealthily and hurriedly leave. Fortunately, its limited range and bombload means that most bombs dropped were the smaller 50kg variety.

On August 21, 1940, unit KG2 was operating Do17z over East Anglia. Based at airfields around Cambrai, north-western France, KG2 were assigned inland targets, including the

The emblem of KG2 'Holzhammer' (mallet). [Wikimedia]

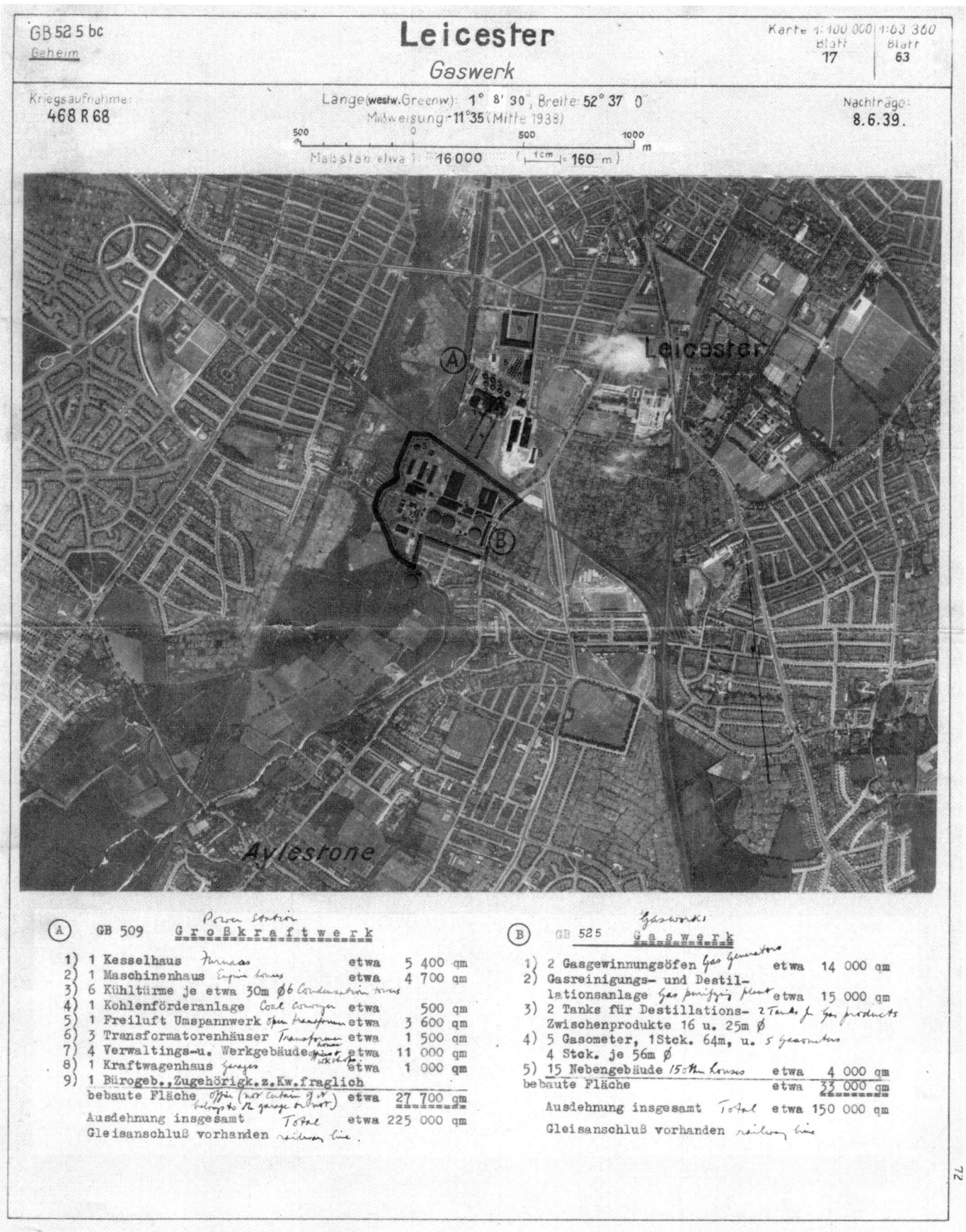

Bomber Command airfield at RAF Wyton, Cambridgeshire, only 10-15 minutes flying time from Leicester. Maybe, taking advantage of the bad weather, one aircraft continued inland. It is most likely that it was a KG2 Dornier that attacked Leicester, but fragmentary Luftwaffe records cannot confirm this.

It has also been suggested two Spitfires appeared sometime later over Leicester – but the

A Luftwaffe reconnaissance target photograph of Leicester gas works, taken on June 8, 1939 – three months before the outbreak of war. [Author]

The view residents of Aylestone Park would have had on the morning of August 21, 1940 – a Dornier Do17z unloads its bombload of 50kg HE bombs. [Via Leicester Mercury*]*

raider had long gone. Ingles wrote, 'Before nightfall, rumour was saying the bomber had been shot down near Skegness.' This type of tale was often spread after raids as a morale booster. But in this case, there might have been a genuine misunderstanding, as several Dorniers were shot down in eastern England, but much later in the day. Most tellingly, an RAF Daily Intelligence Summary stated: 'One hostile aircraft was reported over Leicester and crossed the coast near Cromer. Interception not successful' – suggesting the raider got away.

Ingles added: 'This lone raider had a very sobering effect. We began to realise the fallacy of "there's nothing in Leicester to interest Jerry" had been rudely exploited. ARP took on a far grimmer significance. Now, we suddenly realised WE were fighting this war.' Commander Leonard Lee, in charge of ARP Ambulance services, initially felt the war was unnecessary. 'I saw my first air raid casualties from the Cavendish Road bombing. I went to the scene and the mortuary and saw bodies laid out, some, children. To see these innocent people killed this way altered my attitude immediately.'

The lessons learned from this first air raid blooding would greatly help Leicester's ARP to improve their response for what was to come. Even though the Cavendish Road bombing happened without warning, on a weekday, when most were at work and was over in seconds, it remains the most widely-remembered incident of Leicester's war.

Today, in Cavendish Road, there are still gaps where the bombs fell and although there is still a sign indicating Saffron Hill Road, there are no houses, just a levelled parking area.

With this raid still fresh in people's minds, on August 28, 1940, William Howell, 70, of 11 Dorothy Road, collapsed in the street at the sound of the air raid warning and died.

Saturday, September 14, 1940

Between 8pm and 10pm, one raid of six plus aircraft approached from the North Sea to Cromer. This raid split and sections penetrated to the North Midlands. Ingles recorded: 'Saturday evening was moonlit, but after seven o'clock, a heavy mist spread over the city, yet not thick enough to deter citizens who thronged the streets.'

A preliminary purple warning was received at 8.07pm. At 8.20pm, one plane was seen flying SE over Leicester, changing south. At 8.23pm, flying west to east over the LMS railway, it dropped a shower of IBs and ten 'whistling' 50kg HEs, over six roads, on the north-east edge of Northfields Estate, killing four and injuring five, damaging 28 houses.

The IBs mainly fell on open ground in **Essex Road, St. Ives Road, Huntingdon Road** and **Fairfax Road**. One IB hit a house, 39 **Marston Road**, damaging the roof and ceiling. The occupier, Frank Bassett, extinguished the IB in his garden with a shovel and earth, before the AFS arrived. Another IB hit a bungalow, 12 **Huntingdon Road**, penetrating the roof. The occupants attempted to control the bomb, when the AFS arrived and took over, extinguishing it with a stirrup pump. Elsewhere, when an IB fell through his bungalow roof and lodged in the rafters, as his furniture was being moved to safety, Roland Argyle climbed into the eaves and smothered the bomb with sand.

MoHS scientists believed the 'assumed target' was possibly the brickworks or more likely, the LMS railway. If so, the bomber had released his load a fraction too late.

Bomb 1): Direct hit on party wall between modern two-storey houses, 77 and 79 **Essex Road**, partly demolishing both. Upper floor of both demolished. Remarkably, 10 people in 79 escaped injury, as did two in 77. The *LM* reported: 'Two families were in the house which collapsed like a pack of cards. The families were Mr and Mrs Victor Mills, of 79, and Mr and Mrs Herbert Dick and their son, Robert. The Dicks were in their front room playing cards when the house started to collapse about them. The door was jammed by a collapsed wall and they escaped through the window. At the back, the Mills crouched against the chimney, while the roof and ceiling fell on them. The falling joists rested on the mantelpiece, leaving a hole just large enough for them to escape. They crawled into the garden, shocked, but otherwise unhurt.' A third, empty, house, number 75, had to be demolished. The family were at the cinema and returned to find they had no home.

Bomb 2): Fell between back gardens, leaving a 15ft x 3ft crater. Mrs Goodfellow and her baby were in bed and were injured.

Bomb 3): Fell in a back garden, again leaving a 15ft x 3ft crater. Earth covering and some sheeting removed from empty Anderson shelter. Normally, eight women and children from

12 people had remarkable escapes in 77 and 79 Essex Road when a 50kg HE demolished the upper parts of their homes. [Mike Woolley Via www.wartimeleicestershire.com]

four families would have been in the shelter, whilst the men remained indoors.

Bomb 4): Fell in garden, leaving a 15ft x 1½ft crater, 30ft from back of Sherriff's workshop.

Bomb 5): Direct hit on Messrs Sherriff & Co's works, **Ireton Road**, practically wrecking the garage. HE fell into 4ft deep pit, without striking lorry over the pit, making a 12ft x 1½ft crater. Lorry blown into vertical position but undamaged, except for bent propeller tube.

Bomb 6): The worst incident occurred at 59 **Ireton Road**, the last house in the road, when a direct hit killed four relatives. Louis Ball, 36, and his wife, Irene, 27, of nearby 29 Naseby Road, were visiting the home of Louis' adopted parents, Charles and Emma Pulford, both

A 50kg HE bomb fell through the roof of Messrs Sherriff & Co's garage, on Ireton Road, blowing a lorry into a vertical position. [Via Terence Burford]

The most tragic incident of the night occurred at 59 Ireton Road. Irene, 27 and Louis Ball, 36, were visiting Louis' adoptive parents, Charles and Emma Pulford, both 79, when a direct hit by a 50kg HE killed them all. [Leicester Mercury]

79, as they did on Saturday evenings. They were sitting at a table having supper, when the bomb struck. As the bleak ARP report stated: 'All four dead in immediate proximity to explosion. Two blown to pieces. Recovered at 23.50hrs and taken to Crumbie Stand Mortuary.' Both couples were buried together at Belgrave Cemetery. Directly opposite lived the Pulford's grandson, Ernest and his wife. He found his grandparents' home in ruins and was searching the debris when the ARP services arrived. The Pulfords were the oldest couple to die in the Leicester Blitz. A *LM* reporter reported: 'I saw an ARP Rescue worker retrieve a basket of a dozen unbroken eggs from below a remaining staircase. A neighbour commented "Jerry has left us the eggs."

Bomb 7): Fell in garden. Soft ground camouflet.

Bomb 8): George Morley, of Edgehill Road, recalled he was 'trying to get some interest

An HE bomb struck the pavement in front of 90, 92 and 94 St Ives Road. Toddler 18-month-old Peggy Armer, in the middle house, had a lucky escape. [Mike Woolley Via www.wartimeleicestershire.com]

from my radio. All I got was Lord Haw-Haw's insistent voice, which merged into a military band. Suddenly, there was a whistling noise and a vibration shook the windows and doors. A warden warned us to get under cover, as a German plane was still hovering about.' An HE had fallen on the pavement in **St Ives Road**, leaving a 15ft x 3ft crater, partly demolishing 94, occupied by Mr and Mrs George Barnett and 92, occupied by Mr and Mrs Stephen Armer. The HE tore the roofs off. Mr and Mrs Armer were downstairs in the kitchen, having put their 18-month daughter, Peggy, to bed in her cot in the upstairs front bedroom. The cot filled with bricks, crashed down with the floor into the sitting room. Mr and Mrs Armer, themselves hurt, feverishly removed the debris from the cot and rescued their buried baby. They ran with her into the garden fearing she had been killed. Peggy opened her eyes and, seeing a dog she often played with, began to 'cluck' to it. Peggy was taken to hospital with a slight head injury, and her parents also went for treatment. Mr and Mrs Len Slater, whose adjoining home, number 90, was wrecked, were in the city at the time.

Bombs 9) and 10): In field, leaving craters 10ft x 12ft x 1½ ft.

Alan Boot recalls: 'Boom! "What was that?" Myself and two friends were standing in the street on Thorpewell. There was no air raid siren: if there had been, we wouldn't have been standing outside. A couple of ticks after the boom, there he was – a German bomber, flying south in a hurry. We gave him the double-fingered sign – but not V for Victory!'

The bomber flew south along the LMS, scattering IBs on the railway near **Meadow Gardens**, Saffron Lane. Edward Henfrey remembers 'sitting in our Anderson shelter, as the plane flew over and strafed the railway at the back of our home in Helmsley Road. It sounded like fire crackers.'

The raider continued dropping isolated IBs, with reports from 8.33pm of IBs at Croft Street, **Oadby**; Home Farm, Gartree Road, **Stoughton**; Bassett Street School, Gamble's Farm, Modern School ground, 25 Clifford Street, 50 Clifford Street, **South Wigston**; Peatling Road and Mr Pole's and Mr Page's fields, **Peatling Magna** and Countesthorpe Road, **Peatling Parva**.

Police Inspector Jesse Weston took charge and directed operations in Northfields from an Incident Post until 4am. 'There was no panic,' he stated.' Controller Winteringham reported: 'No red warning was received and consequently, no sirens sounded. In spite of this initial handicap, I am satisfied that no undue delay arose in calling out services.' However, the ARP report recorded it was 10 minutes before the first pump was despatched from Asfordby Street AFS station and 23 minutes before the first Rescue party was dispatched from Uppingham Road depot. Casualties arrived at St Philips FAP at 9.30pm. The all-clear sounded at 9.53pm. The following day, 16 loads of belongings were removed by the Salvage and Removals Service and armed HGs prevented looting.

This attack was part of the Luftwaffe's 'nuisance' raids: with just a few bombs, a single aircraft could disrupt night production and workers' sleep.

Ingles recorded: 'There would be a respite of over eight weeks before Leicester was again subjected to the Luftwaffe's attentions. The sirens sounded many times. Enemy planes roared overhead incessantly. Even though they did not drop any bombs, their presence made the night hideous.'

Sadly, Leicester's ARP suffered another accidental fatality: 'Fred Lock, 44, of Bembridge Close, was fatally injured in a blackout crash while motor-cycling near Kegworth on October 7, 1940, on his way to Derby on ARP despatch duty. At the inquest, Fred Adcock, 32, of Oadby, said he was riding with Lock when he saw the tail light of a stationary motor lorry. He slowed down because he saw another lorry approaching. Lock's machine ran into the back of his, forcing him into the stationary lorry and causing Lock's machine to broadside. Lock was thrown into the path of the passing lorry. Witness was thrown off and afterwards, found Lock, terribly injured. Recording a verdict of accidental death, the Coroner added: 'the public's verdict would be that Lock had given his life in the service of the country.' ARP despatch riders escorted his cortege at the funeral, at St Leonard's church, on October 10.

Friday, November 15, 1940

For the first time since September 7, 1940, London was not attacked. The Luftwaffe realised that strategically, vast resources had been expended bombing the capital for little gain. Midland cities, however, were less defended, more compact targets, with a high proportion of war industry, so Hitler turned his bombers north.

Coventry, only 20 miles from Leicester, had a smaller population, but more arms manufacturing. On this night, under Operation Moonlight Sonata, 449 bombers attacked Coventry. The damage was colossal, with 568 civilians killed. This infamous raid heralded the start of the Luftwaffe's attacks on the provincial cities.

At 9.45pm, Leicester received a Regional Call from **Coventry**. Five AFS cars and pumps, from Dover Street, Church Gate and Great Holme Street sub-stations, plus one regular brigade TL were sent. Six Leicester AFS personnel became casualties. Four days later, five returned, one remained in hospital.

'We were on the flightpath for so many places, like Coventry and Birmingham,' recalls Paul Billings. 'They seemed to circle around Leicester, as if they using the city as a landmark. There were plenty of sleepless nights because we wouldn't get the all-clear until four or five in the morning.' ARP officer Edward Doughty recalled: 'Planes could be seen flying over Leicester towards Coventry like moths in front of the moon. Searchlights would pick them up, then lose them, powerless to stop them.'

Ingles wrote: 'A full moon shed its silvery glow until the streets were lit up like day. The ominous sounds of aircraft never ceased and crimson flashes in the south meant there was a fierce attack some miles away: It was Coventry's sacrifice. As we peered into the crimson sky, the sirens sounded at 9.18pm.'

Previously recorded in published works as two bombers, at 01.35am, a single bomber dropped 17 HEs – fortunately, mostly only 50kg calibre – in a line from Hinckley Road/Fosse Road South to the Cattle Market, killing two and injuring 10. Official reports stated 'small attacks were made on railway communications.' This attack may have been made by a He111 of KG55, who that night made 'scattered raids over the Midlands.'

MoHS scientists recorded: 'Assumed target: Railway, plus electricity and gas works. Bombs in line NW to SE. Medium height.'

Bomb 1): 50kg HE: at junction of **Hinckley Road/Fosse Road**. Blocked by large crater. Broken telephone cables waterpipe. No damage to houses. A man and his wife had a remarkable escape: 'We had been visiting a friend's house and after waiting some time, decided to set for home. We were almost on the crossing, when we heard the scream of a falling bomb. Before I had time to do anything more than duck, there was a blinding flash in front and dirt and stones whistled over us. It was amazing we escaped injury.'

Mrs Ada Coleman, 48, and her daughter, Gertrude, 23, died after 28 and 30 Latimer Street were demolished by a 50kg HE bomb. [ROLLR]

Bomb 2): 50kg HE: At rear of two houses: two people trapped in 40 **Luther Street**. Fifteen houses damaged. Crater: 12ft diameter.

Bomb 3): HE at 27 **Tyndale Road**.

Bomb 4): 50kg HE: Demolished 28 and 30 **Latimer Street**, trapping Ada Coleman, 48, and daughter Gertrude, 23, under debris at number 30. Both died next day at LRI and are buried together at Gilroes Cemetery. Next door, at 32, Mr and Mrs S.J. Wagstaffe, their six-year-old son John, and an elderly couple, Mr and Mrs Bent, had a remarkable escape when half their house collapsed. Mrs Wagstaffe said: 'I was upstairs trying to sleep, when the house fell about my ears. I picked up John. How I found him in the dark, I don't know. There was a strong smell of gas. I rolled down the stairs and staggered out into the street. Mrs Bent, 70, who is blind, behaved wonderfully.' Mrs Stella Bacon and her son, Ronald, were in a downstairs room and were flung several yards. 'We managed to scramble out with a shaking,' Ronald said.

Bomb 5): 50kg HE: fell in the garden of 60 **Ridley Street**, demolishing two outhouses and leaving a 15ft x 2ft crater. Unoccupied domestic surface shelter severely cracked. Mrs Sarah Ann Barratt, 81, was buried in bed by her ceiling brought down by the bomb.

Bomb 6): 50kg HE: On garage of Squires Bakery, in **Briton Street**. Roof blown out. Six of eight delivery vans wrecked. Next door, Mr and Mrs A. Stanion and their two children, plus two other adults, were trapped by debris.

Bomb 7): HE on **Roman Street/Western Road**.

Bomb 8): 50kg HE demolished corner of small house at **Western Road/Briton Street** junction. Large crater. No casualties.

Bomb 9): 50kg HE on Burton's factory, corner of **Gaul Street/Western Road**.

Bombs 10 and 11): 50kg HEs on open ground and gardens across the railway from **Upperton Road**.

Bombs 12): 50kg HE on main stand at **Leicester City Football Ground, Filbert Street**, severely damaging the Double-Decker Stand, kitchens, toilets, gymnasium and boardroom, causing £15,000 [£675,000] damage. Woodwork and seating absorbed much of the blast, housing nearby practically escaped undamaged. Glass ground almost to powder by explosion. The playing pitch, apart from being littered with broken woodwork, was undamaged.

Bomb 13): 50kg HE exploded on pavement in **Filbert Street**, near the football ground, smashing only one window of house opposite.

Bomb 14-15): Two 50kg HE fell on **County Cricket Ground, Grace Road**, damaging a stand. Irene Burdett was in a shelter under Bentley's Engineering, New Bridge Street: 'We could hear the bombs getting closer and one dropped on the cricket ground. It shook a couple of chaps lying on the benches onto the floor! Later, a couple of men from Bentley's came down into the shelter wearing big work gloves, holding a piece of the bomb for us to see.'

Bomb 16): HE on open ground.

Bomb 17): HE caused big crater in **Cattle Market** pens.

A 50kg HE caused £15,000 damage to the facilities at Leicester City's football ground, on Filbert Street. Here are the burnt out changing rooms. [Leicester Mercury]

The 10 injured arrived at Granby Halls FAP at 02.07am and the all-clear sounded at 05.59am. The *LM* reported: 'Considering the noise and the number of bombs, the damage and the casualties are not what might have been feared.'

On the evening of November 17, a request came 'Send one mobile canteen to **Coventry**'. WVS archives record: 'On November 18, at 5am, the Mobile Canteen went stocked with 200 loaves, 1 cwt sugar, 62 lbs ton, milk, margarine, tinned meat, biscuits, cigarettes, etc., carrying 2 milk churns to be filled with water before entering Coventry. Four WVS and two men went. They returned that night, leaving the canteen. On Tuesday, four more WVS went, returning at night. Mrs Burnaby has been with mobile canteen at Coventry all day with Miss Minchin.'

Three days after the Coventry raid, the *LM* reported: 'The Lord Mayor W.J. Cort today opened a fund to relieve distress in Coventry. At a special meeting of the Parliamentary and General Purposes Committee, members subscribed £300 [£13,500]. A deputation were sent to the Lord Mayor of Coventry with the cheque.' They did not know that next day, their attention would be cruelly wrenched back to Leicester…

Tuesday, November 19/ Wednesday, November 20, 1940: Leicester's 'Blitz Night'

That evening, there was little cloud and good visibility. There was also a 'bomber's moon'. Birmingham was the Luftwaffe's main target, under 'Operation Regenschirm' ('Umbrella' – a jibe towards former Prime Minister Chamberlain, the Birmingham MP famous for carrying an umbrella). The attack would see the largest number of sorties flown in one night so far, on a scale as against Coventry. Some 356 bombers, led by KGr100's pathfinders, attacked Birmingham, dropping 403 tonnes of HE and over 29,000 IB, killing 545 and seriously injuring 632. Meanwhile, 47 other bombers attacked 'alternative targets.'

Major W. Blackburn, 32nd AA Brigade Intelligence Officer, realised something else was coming: 'From 19.05hrs-22.48hrs, numerous e/a entered Sector from south, south-east and east, flying irregular courses. Major attack commenced, shortly joined by e/a from the Wash. All raids converging on LEICESTER.'

The yellow warning was received by M/C at 6.49pm, with the purple warning soon after at 7.01pm. Just after 7.30pm, enemy aircraft were reported approaching the city. At 7.41pm, Church Gate AFS sub-station reported: 'Flares over city'.

Pathfinder aircraft accurately dropped parachute flares over Leicester city centre to illuminate the target area. Eye-witnesses state the flares 'turned night into day', as Arthur E. Gardner recalls: 'I was on duty at the Central Lending Library, in Belvoir Street. It was nearly closing. Business was quiet – until a borrower rushed in, announcing startling news that enemy flares were lighting up the city centre. From Market Street, we could see the brilliant glare, from a multitude of magnesium flares. Like clusters of giant chandeliers, they hung in the sky above the town. Slowly, so slowly, they drifted down. Not one of us knew the grim reaper had commenced his back swing, that before morning, death and destruction would be rampant in our city.'

Some didn't get it at first. Mrs G. Bracey, then 12, was walking to her sister's house in Gartree Street: 'I thought they were fireworks. I stood for several minutes watching them.' William Smith, also 12, was playing in Osborne Road with his pals: 'We heard the droning of an aircraft and knew it was German by its sound. It dropped a flare and we saw the swastika on its tail. My brother-in-law came racing, shouting "Get off home to your shelters!"'

Robert Bloomfield, then seven, recalls: 'We rented a house next to Slater Street School, Frog Island. When the sirens were sounded, mother covered me in an eiderdown and took me to the shelter in the schoolyard. When she opened our front door, Leicester was lit up like daytime. I looked up and saw the outline of German bombers, from which came showers of parachutes flares. They made a hissing sound as they hit the canal.'

Marjorie Bishop was an usherette at the Gaumont Cinema, in Market Place. A film called *South of Pago Pago* was being screened to a packed house. Long queues outside the cinema quickly dispersed when flares started descending. Mr Caunt, the manager, asked the audience to leave. John Bamkin was watching the film: 'Although we were informed there was an air raid warning, as this happened nightly, it was disregarded. Afterwards, we came out the foyer into the Market Place, to find the whole place lit up.'

Eileen Wilcox, then 10, remembers: 'We lived at 13, Queen Street. Mother was standing on the doorstep, watching the lights in the sky. A man passing by said: "It's going to be a bad night, me-duck."'

About five minutes later, at 7.45pm, the first wave of incendiary bombers struck. Published histories suggest the firebomb spread was quite broad. However, ARP and FB records reveal initially, the concentration point was from London Road station to Welford Road, spreading to the eastern side of the city centre, before radiating out as far as Aylestone Road gasworks, Stoneygate, even Evington, leaving a general spread south-west to north-east.

Cedric Ashton recalls: 'As we reached London Road LMS station, an incendiary stuck in the booking hall dome, shooting down a shower of sparks. On platform three, we were led to the cellars under the refreshment rooms. They were very dirty, with a sump running the length and a few planks bridging the gap. There we stayed, listening to bombs dropping, but never quite reaching us.'

Doreen Russell, née Palmer, lived in the Campbell Street Railway Hotel: 'My brother Ray, a Royal Marine, was home on leave. An incendiary dropped on the railway horses stabled next door to us. Mother tried to put the fire out with a stirrup pump, whilst Ray managed to get the horses out. The Luftwaffe heavily targeted the railway, but we only lost a window.'

At 7.46pm, the first buildings struck by IBs were the churches of St John the Divine, in South Albion Street and Holy Cross, in New Walk. At M/C, ironically, an ARP exercise was in progress. Minutes later, it became the real thing: between 7.48pm and 8.08pm, M/C received reports of 24 fires.

Charles Murray, then eight, lived on Regent Road: 'The siren on Lewis's sounded, so we went down our cellar. It was musty and cold. We listened to the drone of planes overhead and explosions in the distance and people shouting. We peered out the cellar doors and saw wardens with long-handled shovels and buckets of sand tackling incendiaries, fizzing like giant fireworks fallen harmlessly in gardens. More had fallen on the recreation ground (now Nelson Mandela Park) missing the houses. Later, when we explored the "Reccy", there were numerous incendiary tail fins. The police chased us off, in case of unexploded ones.'

Winifred Moon, then an 18-year-old clerk at Kirby and West dairy, was planning to go with her sister and friend to the firm's annual dinner dance at the Bell Hotel, Humberstone Gate: 'We had been looking forward to going for weeks and had stayed up late the night before putting finishing touches to our dresses.' Excited, the young women caught a bus into town, but were told by an ashen-faced driver that the Tigers' ground had been bombed and he was going no further, so the two sisters returned home and spent the night bitterly disappointed inside their garden shelter, dressed in party dresses.

The IBs left Leicester Tigers' Crumbie Stand 'burning end to end', partially-destroying the city's main ARP mortuary underneath. At 8.40pm, the MOH initiated emergency arrangements to open the reserve mortuary at Aylestone Baths. Before the raid had even properly started, the Luftwaffe caused a major problem for the city's ARP organisation – yet ARP preparations countered this. The Crumbie Stand's central portion was damaged, requiring repairs costing £124 [£4,800]. IBs also came through the roof of the neighbouring Granby Halls FAP, setting fire to two ambulances.

Mrs Harrison's husband, Norman, was in charge of Leicester's Cattle Market and they lived in the lodge there: 'The sirens went and my husband saw the whole city was ringed by incendiaries. He put on his uniform and tin hat and said: "This is it! Get down that cellar with the children and don't come out." He kissed us all and was gone. Would he come back? I could only pray. I made the children comfortable in the cellar, then crept upstairs. Our house stood alone. Bombs started to fall. The house shook from the vibrations. Out my kitchen window, I saw the market was ablaze. I could hear the animals squealing in fright and knew Norman was down there fighting the flames. "Please God, keep him safe," I prayed. All hell broke loose over Leicester. It was terrible and we had no protection. We were not prepared for it. An incendiary landed on my husband's hay loft, where he kept chickens. He saved some, but many were roasted alive. It was a terrible night. About 4am, Norman returned, exhausted – but we were alive.'

Fires reported at:

19.46: House on Upper King St; Victoria Hotel at 101-103 Granby St; Marvin's drapers, 136-152 Wharf St; Midland Counties Garage, Granby St/Charles St; Welford Rd; A. Kemp Ltd, 42 Dover St; Sandy's Warehouse Ltd, 39 Welford Rd; house at 11 Princess Rd.
19.48: St John Divine church, South Albion St.
19.50: Recreation Ground, corner Ashwell Rd/Lancaster Rd.
19.51: House at 4 Turner St.
19.54: Broadbent's Yard; Humberstone Rd; London Rd; Newarke St.
19.55: Big fire on Welford Rd Common.
19.56: Fielding Sarson Leather Goods Ltd, 3 Camden St; Nichols St; house on Kimberley Rd.
19.58: Elton St.
19.59: R. Rowley hosiery, Queen St; Russell Sq; Nichols St; Charles St; Freeman, Hardy & Willis shoes Ltd, Rutland St; Faire Bros Ltd, Wimbledon St; St George St; J.M. Vice Printers, Calais Hill; Moore, Eady & Murcott Goode hosiery, 89 Granby St; Allotments near Aylestone Rd Gasworks.
20.00: Pick Ltd, Wellington St; House on New Way Rd; Highway Rd; House on Kingsway Rd; House on Trueway Rd; Ingham's Farm, Humberstone; Cascelloid Ltd, 234 Abbey Lane.
20.02: House at 8 Newton St.
20.03: back of Wellington St.
20.04: Cattle Market, Aylestone Rd; Park St; East St; Tigers' Stand, Aylestone Rd.
20.05: on railway line at New Walk/London Rd.
20.07: Holy Cross church, New Walk; London Road, off Charles St; Nicholls St.
20.10: Wharf St; houses and Crittall Windows Ltd, Evington Valley Rd.
20.14: Midway Rd; house at Stoughton Rd; G.Gibbons printers, Aylestone Rd.
20.16: Roundhill Garage, Roundhill Rd.
20.26: House on Broadway Rd.
21.02: House on Newby St.

Most smaller fires were extinguished by wardens and the public, but a number of fires developed, some major, the FB and AFS attending 55 fires. So serious was the situation, AFS reinforcement was called from Wigston, Hinckley, Loughborough, Coalville, Market Harborough, Melton Mowbray, Derby, Oakham, Nottingham, Swadlincote, Northampton and Peterborough, arriving in that order, between 10.39pm-02.40am.

Numerous eye-witnesses all state the same thing: the whole city seemed to be on fire. Arthur Gardner recalled: 'From Sparkenhoe Street, the full magnitude of burning Leicester was revealed. Unable to believe my eyes, I dismounted outside Saxby Street church. Looking down Swain Street, it appeared as if the whole city was one massive conflagration, sending volumes of dense smoke pouring upwards. So fierce were the flames, they transformed night into red-rimmed day. Occasionally walls collapsed and flung showers of sparks aloft: a holocaust forming a giant beacon for returning bombers.' Mary Owen recalled: 'I was terrified. I remember going to the top of Avebury Avenue and looking out. I never saw anything like it. I said to my husband: "The other night we were saying 'Poor old Coventry", but it's poor old Leicester tonight.'

The raid started nine minutes before the sirens sounded at 7.49pm. Tragically, 56-year-old warden George Ainsworth, of MacDonald Road, was fatally injured before even a single bomb fell. He collided with a van at the corner of Belgrave Road and Law Street, after seeing his wife safely across the road.

7.56pm: Horace Jarvis was on fire watch at Joseph Frisby's boot factors, opposite Freeman, Hardy and Willis, at the corner of Rutland Street and Humberstone Gate. At 7.45pm, while playing cards and drinking tea with his mates, he heard aircraft overhead. 'We heard what sounded like tin cans falling on the roof opposite. At first, we ignored it, but it continued, so I investigated.' Mr Jarvis climbed the firewatch tower and to his horror, saw hundreds of small fires springing up. 'Within minutes, the whole east side of the city was alight. But the sirens stayed silent. Minutes later, the Freeman Hardy Willis factory was surrounded by water pumps and AFS personnel. Things happened so quick, no-one had time to think. For the first half hour, it was absolute chaos. But the services did a marvellous job. Incendiaries stuck in gullies on the factory roof: it was soon ablaze and burned down floor by floor, hour by hour. The Germans caught us with our pants down. It was a lost cause from the start. Firemen battled through the night and next day. A terrific flash the following evening told them the fire had reached the basement, where polish and coal were stored. The fire had won.'

This was the night's most serious fire, involving a block of property from **Wimbledon Street to Rutland Street,** including the large Freeman, Hardy and Willis shoe works and Faire Bros Ltd, shoe mercers, at St George Mills.

The MoHS reported: 'OB, plus IBs and HE: Boot and shoe warehouse: 4-storey steel-framed building. Bomb pierced all floors, spraying burning oil and set fire to contents practically simultaneously. Premises gutted, but exterior walls standing. HE bomb fell during fire-fighting. Production stopped.'

Fire watchers on duty tried to tackle this impossible task before the FB arrived. The large burning buildings acted as a magnet to bombers as the AFS strove desperately to control the fires. Chief Fire Officer Winteringham reported: 'This had to be dealt with as one occurrence, bombs being dropped each end of the block, causing the largest fire. Within an hour and a half, this was being well held, but the explosion of an HE and [OB] in the centre of the building caused it to go up again. The top floors of Faire Bros, in Wimbledon Street, were fired by the heat opposite, but was kept in check.'

The fire was so serious, a FB Regional Call was issued. Appliances from Wigston, Market Harborough, Melton Mowbray, Oakham and TLs from Derby and Nottingham, plus Leicester's regular fire appliances 1, 2, 3, 4 and 6, gave valuable assistance.

Police Sergeant Smith established an Incident Post at the weighbridge on Humberstone Gate. At 01.34am, he reported 'Freeman, Hardy & Willis gutted and Faire Bros burning fiercely, but fire in hand.'

Fireman Thomas Harris recalled when Freeman Hardy and Willis' was hit, he and his chief had only just emerged from it after seeing how best to tackle the roof fire, when a second bomb struck: 'The whole building went up like a tinder box.' Fireman Jack Ward had a narrow escape. He had been hosing the fire, when his senior shouted to him to go further into the building, as the girders were red hot. He was about to, when a large part of the building collapsed.

There was one fatality at Freeman, Hardy and Willis. Post-war histories simply mention an un-named 'nightwatchman'. However, he deserves naming, as he was a very brave man, as A.E. Hendry, Director of Freeman, Hardy and Willis, made clear in a report:

'Fred Coe: age 59, of Rendell Street. Head Caretaker of our warehouse in Rutland Street. He had just left the building, when the alarm was given and immediately re-entered and assisted the firemen within to deal with fires on the top storey, caused by a shower of incendiaries. He was last seen at 7.45pm, still on the top floor, by one of our firemen, Mr F.G. Allen, when the place was well alight and full of fires. In spite of every effort made by Mr Allen and other firemen, Coe could not be found, and they were forced to abandon the building.' Frederick Allen stated: 'I went to the top storey with Fred Coe, who I knew personally. We discovered the fire. Mr Coe endeavoured to seek another staircase and I returned by the original staircase to seek help. I never saw Mr Coe again.' Mrs Coe stated: 'My husband

The morning after the Blitz Night, firemen damp down the smouldering ruins of Freeman, Hardy and Willis' warehouse, on Rutland Street. Behind them, the upper floors of Faire Bros also still smoke. On the right is the old Coffee Stall. [Leicester Mercury]

The distinctive burnt out shell of Freeman, Hardy and Willis stands out against the skyline at the corner of Humberstone Road and Rutland Street. It would be another nine months before the body of caretaker Fred Coe would be found inside the building's ruins. [Leicester Mercury]

left for the warehouse at 7.35pm, wearing a grey overcoat, grey sports jacket and grey flannel trousers. This was the last time I saw him alive.'

She would never see her husband again. His 'badly burned and unrecognisable' body was recovered from under the great pile of debris cleared nine months later, on August 26, 1941, '10ft in from building line, opposite 8 Humberstone Gate corner. His remains were taken to Aylestone Baths Mortuary.'

Fireman Douglas Dickens recalled in Carswell: 'The WVS brought a mobile canteen and positioned it close to the Odeon. They'd got big tins of corned beef and stuff, but no one had a tin opener, so I opened them with my fire-axe!' Afterwards, two Loughborough WVS members, both of Cheveney Road, Quorn, were commended in the *London Gazette* for their services 'during a raid on a Midlands town'. 'Mrs Hanford was driver of YMCA "S.H.B. Livingston" No.1 Tea Car, and with her helper, Mrs G. Paulson, also, displayed great devotion to duty.' They both received a letter from Regional Commissioner Lord Trent: 'Mr Morrison felt your devotion to duty in running a mobile canteen under dangerous conditions throughout the night was most praiseworthy. The matter was brought to the notice of HM the King, and I have pleasure in informing you, at the request of the Minister, that his Majesty has been graciously pleased to give orders for the publication of your name as having received an expression of commendation for your services.'

Fourteen-year-old AFS volunteer Kenneth Jordan spent three hours spraying the burning Freeman, Hardy and Willis building with a hose. Later, he was sent to Melton School, in Wharf Street, for a rest. No sooner had he sat down, he had to duck under a table when a bomb fell close by. As he emerged, he was horrified to see an old woman come in carrying an unexploded incendiary in her basket. Quick-thinking Jordan grabbed the bomb and dropped it in a water tank outside.

For local residents, it was an unforgettable night. Iris Smith recalled: 'I was 11, living in Grafton Street. Mother sent my sister and me to the Lee Circle shelters. Mother was a first-aider and had to stay at home. There were four entrances to the shelter. They all sloped down and linked underground. There were passageways with seats on the side walls. A crowd of us watched the blaze in Marvin's drapers, on Wharf Street, which then caved in. We heard a noise like machine-guns and in the rush for cover, my sister was knocked over. Fortunately, she was unhurt.' Next morning, burnt invoices and shoe fragments littered backyards. The following afternoon, weary school children were allowed to sleep at their desks.

Mr D. Hall: 'My father worked at the Coffee Stall, actually an old bus, on Humberstone Gate, by Freeman Hardy, and Willis. The stall was still open when Freeman, Hardy and Willis was bombed, an incendiary actually glancing off the stall and burning out on the pavement! My father hurriedly packed up and got a lift home. He joined us in our Anderson shelter, still with his apron on and the night's takings in the pocket. Chris Foster opened the stall next day to serve firemen still fighting the fire.'

8.14pm: Two 50kg HEs fell in **Holmfield Avenue**. One made a shallow crater in the road, causing blast damage. The other burst in the roof space between two semi-detached houses at 20 Holmfield Avenue. Miss R. Parr, her sister and mother escaped unharmed.

The first ARP fatality due to enemy action that night was warden/telephonist of 'E' DRC, Bernard Alderson, 33, who was rushing from his home at Aber Road to his wardens' post, in a garage at 7 Holmfield Avenue. As he crossed the road to his post, he was sandwiched between the two explosions, taking the full blast and a bomb splinter. ARP records state: 'compound fracture left leg and penetration wound to lower abdomen.' William Horner, was an ARP Ambulance driver: 'My first call was to Holmfield Avenue. We found an injured warden and took him to St Philip's FAP and to the City General Hospital, where he died the next day.'

Noel Rudkin lived on Aber Road: 'Eventually, the 'all-clear' sounded. In the morning, on Holmfield Avenue, folk were discussing that our local warden had been killed whilst patrolling. There was a large puddle on the pavement, stained red with blood. Murmurings of onlookers was that it was here the warden died. Such were the stark realities of war.'

8.16pm: An SC 250kg HE crashed through the **Town Hall** roof and penetrated the basement without detonating. The Town Hall's stirrup pump party extinguished the resultant fire. 'The bomb passed through the Planning Department on the second floor, the Lord Mayor's Secretary's Office on the first, the fire watcher's off-duty room alongside the entrance on the ground floor, before reaching the basement. On each floor was a neat hole marking its route. The bomb landed vertically, on its nose, neatly positioned beside a gas meter. The firewatchers discovered a split in the bomb through which the explosive was spilling out.'

Former ARP officer Edward Doughty recalls: 'The bomb caught the building's façade, ricocheted into councillors' cloakroom, smashed the furniture and floor to matchwood, shed its tail fin and became embedded in the basement. It was possible to look inside the bomb like looking into a dustbin. When the BD officer came along the next morning, the air was blue with his language, because Town Hall staff had lifted it out very neatly. The officer wanted to know why and they replied: "Well, you see sir, we had to sweep just there."' Chris Chettle reveals it may have been his grandmother, Lucy Chettle: 'She worked as the cleaner. There, amongst the rubble, she saw the UXB and set about cleaning it! An anxious warden yelled at her to get out quick. Lucy finished her job, then left quite calmly. This was her way of sticking two fingers up at Adolf!'

This was indeed very fortunate: aside from almost losing one of Leicester's finest buildings, all those who came in contact with the UXB could have lost their lives. Although the bomb was visibly sectioned, BDS viewed damaged bombs as dangerous as live ones. No. 42 BD Section recorded: 'Bomb removed from Town Hall basement at 11.10hrs. Case made of sheet metal with heavily welded nose. Filled with loose TNT. Fuze and fuze pocket torn. Only part of fuze recovered.'

8.17pm: A medium HE fell in the yard of a house in **Fitzroy Street**, at the corner of King Richards Road, demolishing a fish shop. Damage to houses and gas mains.

8.20pm: HE and UXHE fell on Surridge Dawson's, newspaper distributors, in **Great Central Street**. UXB destroyed front of building. Road strewn with debris. UXB caused extensive evacuation and closed main road. Another UXHE was discovered on **Great Central Street** at LNER and Downing's.

A rare photo of the unexploded SC 250kg HE bomb resting in the basement of the Town Hall. The rear of the bomb has separated as it has passed through several floors and the fuze pocket can be seen top right. Had it detonated, Leicester could have lost one of its finest public buildings. [Leicester Mercury]

8.26pm: A heavy HE, c.500kg, caused serious damage to south side of **Quenby Street**. Edith Sills, 56, of 7 Quenby Street, was killed and two injured. ARP services were impeded by fire. Mrs O. Abbott recalled: 'My father, Eric Turner managed the Shaftesbury Cinema, in Overton Road. Mother and I were in the audience when a bomb exploded behind the cinema, partly demolishing a row of houses in Quenby Street. The cinema shook and the picture shot from the screen onto the ceiling. Father managed to evacuate the cinema without panic, but a few people chose to remain. Mother and I stayed with father, sheltering beneath the projection room, which had a six-inch concrete floor.' Fred Groyne and his brother left the cinema and set off quickly along Overton Road: 'From nowhere, an old lady wearing a pinafore and plimsolls sped past, holding on to her hat and shouted: "Good night, me-duck!"'

8.27pm: Mere Road, by Twycross Street: A large UXHE buried below the bay window of 213 Mere Road, opposite the post office. On November 24, No. 42 BD Section commenced work on the UXB with AMPC and Leicestershire Regiment personnel. Each time they dug in the sandy soil, the UXB sank further, so they had to suspend it with a rope. Eventually, at 24ft, they uncovered a sky blue-painted SD 1400kg 'Fritz' HE. The only marking on the raised fuze was a Roman 'II'. Due to the obscurity of this type of bomb, it was removed – still live, without defusal – on December 16, supervised by Major McCartney and Lt Lee. Assistance was given by a Derby BD Section who, remarkably, drove the huge bomb away, live, through Leicester's streets! Afterwards, lights could be used again, but only at two-thirds power.

G. Morton recalled: 'I put my two children under the stairs, but the warden came and said we had a UXB outside, so we moved to the shelters on Spinney Hill Park, where we spent the night with lots of Londoners who had come to escape the capital's bombing – so they weren't happy. Every time a bomb dropped nearby, we were all wet

A rare photo showing a ladder disappearing into the 24ft excavation dug by RE bomb disposal personnel in front of 213 Mere Road, whilst they retrieved a large unexploded SD 1400 'Fritz' HE bomb. Although the bomb did not explode, the force of its impact smashed surrounding windows and required the house to be shored up. [Via Terence Burford]

by the condensation from the shelter roof. When the all-clear sounded, we found we weren't allowed home, because of the UXB.'

8.35pm: One of the most tragic incidents of the night: Four large HEs fell on **Frank Street** and **Humberstone Road**, demolishing 319 and 321 Humberstone Road, plus 18 and 20 Frank Street. Some 20 houses were seriously damaged. Previously published as seven killed, the fatalities were actually almost double, at 13 dead with 20 injured.

This developed into a major incident. ARP records state: 'Many trapped and Humberstone Road blocked'.

'21.13hrs: Police IO, Sgt 17, reports 2 houses at the corner of Humberstone Road down and 3 or 4 people still under wreckage. 1 FAPy, 1 RP and 1 AFS party at incident. Intense smoke forced firemen to need smoke masks. Another RP requested.

'23.12hrs: Police IO reports 3 women and 2 children in 319. One rescued. There was difficulty owing to fire. Ample services available. 6 persons trapped under 18 and 20 Frank Street. Three now rescued, other 3 comfortable. Many houses in Frank Street badly damaged. IP opened at Wardens' Post, Newby Street.

'23.40hrs: Police IO reports 'Persons still trapped, believed dead. Fire still burning, water playing on it. Three still trapped in Frank Street. Work continuing. Gas escaping.'

Remarkably, the surface shelter at the corner of Frank Street remained standing, though cracked, despite a bomb landing by it. Work continued for days, with relays of FAPys and RPs. Clothing blown into trees remained for months.

The most fatalities occurred at 319 Humberstone Road. Mrs Dorothy Lock, 37, her son Harold, seven, daughters Sylvia, six and Theresa, nine, were all trapped under the rubble. Poor Albert Lock had to claim his wife and three children from the mortuary. All are now buried together at Gilroes Cemetery. Mrs Iris Pardoe, 20, Mrs Hilda Wilmott, 42 and widow Eliza Smith, 67, also died here under the rubble. Some of the fatalities were taken to Spence Street FAP, where they were pronounced dead. Next door, at 321 Humberstone Road, Mrs Annie Alexander, 49, and her son, Thomas, 13, also died under the rubble. Both are buried together at Saffron Hill Cemetery. Walter Mosley, 73, also died here.

At 18 Frank Street, an off-licence, owner Mrs Alice Baker, 65, plus twins Elsie and Clifford Stubley, 28, were killed by blast. Clifford's body was recovered at 28 Frank Street, wearing a blue pin stripe suit and a lucky charm. Brother and sister are buried at Gilroes Cemetery.

Blast from this incident may have caused the damage noted by a HO report: 'Damage to Factories Engaged on Work of National Importance: George Deacon & Sons, Forest Road: Engaged upon socks. Factory intact, but warehouse damaged. Uncertain of socks lost and damaged for Government and Admiralty.'

Terence Cartwright recalls: '8pm: Grandmother, who had just returned from a visit to her sister and cousins in Frank Street, decided to go to Ash Street communal shelter. The shelterers heard an enormous explosion. A few minutes later, a "clown" – only way to describe him – of a warden stuck his head through the door and shouted "Frank Street's gone!" Many in the shelter had friends/relatives living there and the stress caused must have been horrendous. It was not until the next day, grandmother found her twin cousins, Elsie and Clifford Stubley, had died. Grandmother's sister, was dug out the next day. She never recovered from the shock and died later.'

Ruby Lawrence knew instinctively her grandmother Mrs Elizabeth Dobney's home, at 20 Frank Street, had been hit. Three elderly women lived there. When Mrs Lawrence and her brother arrived, they discovered the three were buried under rubble: 'We removed the bricks with our bare hands, discovering grandmother and the other two alive – but we couldn't get them out. A warden instructed us to go to the shelter on the corner of Frank Street and Humberstone Road. The three elderly ladies were rescued at daylight, miraculously, sustaining only cuts and bruises.'

Possibly resulting from this incident, in April 1943, 'Squad Leader David Midglow, at Humberstone depot, was presented by Controller Worthington with a badge inscribed "For Brave Conduct". Mr Midglow, of Gresham Street, was recommended for the award for bravery. His squad entered two burning houses at great risk and rescued people and removed dead, at the same time putting out the fire which was in immediate danger of affecting people trapped in the debris.'

Post-war, during the Charnwood Street slum clearances of 1968, Frank Street was demolished and no trace of it remains today.

Numbers 319 and 321 Humberstone Road were destroyed by a heavy HE, killing ten people. Fortunately, although cracked and covered in rubble, the communal street shelter, right, survived intact, protecting its occupants. [Leicester Mercury]

A UXHE was reported in **Humberstone Road** coal wharf. Then came an hour's lull.

9.30pm: HE and UXHE reported in roadway at LNER Station, **Great Central Street**.

Another UXHE was found in the LNER Goods Yard, **Eastern Boulevard**, possibly from the same stick of bombs. On November 30, 1940, No. 42 BD Section commenced work on the UXB with AMPC and ITC Leicestershire Regiment personnel. The UXB was near the goods yard, in allotments. On December 4, operations were suspended: 'Excavation below level of nearby canal and water pouring into hole faster than can be dealt with', so the UXB was left for over four months. On May 9, 1941, 'operations commenced'. Reports cease after this – does this suggest the UXB was not recovered?

Jack Brooks, then 10, lived in Filbert Street: 'A distinctive whistle of three bombs was heard. The next day, we could see two large craters on the strip of cultivated land between Filbert Street and the recreation ground, now a car park. Discussion began about what had happened to the mysterious third bomb. The military arrived and dug at various sites: near the craters, at the back of Bede House bathing station and the allotments across the canal. The canal was dragged, but only rubbish found. I think it was concluded that if the bomb was underwater, it would never explode and the search stopped.'

AFS telephonist Margaret Hatton was based nearby at the AFS Divisional HQ on Great Holme Street: 'I had gone to the Savoy Cinema, on Belgrave Gate, with an RAF chap. It said on the screen the alert had sounded. I was just in my civvies and had heels on, but had my helmet, so said "I have to go" and left him at the cinema. I partly ran and walked all the way to the Div HQ. It was a brilliant night with a full moon, but it looked like the whole city was on fire. It was quite frightening, but I was more concerned about reporting for duty.

Margaret Hatton, née Hall, in her AFS office overall, late 1940. [Margaret Hatton]

'The fire pumps from Lancaster Road fire station were dispersed around the city, so they wouldn't all be wiped out by one bomb. We had the turntable ladder stationed at Great Holme Street at the alert. Three of us took telephone messages onto pads and also made up the logbook. The public called Lancaster Road station, who passed the message to us, where the Divisional Officer decided which fire engines should be sent from which local sub-station in our control, either Winstanley Road or Glenfield Road. We had quite a busy night with calls coming in. At one stage, we heard bombs coming closer so left the telephones and dived under a table for shelter – which was a joke, as it was made of plywood! I remember counting the bombs falling closer and the last one crashed on the marshalling yards by Braunstone Gate. We were very lucky because we were next in line had there been an extra bomb!

'I went for a quick break and joined the picket standing outside. We looked up and saw a German bomber fly down the whole length of Great Holme Street: it was low enough that I could see the form of a German airman in it. Thankfully, he didn't drop any bombs on us!

At 2am, a mobile canteen arrived and gave us corned beef sandwiches. Then, at 5am, my mother arrived with more sandwiches, to see I was alright. I went straight to work in the morning, but was so tired, I went home at lunch and didn't go back in the afternoon.'

9.31pm: Four 50kg HEs fell in **Mansfield Street** and **Gravel Street**, damaging Pollard's Mineral Waters and the Co-op Printing Works. At 1.29am, fire broke out in Pollard's and FB responded.

9.33pm: An HE fell at the rear of a house and shop at 127 **Brunswick Street**, causing a fire. No casualties.

9.49pm: An HE fell in the middle of the road in **Denman Street**, damaging houses, gas and water mains. Pete Howe, then seven, recalled: 'We lived at the off licence. The sirens went, so Mum closed the shop. We'd been sitting in the living room, when Dad ran out of cigarettes, so Mum went into the shop to get some. She just returned when bang! – a bomb dropped right outside the shop. I fell off my chair, Mum grabbed me by the scruff of my neck and dragged me out the backdoor with Dad following, hot-footing it to the Anderson shelter in the communal gardens. If Mum had gone for Dad's fags a moment later, she would have been buried under the tins off the shelves. Having scrambled into the overcrowded shelter, thanking them for allowing us in, Mum counted how many were there: 13. Mum, being superstitious, wanted to get out, which no one would allow. Afterwards, my parents decided our home was not fit to stay in: Mum could stick her hand through the cracks in the outside wall.' ARP records state a UXHE was found in the middle of **Denman Street**, but it is not recorded in BD records. However, Vera Taylor says the walls of her parents' pub, The Talbot, were split when a UXB landed outside.

9.55pm: The night's worst incident, with the heaviest death toll. Three heavy HEs, c.500kg, fell across the **Highfield Street/Tichborne Street** crossroads, destroying seven large boarding houses. The large, three-storey Victorian terrace houses proved unforgiving to those sheltering in their cellars: the bombs brought the whole building down on them. As they were mainly boarding houses, casualty figures were higher. Previous published figures state 41 dead, but a new count reveals 45.

On the southern side of Upper Tichborne Street, 41 and 49 (now Trinity Life church) were demolished. On the corner opposite the Synagogue, at 27, The Ritz boarding house was levelled, killing five: Mrs Jeanette Rippon, 25, and her son, Philip, 16 months – the youngest victim of Leicester's war. Likewise, Mrs Cissie Kirby (aka Bunting), 29, and her daughter Pamela, 4, were killed. Both mothers and their children were buried at Saffron Hill Cemetery. William James (aka Hill), 34, was fatally injured, dying three days later at the LRI.

Round the corner at at 27 Highfield Street, six died: piano teacher Miss Dora Jewsbury, 50, widow Mary Jewsbury, 75, her daughter Mrs Gwendolyn Norman, 43, Gwendolyn's husband, Harold Norman, 43, and their son, Christopher, 12. All are buried together at Welford Road Cemetery. RAPC Private Lionel Cohen, 23, died here, too.

Next door, at 25 Highfield Street, the greatest loss of life occurred with 12 killed. Mr J Spiro had evacuated his mother Annie, 58, his wife, Rose, 35, and two sons, Gerald, 2 and

Numbers 41 and 49 Upper Tichborne Street, Highfields, were destroyed by a medium HE bomb, fortunately, it seems without fatalities [Via Terence Burford]

When a heavy HE struck the corner of Upper Tichborne Street and Highfield Street, five people were killed in The Ritz boarding house, left, and six people in the building that stood on the right. [Leicester Mercury]

Gordon, 4, from the bombing in London: Mr Spiro lost them all and they were buried in Gilroes Cemetery. Other London evacuees killed here include Mrs Iris Marks, 25, widow Rebecca Steinberg, 70, her daughter Esther Marsden, 40, and Esther's husband, Nathaniel Marsden, 40, Mrs Lea Sietz, 43, Michael Tate, 7 and Miss Mary Warner, 65. Mrs Elizabeth Stevens, 60, was fatally injured, dying on December 12, 1940.

Opposite, on the western side of Highfield Street, between Tichborne Street and Gotham Street, a large bomb destroyed number 28, the Argyle Hotel, killing nine: Russian nationals Isaac Berezin, 35, and his wife, Sinaida, 30, Mrs Lily Cowie, 37, plus RAPC soldiers Private William Giles, 28, Private Frank Harvey, Private Sidney Saxton, 28, Private Frank Wheeler, 22. Private Albert Luesby, 24, was discovered on Tichborne Street corner. All were in uniform. A 'male torso, in a ripped blue stripe shirt, with parts of arms and legs' was recovered four days later and buried as 'unidentified, No.72'.

Next door, at 30, three died in the Lorne Hotel: The boarding house owner's son, William Fleming, 37, and his wife, Iris, 22, were recovered four days later and buried together. The body of married Polish refugee Samuel Gelbard, 30, was 'not recovered' and may be the unidentified body 'No.72', above.

Three people were killed in the Lorne Hotel boarding house, left, at 30 Highfield Street. Next door, at 32, the Victoria Hotel boarding house, right, seven people, mostly RAPC soldiers, were killed. Their comrades, bottom right, take a break whilst clearing the rubble. [Via Terence Burford].

As many as seven were killed at number 32, Victoria Hotel, mainly a RAPC billet. All were described as 'unidentifiable': Private Harry Attwood; Private Francis Johnson; Private Herbert Tindsley, 26 and Private James Willey, 24, whilst Private John Kirkpatrick, 22, was found in Upper Tichborne Street. The remains of Private Harold Briggs, 25, were uncovered four days later, in uniform, with a prayer book. Government trainee Leslie Hurdell, 30, also died here.

It seems some may have been caught in the street. Married travelling salesman, William Main, 38, of Somerset, was discovered on Highfield Street, later identified by a 'business acquaintance'. Married factory manager, Alfred Sklar, 35, of 42 Eastfield Road, was injured and died four days later in LRI. Interestingly, on January 4, 1941, magistrates withdrew a case against Sklar for a blackout offence at his home three days before his death. ARP records also note: 'Lady's and soldier's feet: owners found and remains disposed of.'

So serious was the incident, RPs were sent in triplicate. From M/C, MOH Dr MacDonald telephoned ARP Depot Senior Medical Officer, Dr Duncan Porteous, stating: 'There's some trouble in Highfield Street – will you go and take charge?' At 10.05pm, Police Inspector Weston also arrived and, being IO, took control of ARP operations – for the next 20 hours. Dr Porteous recalled: 'He was everywhere, never in a hurry, but never wasting a second.' Two months later, Inspector Weston was awarded the OBE, the LEM reporting: 'Police Hero's Task Amid Rain of Bombs: For 20 hours, Inspector Jesse Weston [of 58 Peter's Drive], wearing a white incident officer's smock, directed during an air raid. Although bombs were falling around him, he remained standing, exhorting everyone else to lie down. He was an inspiration because of the extremely calm and collected way he organised his men and directed Rescue parties.' Chief Constable Cole said: 'He was in control where the heaviest bombing occurred, directing operations, without break, from 7pm until 3pm next afternoon.' This was not Inspector Weston's first gallantry: during the previous war, he won the Military Medal for single-handedly attacking a German machine-gun post at St Quentin in 1918, while serving with the 1st Battalion, Leicestershire Regiment. He joined Leicester police in 1919 and was in charge of Eastern Division.

Mr A.J. Harris, of 86 Stoughton Road, in bowler hat, leader of a Leicester Rescue squad, with his wife and son and Inspector J.S. Weston of the City Police, with his wife and two sons, after both men had received the OBE at Buckingham Palace in March 1941. [Leicester Mercury]

ARP Rescue squad leader Alfred Harris, of 86 Stoughton Street, was also awarded the OBE. Harris and his squad rescued 20 casualties, working for 10 hours until exhausted. 'It was due to his splendid leadership and disregard for his own safety, his squad was so successful in their efforts,' read his citation. In March 1941, Harris and Weston received their OBEs at Buckingham Palace for 'bravery in a Midland air raid.'

But it is clear there were also many unpublished heroes. For example, George Bernard Emmett, 45, of 43 Medway Street, was Group Warden for Highfields. Like Weston, he had given distinguished service in the First World War. As a corporal in the 1/5 Leicestershire Regiment, Emmett was awarded the Military Medal 'for gallantry and dedication to duty', leading troops after their officer was wounded during the penetration of the Hindenburg Line, France, in 1918. On this night, Emmett was in the epicentre of this incident and was blown over the railings of the Synagogue, damaging his shoulder. Emmett tended the garden of Richard Corah, of Corah's hosiery, and Mr Corah paid for him to go to London to have his shoulder treated. Emmett's wife also became a warden. Three months later, Emmett received a typed letter from Chief Constable/Chief Warden O.J.B. Cole: 'As Group Warden in the area most heavily damaged, you worked with untiring energy in organising your wardens and during the greater part, you were under fire. Your difficulties were increased by the fact that telephones at five of your posts were out of action. I am aware you absented yourself from work the day after the raid, so you could continue duties as warden. I shall be glad if you will accept not only my personal thanks, but also those of the citizens of Leicester, for the splendid way in which you carried out your responsibilities as a warden. I consider myself very fortunate in having such men as you and those who work under you in the Wardens' Service.'

For Dr Porteous, 'As the bombs whistled down, to see the young ambulance girls, without a smile, but without showing fear, impressed me more than anything else. They came to Highfield Street, waited for casualties to be loaded, then took them to St Philip's FAP.' Aged 18, Joyce Chapman was one such 'young ambulance girl': 'I was at my grandparents for tea, when we heard the sirens, which meant I had to report for duty. So I bicycled to the College of Arts depot. My driver, Mr Hardiman, was in his thirties. We got on well. In those days, you were respectful of your elders, so I called him "Mr Hardiman": he called me "Joyce". Our "ambulance" was a requisitioned car towing a trailer with a green canvas top. We got the call and heard Highfields was getting badly hit, so went up London Road. Half way up, a bomb exploded nearby, blowing our car across the road and lifting it. Mr Hardiman was a good driver and got the car back on course. We got to Highfields and Rescue were digging people out. We picked up casualties and went to Granby Halls FAP. I'd been in the ambulance trailer with a woman with bad head injuries and rested her head between my knees. When I got back to the depot, I had blood all on my hands. When the girls in the office saw, they went rather green!'

Many who acted with gallantry will never be known. Dr Porteous found one terrified young girl in a bombed house, at the end of a tunnel of bricks: 'A young man volunteered to rescue her and inched his way through, then brought the child out. This was one of the night's most outstanding acts of courage.'

It is apparent rescue operations were very difficult and gruelling: the following afternoon, London evacuee, Isaac Blaskey, 47, was discovered below the rubble of Victoria Hotel, at 32 Highfield Street: 'Rescuers working on the debris of a three-storey boarding house heard what they thought were human cries, and after strenuous efforts, released a dog. They carried on day and night to reach the wrecked cellar, and at 10am today [November 22], one of the squad heard a faint voice. He eventually located the voice at the bottom of the fireplace. A hole was knocked in the wall and words came clearly: "I'm here." The rescue squad shouted, "Hold on, can you?" and intensive efforts started to free him. The rescuers were faced with insuperable difficulties. They were sandwiched between a tottering 50ft chimney stack and walls of three-storey houses which wobbled as they worked; they had hundreds of tons of debris, including floors to remove. Meantime, the man was trapped with dead colleagues either side of him. Blaskey had gone to the cellar shelter on the alert, but was trapped when the building collapsed. He was lying on a bed with his feet trapped, but his arms and head were free. He had been lying for 64 hours in the dust, dark and debris, while several other alerts and raids took place. Despite the wobbling walls, over 50 rescuers cleared the debris. Ropes were used to lift floors out the way. Corrugated iron protection was placed over Blaskey. He calmly gave instructions as to the best way to free him. Through a hole in next door's fireplace, hot drinks and stimulants, a steel helmet and blankets were passed to sustain him during the last stages of his ordeal. Blaskey was so anxious to help his rescuers with his arms – the rest of him was trapped – doctors had to warn him to keep quiet, lest his strength gave out. Blaskey was reached, splinted and bandaged. He had shown marvellous endurance and good heart, but despite all efforts, he died a few hours later.'

ARP Ambulance Officer Leonard Lee later received a commendation for brave conduct and devotion to duty at this incident: 'Two days after the raid, Mr Lee, at considerable risk, gave first aid to a man still buried. Mr Lee crawled beneath the debris, showing great courage and keenness.' Mr Lee also received the Order of St John from the Duchess of Gloucester.

RAPC soldiers also helped in Blaskey's rescue, as Colonel C.J.K. Hill wrote in *Pay Parade*,

Highfields Group Warden George Emmett, received a letter of commendation from the Chief Warden/Chief Constable O.J.B. Cole for his 'untiring energy' whilst under fire. [Mary Pepper]

Left: *This remarkable pair of photographs capture Isaac Blaskey's rescue. We see a RAPC medical officer lieutenant, looking at the camera, passing bandages to a St John nurse, her face hidden by the black helmet. Blaskey lies buried beneath the corrugated iron sheet, right* [Leicester Mercury].
Right: *Then the moment of rescue: Isaac Blaskey's face can be seen, bottom right, as he lies on a stretcher covered in blankets, surrounded by RAPC officers. The St John nurse stands at the back, her work done. Sadly, despite surviving buried alive for 64 hours, Blaskey died on November 22, 1940.* [Leicester Mercury]

Leicester's RAPC journal: 'A particularly stout ARP official directed the rescue of one poor chap. He led a devoted gang of our RAPC. During the tearing suspense of those unendurable hours, Lt England and Private Dick particularly distinguished themselves, whilst our genial and popular MO, Lt Widman, performed prodigies of medical ingenuity.'

Blaskey was one of many Jewish refugees who had fled to Leicester, as recorded in Adam: 'Many Eastern European Jews had escaped Nazi persecution before the war to London. Many fled the Nazi bombs to Leicester and lodged in guesthouses in Highfield Street, because they were near the Synagogue and the local Jewish population. Unfortunately, bombs dropped around this Jewish quarter and killed several families who had just come from London the day before. The Synagogue remained largely intact, though suffering broken windows and the chandelier fell. It would be two years before it reopened. The community recovered and in 1953, a Jewish community centre was built on the bombsite at the corner of Tichborne Street/Highfield Street, where Jews had died.'

Twelve young RAPC soldiers, in their 20s, were killed: 'The RAPC were billeted in guesthouses in the Highfield Street area, near to their workplace at the Edward Wood Hall, 151 London Road, opposite the London Road/Highfield Street junction.' It is said the 12 RAPC dead were temporarily laid out in the bar of the Princess Charlotte pub, on Oxford Street, near the RAPC's offices on The Newarke.

Colonel C.J.K. Hill wrote: 'We've been through the ordeal by fire. I can only hint at the job taken on by SSM Thornton. If I mention identifications and next-of-kin, you will know roughly what I mean. Our erstwhile Great Central Street canteen NCO, Cpl Best, was caught at the top of the cellar stairs of his billet. Best fought his way out the wreckage in inky blackness. This took about 15 minutes – think of it. Then, he went back and helped nine others trapped in the cellar. He then joined the rescue work whilst the raid continued, earning him the Chief Constable's commendation.'

Locally-billeted ATS women also carried out 'invaluable work. Section Leader Swift and her swallows flitted around with hot drinks and cigarettes for the inner man and cold fingers and iodine for the outer. For hours, they were the pleasantest sight on the site. The next best was a pathetic little Scottie dog, dug out after two days, too weak to stand: his eyes eloquent, his voice silent. His owner, very distressed, now has him.'

George Cox, then 11, was walking past a bombed house in Highfields, with its front torn away. Inside, he saw a family playing cards around a table, like nothing had happened. Only at closer glance did he release they were all dead – killed by blast. Inez Henson recalled: 'My mother-in-law, on nursing duty at St Philip's FAP, saw dreadful sights. Soldiers in cellars in Highfield Street were killed by blast: One was found sitting on a form still holding a cup of tea.'

David Black: 'I was in the Leicestershire Regiment. Next morning, our platoon was sent to Highfield Street to dig for bodies. I uncovered the torso of a young blonde woman, which upset everyone. Remarkably, the Jewish tabernacle remained intact, managing to shout defiance at the Nazis.'

Harry Haines: 'It was my 22nd birthday. I was in the Army at Tewkesbury. I was summoned by the commanding officer, who informed me my sister and brother-in-law had been killed in the Coventry raid. I was sent on immediate compassionate leave to Leicester, to attend the funeral. Arriving at the Midland Station, I stepped into devastation. The sky was red with fires. I started walking home to Staveley Road, accompanied only by the drone of aircraft and falling bombs. I was in the centre of a terrifying nightmare. As I walked up London Road, I saw houses hit and others in ruins. I suppose this walk was sheer stupidity, but I didn't fully realise the situation's seriousness. I eventually arrived home: my body unhurt but my mind in turmoil – a walk I will never forget.'

A UXHE was discovered in **St Peter's Road**, near Welland Street.

10pm: An HE fell on **Coleman Road** waterworks, damaging the mains.

10.12pm: An HE fell on **St Denys Road**, damaging a water main.

10.14pm: A PM fell near the corner of **Tollemache Street and Sudeley Avenue**, just missing the LNER railway, leaving a large crater in the road. Mrs Winifred Harris, 30, of 8 Tollemache Avenue, was killed and 26 injured. Twelve houses were demolished, with extensive blast damage in Sudeley Avenue, Tollemache Street, Egerton Street, Downham Avenue and Abbey Lane. Over 400 houses were damaged. Several fires broke out. All local Anderson shelters remained intact. The LNER reported 'line blocked by debris for eight hours.' IO Sergeant Hallam established an IP. By 01.40am, the situation was in hand.

For 30-year-old Bernard Harris, it would be a night he would never forget: 'I went to take my wife, Winnie, to the Anderson shelter I'd built in the garden. She was sitting knitting a baby's shawl. I told her to "come on" and she walked towards me. Then, for some reason, she stopped. I put my arm round her, kissed her.' Mrs Harris went to the kitchen to collect a coat. Bernard followed her. As he reached for his coat, a massive mine detonated less than 40ft away.

'I felt a push in the stomach,' said Mr Harris. 'I didn't feel or hear anything. It was a strange sensation, more like a dream. I don't know how long I was out. I came to, on my back with my left hand stuck on my face. My right hand was outstretched. I soon realised my whole body was trapped. I couldn't move at all. At last, I heard a voice and called for help. It must have been the fire brigade. Someone answered, "Sorry, we'll have to put the fire out before we can help you." I was helpless. I thought, "Oh God, the place is on fire on top of me." It seemed ages before a voice told me to keep talking, so they could find me. It was a friend, Harry Hearth, who shouted: "Come on chaps, he's a mate of ours." The ARP Rescue party was made up of builders. I was foreman at Moss's Builders, Loughborough. Harry worked frantically to free me. He almost had me clear, when the rubble caved in and he had to start again. I felt no pain when he tried to drag me out. Although the left side of my face and one hand were smashed, I managed to hook my arms around a rescuer's neck, while he

The remains of a pair of semi-detached houses on Tollemache Avenue destroyed by a parachute mine, which demolished 12 homes and killed Mrs Winifred Harris, aged 30. The presumed target, the LNER railway line, runs behind on the embankment. [Via Terence Burford]

It was reported that all local Anderson shelters remained intact – even if the homes didn't. Again, the LNER railway can be seen running behind these homes on Tollemache Avenue, near its corner with Sudeley Avenue. [Leicester Mercury]

hauled me out. I'd been blinded and could only lie helplessly on a stretcher, while I listened to men attempting to rescue my wife. I woke in hospital. I just lay in blackness. I'd no strength and was powerless to move. My first visitors were my brothers. They told me I was in the General and that Winnie was in the Royal.' It was days before Mr Harris learned his bride of two years had been killed by the blast: 'A sister came and drew the curtains around, saying she was going to tell me something. I sensed what she was going to say: the dreadful news Winnie was dead.'

Ronald Shaw, 19, lived at 9 Tollemache Avenue: 'I'd been to the Colosseum Cinema. We heard the bombers coming. When I got home, the family were huddled under the table in the living room. There wasn't room, so I kipped down on a rug. Then, the landmine fell. The table took the full force. Although mother was bruised, my sister and brother were unhurt. I was buried in rubble with a joist across my shoulder, paralysing my right arm for three months. I came round to hear rescuers saying they couldn't find me and realised they were standing on the bricks above my head. They took me to the General, where I stayed for four weeks.' Undaunted, after he married two years later, Ronald set up home in Tollemache Avenue and volunteered for RAF Bomber Command, becoming wireless operator/air gunner: 'I wanted to get my own back…'

The bomber had clearly been aiming for the LNER railway, as the houses backed onto the embankment. Gwen Walthoe was at Great Central station: 'They fetched us out the station canteen and made us go under the platform. The bomber had followed the Nottingham to Leicester train. The driver managed to pull into the station, but was badly shocked. We dealt with him and took him to the Infirmary.'

After this incident, Mrs Winifred Flewitt, of 61 Sudeley Avenue, an ARP telephonist, received a commendation for brave conduct and devotion to duty. She remained working at her post, 'under difficult circumstances', when she knew her street had been hit: 'she received reports of damage and casualties, but acted promptly throughout the night. Afterwards, she found her home almost completely wrecked. She insisted on returning to her post, with calmness and courage.'

c.10.15pm: An HE fell **between Bell Lane signal box and Humberstone Road LMS station**, overturning the locomotive of the 14.20 freight train from Rugby, injuring the crew. Home Guard Tom Downs recalls: 'We went onto the railway bank, over Uppingham Road, to Belgrave Station. We'd got a pillbox there, where we could shelter. We sat playing cards. All of a sudden, we heard bombs coming nearer. One dropped very close. When we went onto the bridge over Uppingham Road, a train had been completely lifted off the line and put by the side of the track.'

10.16pm: An HE and IBs hit Browett's Garage, **Dover Street**, causing a large fire. It was believed a UXHE had landed in the road within 100yds of the AFS sub-station, causing serious disruption. It was found to be a manhole, with the lid blown off. As firemen were fighting a blaze at neighbouring Kemp's hosiery, another HE fell into the fire, completely gutting the building. This fire was viewed particularly seriously by the HO: 'Damage to Factories Engaged on Work of National Importance: Arthur Kemp Ltd, Dover Street: contracts for socks, vests cotton, woollen and summer, jerseys pullover and socks hospital.'

Below: *A fireman and workman survey the damage to Kemp's Hosiery factory from the top of a ladder on a Merryweather turntable appliance, at the junction of Dover Street and Albion Street. Factory owner Roy Kemp, in the suit and trilby hat, immediately to the left of the appliance looks on. The manhole cover right of Mr Kemp may well have been what was mistakenly thought to be a UXB.* [Leicester Mercury]

A further UXHE was discovered in Browett's Garage. Chief Fire Officer Winteringham reported: 'One of the largest fires was at Messrs Kemp. It was impossible for the Brigade to make any save. Owing to heavy draw on the mains, difficulty was experienced getting water for this occurrence. This necessitated the men running hose for a greater distance. Fortunately, this meant men had not got inside the building by the time the HE exploded, otherwise, we may have had some serious casualties.'

10.19pm: An HE fell behind houses on the corner of **Fairfield Street and Eggington Street**, damaging several. One person injured.

10.20pm: A heavy HE fell at the rear of Willson's printing works, **King Street**, destroying several buildings and causing considerable damage to property, including head offices of Wolsey Ltd.

10.21pm: An HE and OB fell in **Main Street, Humberstone**, starting fires.

10.25pm: Another major incident. A PM fell in **Grove Road**, by the Vulcan Road junction. Originally reported as 10 dead, four were killed and 14 injured. Twelve houses demolished and many others blasted. IP corner of Vulcan Road and

A police officer, possibly Inspector Weston, surveys the mountain of rubble, all that is left of the houses on the north side of Grove Road, after a parachute mine levelled them. [Leicester Mercury]

Sherrard Road. ARP parties worked many hours to free the trapped.

MoHS scientists recorded: 'Crater 75ft x 19ft, centre of building line of two-storey terrace houses. Domestic surface shelter 62ft from crater, struck by debris and badly shaken by earth shock. Occupants: 8 injured, 1 hospitalised. Neighbouring shelter: roof blown off, almost completely demolished.'

Warden William Pratt, 65, was killed patrolling this sector. His body was not recovered for 13 days, under 6/8 Grove Road. Amongst his ARP kit, a lucky charm was found. Mrs Ivy Sheen, 40, of 2 Grove Road, and her daughter Joan, six, were killed next door at number 4 and were buried together in Gilroes Cemetery. Mrs Margaret Chandler, 50, also died here.

On the other side of the street, several houses were demolished. Debris tore holes in roofs in adjoining streets. One woman said the bomber flew down very low before releasing the mine. It was rumoured the mine's parachute caught and pulled off the weathercock on St Saviour's church, diverting the mine on to Grove Road. Another version even claims the mine landed at the top of Grove Road and rolled all the way down before detonating. Both seem far-fetched: it's more likely the weathercock was blown off in the explosion.

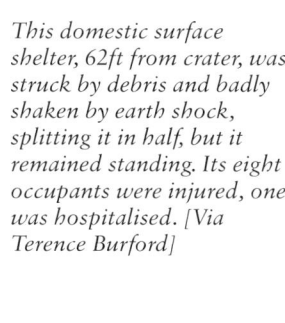

This domestic surface shelter, 62ft from crater, was struck by debris and badly shaken by earth shock, splitting it in half, but it remained standing. Its eight occupants were injured, one was hospitalised. [Via Terence Burford]

In 1950, the *LM* reported: 'Ten years after his death, comrades of Warden Pratt attended a memorial service at St Saviour's church.' A service had been held in his honour every year since then. Members of 'A' Division Wardens Old Comrades Association were led by Mr C.T. Johncock, formerly Divisional Warden. Conducting, Rev. J.M. Holderness, also an 'A' Division Warden. A wooden memorial lectern to Warden Pratt was donated to St Saviour's church. Sadly, it was badly damaged when vandals broke into the disused church in 2010. A small memorial urn, bearing the inscription 'In Loving Memory of W.H. Pratt, ARP Warden, died Nov 19th 1940' stands in Welford Road Cemetery.

Both affected sides of the street were rebuilt after the war and the differing style to the Victorian terraces is apparent.

10.25pm: An HE fell at the rear of houses at the corner of **Evington Street and Oxenden Street**, causing serious damage to six houses. A widow, Mary Johnson, 70, of 53 Evington Street, died of shock. One injured.

Miss C. Aston, then five, recalled: 'We lived at 49 Evington Street. Dad was a warden, getting ready to go on duty. He said to Mother: "I think you'd better both go in the shelter, it looks like being a nasty night." We had a brick surface shelter in the backyard. It had a bench and bucket. Dressed in warm clothes, with a small lamp and something to eat, Mother and I settled down in the shelter. The raid became worse. Mother was worried about the family next door, who had no shelter. When Dad looked in on his beat, mum asked him to fetch them to our shelter. The husband was in the Army. The lady and little boy came in, but the two teenage girls wanted to stay in the house. However, as the raid got worse and their mother got more worried, next time Dad came round, they consented to come in.

'We could hear the bombs whistling down and every time, the mothers would grab us small children and tuck our faces into their coats, so the blast should not suck our breath out. Mother had her fur coat on – I can still feel that fur on my face. After every bomb, the little boy would pop out and say: "That one missed us, Mum!" Then came the one that didn't: it landed right on their house next door. There was a great crash and the whole shelter rocked. The blast ripped the door off and stood it neatly against the house.

'Dad was in the next street, lying in the gutter, with bricks bouncing off his tin helmet. When he heard "a bomb in Evington Street", he came rushing and saw his own house with no roof and windows and the entry full of bricks. He scrambled over the bricks, shouting: "Emma, are you there?" He said he had never been so glad as when mum shouted: "We're all right." In the rush to get to the shelter, we'd forgotten the budgie. Poor Joey was lying on his back. Then, Dad heard a "chirrup" and there was Joey, up on his swing! He'd just been knocked out and lived for several years after. Dad found a piece of the bomb in the front room wall.'

At the same time, an HE fell on 98 **Sparkenhoe Street, at the corner of Gopsall Street**, killing two. Anthony Lloyd, 11, was buried under the wreckage. His brother Derek, eight, was rescued, but died three days later in the LRI.

A letter survives in the *LM* archives, written by the Lloyd's parents following the incident, addressed to 'The Editor':

'Dear Sir,
c/o 6 St John's Road, Leicester

I write to thank you for the kindness and help you have given us. My husband heard from Mr Bream and he kindly gave us the sum of £10 [£425]. I just cannot find words enough to thank you. Yours is the only outside help we have ever had, but believe me, you will always have our life long gratitude.

Yours very sincerely, F & B Lloyd, late 98 Sparkenhoe St.'

Dr Eric Adderson, then 14, was a member of 23rd Leicester Scout Troop, which met in St Peter's parish room: 'We were disturbed by a man coming in who said "I think you should look outside." We were amazed to see the town brightly illuminated by parachute flares descending. We went to the nearest shelter, St Peter's School, in Gopsall Street. Although not bombproof, its ground floor was shored up with steel girders, its windows protected with sandbags or brick blast walls and thick curtains to catch shattering glass. Over 100 spent the night in the school, from babies to elderly. Most came without food or drink. Water was from a tap in the lobby. The only sanitary provision was screens surrounding buckets. Bombs fell close by: a frightening shriek and a loud explosion. The building shook and more than once, a crash of glass and the sound of window fragments sliding down the protective curtains. The nearest bomb fell 100yds away. The west door of St Peter's church and its surrounding stonework were pitted with cavities. Later, a boy [Derek Lloyd] was carried into the school, badly injured. Some people screamed at the explosions, but mainly, reactions were stoical. There was a lot of noise, including children crying. There were periods of quiet, when everyone relaxed, only to be aroused by further explosions. Some tried to sleep, stretched out on benches or the floor. One of the most frightening events, which nearly caused a panic, was an explosion followed by darkness. I realised the mains had been cut. Fortunately, I had a torch and matches for the oil lamps suspended from the ceiling. I lit some and calm was restored.'

HE bombs fell along **Sparkenhoe Street to Gartree Street**. A large crater blocked the road and pavements. Several houses were demolished. All services and cables were damaged, including telephone cables to Evington, Stoneygate, Oadby, Humberstone, Derby and London.

Clifford Hall recalled: 'I was eight and lived in East Goscote Street. In the street was the shelter, with a thick concrete roof. The local warden, Dicko, was in charge. We were all in bed but tumbled down the stairs, out the front door, into the shelter. Dicko had the door open and counted us in. We sat in semi-darkness: the only lights, hurricane lamps. The grown-ups were trying to keep cheerful in front of us kids. "It's probably just a false alarm," they were saying. But this was no false alarm. We heard the bombers go over and the crump of bombs. Next thing, the lanterns went out. We were in darkness. We clung to each other as each crump went. I was terrified, so was everybody else. Eventually, Dicko managed to light the lamps again and some kind of sanity returned. The grown-ups were trying to reassure us that all was okay – but this was fear talking: you could see from their faces that even they didn't believe it. Eventually, I went to sleep. When I woke, the shelter doors were opened and we all went outside. The smell as the doors opened, wafted in: smoke, burning: these smells have never left me. One side of Gartree Street was gone. It was like looking at my sister's doll's house. You could see right inside. Furniture hung down, burning. The scene is imprinted on my memory.'

Looking up Sparkenhoe Street, with Gartree Street on the left, it's clear how bomb blasted this part of Highfields was: every building has some form of damage. [Leicester Mercury]

Two other HEs fell in **Conduit Street** and **Andover Street**, injuring six.

Winifred Goodwin was a FA volunteer: 'At the Swain Street (Hillcrest) FAP, the bombs were dropping so fast, staff and casualties were arriving at the same time. One elderly woman said: "Don't let the doctor examine me, I've only got my old corsets on." It was really pathetic, as she was covered in plaster debris. Later, I thought she was talking to herself, but she had her hands together under the blanket and was praying. Tears still come when I think of that grand old lady's courage. We were near the railway, so were in the target area. The doctors told us to move patients not too badly injured under the tables. One man was far too ill, so Sergeant Grills stood by the stretcher and held his hand all through the bombing. He had been in the Royal Navy during the First World War and ran the FAP like a ship. If he gave an order, everyone obeyed. When we came out of Swain Street next morning and saw the damage, we wondered by what miracle we were still alive.'

10.27pm: A small HE landed in **Castle Gardens**, near Morgan Squires' stores. Road strewn with glass. Two injured.

10.28pm: Two 50kg HEs fell in **Trinity Hospital Gardens** and **Castle View**, damaging the historic Tudor Chantry House and strewing The Newarke with glass. The *LM* reported: 'Bombs dropped either end of a hospital for aged people [Trinity Hospital]. The 39 occupants had miraculous escapes and none was hurt. The old lead lattice windows were shattered at one end, where Miss Pauling had just entered her room with a flash lamp: "I suddenly saw a bright glow through the blackout curtains and dashed behind the door. There was a terrific explosion and the glass came in." Her presence of mind probably saved her from injury. Damage was done to two historic houses, but valuable museum pieces escaped. A college [College of Arts] had many windows broken.'

Shop windows were damaged by blast from an HE in **Uppingham Road**.

10.35am: An HE fell in **Evington Drive**, above Kilworth Drive, demolishing a house and leaving a big crater in the road, damaging telephone cables.

10.40pm: It is clear the focus of the raid was gradually shifting eastwards, away from the railway station, deeper into Highfields.

Fire services, FAPy and rescue squads were at full stretch, when a salvo of three heavy HEs fell on **Saxby Street**, near the corner of Sparkenhoe Street. One hotel, one shop and four houses were demolished. Direct hits were also made on 59 **Sparkenhoe Street**, the eastern, southern and western corners of the crossroads, destroying several houses. Water, gas and telephone cables damaged.

The three bombs appear to have fallen diagonally, with the Saxby Street hotel centre. MoHS scientists recorded: '1 hotel, 1 shop and 4 houses demolished; practically direct hit on ARP depot. Casualties 13 killed, 13 injured (2 ARP personnel).' This figure has since been accepted in published accounts. However, a clarification in the *LM* later in the war, pointed out: 'Up to 40 personnel were in the depot, in the Wesleyan chapel schoolroom, when it was wrecked by blast. It was the church that had a direct hit. Amazingly, most of the ARP workers escaped with just minor scratches. Two were severely hurt: Deputy Superintendent Mr D.A. Peel, who had a face injury, and Mr P. Baker, a FA man, a broken collar bone. The rescue and FA kit was destroyed.'

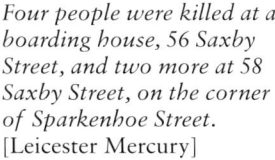

Four people were killed at a boarding house, 56 Saxby Street, and two more at 58 Saxby Street, on the corner of Sparkenhoe Street. [Leicester Mercury]

Blitz victim: Kathleen Tilley, aged 27, was killed at the boarding house at 56 Saxby Street. [Leicester Mercury]

Although the ARP depot, a post office and houses had been hit, the main area of concern was on Saxby Street corner. Four were killed at 56 (boarding house): Joseph Pertzin, 32; Miss Kathleen Tilley, 27; Mrs Frances Taylor (aka Fowkes), 29 and Harry Taylor (aka William Johnson), 48. Mr Taylor was found smartly dressed, with kid gloves, gold cufflinks, diamond rings, watch chain and medal, brandy, tobacco pouch, keys and £125 [£5,500] cash. Two were killed at 58 (apartments): Sidney Harper, 34, and Arthur Wood, 37, of Birmingham, furniture department manager of Lewis's, Leicester.

The 18 personnel of Bond Street Mobile FA Unit, under 40-year-old MO Dr Ernest Berry Garrett, were dispatched in their converted bus, the first time it had been used. Parking just in Stoughton Street, the party took over the kitchen of 80 Sparkenhoe Street as an emergency dressing station, opposite the incident. They started to attend the first casualties 'with great coolness and endurance'. Joan Howes lived at' 80 Sparkenhoe Street: 'The bombs began

More HE bombs demolished properties directly opposite the Saxby Street incident, on the Stoughton Street junction, with Sparkenhoe Street running left to right. [Via Malc Tovey]

falling and I went to the cellar. Shouting outside brought me running out and I helped pull two injured people from a cellar opposite to our cellar. Shortly after, a doctor and ARP people crowded in. A room above was fitted with wooden shutters as a temporary casualty station. Shortly, a bomb dropped at the front gate on a medical bus parked there. We were instructed to get out quickly. As I ran from the cellar steps, I looked towards the front of the house, to see a huge wall of flames. Unfortunately, the nearest shelter had been cracked by the blast and we had to move to another shelter. After the all clear, we returned to find all three corners of the crossroads down, with the exception of ours. Number 80 was still standing: marble fireplaces lifted, doors blown off, windows and china shattered and the bedroom a sea of mud from hoses. Next day, everybody was exhausted. Removal of our damaged property was delayed because the steeple of Saxby Street church was unsafe, preventing traffic. Later, it was brought down by explosives.'

The burnt out remains of Bond Street ARP MFAU bus after it was struck by an HE bomb in Stoughton Street. The bomb blast flung it against this brick surface shelter, badly cracking it. The white cross marks the emergency exit. [Via Terence Burford]

No doubt attracted by the fires, this second salvo had fallen on the eastern corner of Stoughton Street/Sparkenhoe Street. The MFAU immediately blew up and was destroyed by fire. Detective Constable Jock Joiner, then 24, witnessed it.

'Earlier, Jock and his pal, DC Brian Hawkes, had been sent up on to the flat roof of Charles Street police station on fire watch, as the hailstorm of incendiaries came tumbling out of the darkness: "We were surrounded by the buggers. My shoes were burning from kicking them off the roof. We were on that bloody roof two-and-a-half hours."

'No sooner had the pair flopped into the canteen for a break, than they were being sent out again. "Inspector Poole came in and said, 'You, you, you and you', pointing to me, Brian Hawkes, Len Norman and George Trump, 'I want you to go up to Highfields. It's taking a right hammering.'" Their job was to set up an incident post. They had not long set up their blue police lantern, when it was smashed by a nearby explosion. "A bus carrying medical supplies was blown up in front of my eyes."

'Jock and George were sent back for another lantern and set it up again: "We helped fetch the dead and injured out of houses in Saxby Street. You could hear whistles of the bombs coming down. Jets of flame shot from a fractured gas main in Sparkenhoe Street. The whole place was lit up like Piccadilly. You could almost wave at the bomber pilots. There was no ack-ack, so the pilots came as low as they liked." Shrapnel smashed into one man's gas mask case. He instinctively put his hand up to his chest and it took his finger off.

'Suddenly, a blast smashed the breath from Jock's body: "All I remember is a searing orange

DC Brian Hawkes, killed by a bomb at Stoughton Street. [Leicester Mercury]

Dr Ernest Berry Garrett, MO in charge of the Bond Street MFAU. [Mary Maynard]

Though concussed by a bomb explosion and falling debris, St John sister Ivy Marsh attended to fatally injured DC Brian Hawkes. For her 'coolness' and 'bravery' under fire, she received a St John Certificate of Merit. [Author]

St John officer Carrie Wells found and rescued a fatally injured boy, Frank Thorp. She then carried him a quarter of a mile to the nearest FAP, whilst bombs were still falling. She received a St John Certificate of Merit for her courage. [Author]

flame and gliding through the air, mouth wide open. It all seemed in slow motion. Oblivion." Jock's escape was miraculous. He had been standing inches from his fellow officers: "I was hidden under debris." Jock suffered from shock. Shrapnel blew a hole in his steel helmet and the right side of his head was numb for months. It was two years before he could taste food. Widower DS Leonard Norman, 34, and DC George Trump, 26, were killed instantly, but DC Brian Hawkes, 26, died at 5am in the LRI. PC Horace Burks was badly injured by bomb splinters and was off duty for six months.'

This time, the IP was moved right out the area: '11.45pm: Incident Post out of action: moved to corner Highfield Street and London Road.'

Mary Maynard, Dr Garrett's daughter, recalls: 'I remember father coming home. He was a tough man who didn't suffer fools but he looked pale, the way he used to after attending bad road accidents. He was grey with dust and his smart leather doctor's shoes were cut to ribbons by broken glass. The MFAU was a converted single-decker charabanc, with an emergency operating table. My father was very proud of the bus and was very upset about losing it, as he had put a lot of work into it. Father said the policemen were discussing the incident, when they heard a bomb falling: some dived one way, the others the other way and were killed.'

On January 31, 1941, the Duchess of Gloucester, Deputy Commandant-in-Chief of the Order of St John, visited Leicester and inspected the FAPs. At Granby Halls FAP, she presented certificates of merit to members of the Bond Street MFAU. They were: Dr Ernest Garrett, divisional surgeon, of 257 London Road: 'Regardless of danger, Dr Garrett went to the assistance of casualties lying in the street. He again established his Post with equipment he had been able to save, in a surface shelter in Saxby Street, and, amidst further bombing, freed casualties covered by masonry to render first aid and remove them to Swain Street FAP. The work of this Officer and his unit was exemplary and deserving of the highest commendation. They displayed the utmost gallantry and devotion to duty in most trying circumstances.'

Although off-duty, Miss Ivy Marsh, of 35 Portland Street, a St John Ambulance Sister of the MFAU, went with her unit in civilian clothing to the incident. Although in great danger, stunned by an explosion and half-buried under a fallen door, she worked while bombs exploded, attending injured DC Hawkes. She remained with him, until he was removed by ambulance. Her 'coolness, pluckiness and bravery' was recognised by the Watch Committee, who presented her with a certificate for bravery, and by St John Ambulance, from whom she received a Certificate of Merit. The Chief Constable stated she displayed 'signal gallantry and courage.'

Miss Carrie Wells, senior FA officer, of 104 Barclay Street, heard a child crying for help. By light of the burning MFAU, she found the child in the street. The boy, Frank Thorp, 15, was dragged away from the burning vehicle, and with the assistance of a soldier and two wardens, she applied improvised tourniquets to the boy's arm and leg and carried him on a deckchair to Swain Street FAP, a quarter of a mile away. Here, she gave what assistance she could, then returned to the incident, where bombs were still falling, to find Dr Garrett, where she reported again for duty. 'Her courage and resource in the face of great danger were most commendable.' Sadly, Frank Thorp died next day at the General Hospital.

Mrs Hilda Hefford, of 5 Royal Road, was with Dr Garrett's unit and, after escaping from 80 Sparkenhoe Street, 'showed courage in re-entering the house to help find morphia and instruments. She took part in the rescue of trapped men and twice entered the house, only leaving when ordered owing to the danger of fire.'

Widower DS Norman left two children under 16. His funeral was held at St Hilda's church, Melbourne Road, on November 23, 1940. Neighbours lined the streets as the hearse bore his coffin to the church. Six colleagues acted as bearers and a guard of honour of 20 sergeants and constables formed outside the church. The Chief Constable and Deputy attended. DC Trump left a widow with one child. His funeral took place in his Midland home town. DC Hawkes left a wife with no children. He was buried in St Deny's churchyard, Evington. The Chief Constable, Deputy Chief Constable and various other police lined the church entrance. In 2008, a new headstone was placed on his grave by Leicestershire Police Federation. In *Upbeat*, their in-house magazine, Jock Joiner said: 'Hopefully, people will read about those lads who lost their lives in the line of duty. It's important people remember.' Deputy Chief Constable David Lindley paid tribute: 'Brian, George and Leonard demonstrated enduring qualities including courage and commitment, service to community, putting others before self, regardless of risk and consequences. This is what we should remember them for.' Their names appear in a roll of honour at Leicestershire Police's force headquarters.

10.44pm: Just minutes after the first stick of HEs hit the Sparkenhoe Street/Saxby Street junction, **Highfield Street** was again hit, this time at the crossroads with **Severn Street**, where up to four HEs destroyed two houses on the south-western corner, including 31 Severn Street, killing six people: the owner, widow Mrs Eliza Knew, 76; Mrs Ethel Brown, 35 and her son, Frederick, seven; Mrs Muriel Curtis, 41, Miss Susannah Thompson, 73 and widow Mrs Frances Freezor, 65, who died three days later at the LRI. Five people were injured.

Though the time is slightly different, amazingly, it appears we may now know the type of German bomber, its unit and ordnance it dropped at this incident. German records reveal a Ju88 bomber of LG1 (Lehrgeschwader 1), a mixed unit comprising instructors, based at Orleans/Bricy, France, reported: 'Flieger Korps IV: Leicester: I/LG 1: durch 1 Ju 88 um 22.00 Uhr mit 1 SC 500 [HE], 1 SC 250 [HE] und LZZ 250 [delayed action HE]. Wirkung nicht beobacht ['Effect not observable'].' Fire broke out and ARP services were considerably obstructed by the presence of a delayed action in the crossroads, which exploded at noon next day, leaving a large crater.

Len Weir was sheltering with his parents in a basement next door at their hotel, The Severn Hotel, at 27-29 Severn Street, together with 15 guests: 'A guest went up to her room to get something she'd forgotten. On returning, she said there was a hole in her bedroom wall. I was thrown out my hammock when the house next door received a direct hit. It was particularly sad, because the house belonged to the mother of a warden who had taken his wife and son there, as he thought they would be safer in that large house.'

On the opposite side of the crossroads, at 41 Highfield Street, terrified 10-year-old Rodney Bates and his brother, Geoffrey, seven, had retreated to their cellar in pyjamas and dressing gowns when the bombs started dropping. The two boys, their parents, plus a lodger and her baby, listened to the drone of planes, the crump of bombs and then the crashing of houses collapsing nearby: 'All the lights went out after a bomb came down in Sparkenhoe Street. Soon after, another stick fell – and the last one hit us and number 43. Dad held us both down as the house collapsed above us. The plaster ceiling fell on us, the cellar window blew over us and our candles went out. I thought we were going to die. Dad wanted to go upstairs: he was worried the ashes in the grate would start a fire. I cried: "Don't leave us". Suddenly, an ARP officer in the house above us, shouted "Is there anybody in?" "Yes" Dad called. "Are you all alive?" he shouted. "Yes," said Dad again. It was amazing: we were all okay, though

St John nurse Mrs Hilda Hefford, after escaping from 80 Sparkenhoe Street, 'showed courage in re-entering the house to help find morphia and instruments. She took part in the rescue of trapped men and twice entered the house, only leaving when ordered owing to the danger of fire.' [Author]

An ARP ambulance car and trailer lie smashed in the centre of the crossroads at the junction of Highfield Street and Severn Street. Six people were killed in the building on the right, 31 Severn Street. An AFS Coventry Climax light trailer pump appears in the foreground. [Leicester Mercury]

people died opposite. "Come out as quickly as you can," said the warden. "There's a bomb in the crossroads that hasn't gone off."'

Dr Duncan Porteous recalled: 'As were dealing with the incident, Inspector Weston said: "Doctor, there's a little round hole in the road. Was there a manhole there?" I replied: "Not to my knowledge". "Well, it must be an unexploded bomb: we'll evacuate the district", he said.' Inspector Weston recalled that when he gave the order to evacuate, there was 'no panic amongst anybody: After all they had been through, it surprised me. They'd had such a hammering and I thought some would be hysterical. Absolutely nothing.'

Buses were brought up through the raid, each with a policeman on board, to evacuate residents. Hundreds more walked up London Road to Victoria Park, where it was hoped they would be safe. Mr H.W. Peek recalled: 'I was one of four City Transport drivers who answered the call to drive a bus to evacuate people. I took the first load to East Park Road WMC rest centre. The next load was taken to Queen's Road Club rest centre. I've often thought of the person playing a piano in a house in Saxby Street with the windows blown out.'

Mr D.J. Paynter lived in Sparkenhoe Street, opposite St Peter's church: 'The bombs fell before the sirens sounded. It was said the ARP had to telephone Coventry and Birmingham to ask permission. The bombing shredded our washing and blew it over our lilac tree. We took shelter on our cellar steps. We were there until 12.10am, when we were turned out our house because the situation was getting worse. Doors had been blown off their hinges, windows blown out, a piece of shrapnel had gone through the bay window along a wall, a door, then another wall and landed in the hearth, taking a line of wallpaper and paint off. Outside, a Corporation double-decker bus was covered in holes. The opposite side of the road had been completely flattened. We went to Medway Street School, where we were packed into the playground until 5am, when a bus took us down Humberstone Road to a hall. The bus driver was from Birmingham and didn't know his way – we nearly finished up in a crater.'

Leicester Corporation bus 266 was caught in a bomb blast on Sparkenhoe Street which shattered its windows and pockmarked its body with shrapnel. Fortunately, all aboard had taken shelter just moments before. [LTHT]

Back in Severn Street, Len Weir recalled: 'After a while, we were told to vacate our hotel's basement because there was a UXB nearby. As we were leaving, mother got caught up in telephone wire brought down with the bombs. We were taken to a shelter in Stoughton Street. Buses eventually came to move us to Clarendon Park. As we were going down St Peter's Road, there was a loud bang: the bus behind received a direct hit.' A *LM* reporter noted: 'The Corporation bus was was evacuating people at Saxby Street corner. Everyone took shelter, the driver and conductor in a basement. I spoke to Stafford (Transport Manager) who said the bus was in service again four days later. The driver was unharmed.'

An unusual event was reported almost three decades later, when Leicester's last war damage claim was finally settled in July 1968: 'Since 1940, Mrs Alice Lawley, 72, has been trying to claim compensation for damage done to her home, 45 Highfield Street. The house next door was bombed, leaving one side of her house without protection from the weather. As a result, she has since been unable to use her downstairs room because of damp.'

10.45pm: An HE demolished 79 **Evington Drive**. Gas, water and telephone services damaged.

10.46pm: An HE in **Gwendolen Road** damaged two houses, started a fire and burst a water main.

10.48pm: A 'direct hit' by a c.50kg HE on Woodville, 'a large, private house of the best type' at 14 **Knighton Park Road,** on the corner of The Avenue, killed two people, Mrs Lillian Miller, 40, and Bertha Phillips, 60, plus injured one. The house has since been rebuilt to the original style. ARP volunteer Alice Lomax, of 69 Stoughton Drive North, may have walked past this incident: 'Miss Lomax, a Wyggeston Girls' School teacher, received a telephone call at 10pm to give a blood transfusion at hospital. Although bombs were falling, Miss Lomax walked about 1½ miles to hospital, and after the transfusion, walked home. She showed great determination to get to the hospital, despite risk to life.' She later received a commendation for brave conduct and devotion to duty.

A medium HE bomb caused a large crater in land behind houses on Gwendolen Road, throwing up much rubble which damaged surrounding roofs and windows. [Via Malc Tovey]

10.59pm: An HE fell at the rear of houses on the north side of **Diseworth Street**, at Mere Road, close to a shelter, but only one person was hurt.

11.03pm: HE and IBs fell in **Holmfield Road** damaging houses, trapping some. The *LM* reported: 'Mrs P. Dear, [of 4 Holmfield Avenue], had an extraordinary escape. A large piece of bomb came through her window, just where she had been standing. The same district experienced a hail of IBs. Some fell in houses, others in the roadway. In a few seconds, the interior of a house was ablaze. One man called the owner, Mr T. Holmes, [of 60 Holmfield Road], from his shelter, from which he had to dig himself out. A neighbour, Mrs J. Fortune, [of 2 Holmfield Avenue], and Special Constable Knight, together with Mr Holmes, ran into the burning front room, tore down the curtains and

At 10.48pm, the smart Victorian property Woodville was struck by a 50kg HE bomb, causing several floors to collapse, killing Mrs Lillian Miller, 40, and Bertha Phillips, 60. [Via Terence Burford]

smothered the burning furniture with the carpet. Their presence of mind saved the house. Meanwhile, Mrs H.G. Leif was alone [at 71 Holmfield Road], when a neighbour rushed in to tell her an IB had fallen through her roof. A party armed themselves with buckets of earth, plus a stirrup pump, and put the fire out.'

11.24pm: Two HEs demolished 27, 29 and 34 **Norwood Road**. Two UXHEs were found: one at the rear of **113 Evington Lane** and another at rear of **10 Evington Drive**, possibly from the same stick. Both spontaneously exploded next day before BDS could attend.

11.34pm: Two houses, 133 and 92 **Evington Drive** were badly damaged by blast: 92 had to be demolished. Public services damaged and three hurt. The road was blocked by a large crater.

11.45pm: An HE fell on the LMS railway embankment behind 109/111 **Cobden Street**, but caused no damage.

11.54pm: A large HE made a very large crater in **London Road**, at Stoneygate Road, completely blocking it. Water, gas and electricity mains cut, tram tracks uprooted and telephone cables destroyed. One injured. Damage was caused to houses in Albert Road, Avenue Road, Stoneygate Road and London Road. The telephone service in Stoneygate failed. Communication between M/C and 'F' Division was very difficult. Repairs were impossible for several days because of UXBs nearby at Albert Road; Rudd's Playing Field (Stoneygate School); Avenue Road, 60 yds from London Road and opposite 55 Avenue Road Extension.

PC John Pomfret was sent on his bicycle, with blue steel helmet and gasmask, to search for UXBs. He arrived at Avenue Road. As best he could in the blackout, he began checking roads and gardens for UXBs. Instead, as he neared Holmfield Road: 'I found a hole big enough for several double-decker buses in the middle of London Road, between Albert Road and Stoneygate Road.'

On November 24, 1940, No. 42 BDS commenced work on two UXBs at London Road and one at 55 Avenue Road Extension, with AMPC and Leicestershire Regiment personnel. On November 30, a 50kg UXHE was defuzed and removed from the rear of 312 London Road. It was sent to Company HQ, on account of its unusual locking ring. A similar UXHE was also dealt with at Avenue Road. Both had No.15 fuzes. On December 1, Lt Lee defuzed a 50kg UXHE at the front of a house in London Road. It also had a standard No.15 fuze.

11.55pm: An HE fell in the middle of **East Park Road**, at Bradbourne Road, damaging the tram track and cable, caused a complete roadblock. Houses suffered blast damage and two people were injured. Graham Francis recalled: 'In the moonlight, I saw an enormous crater in the road outside the butcher's. Paving stones were on the roof and shop windows had disappeared, whilst in the crater, remains of a saloon car were enveloped in twisted tram rails. The huge crater caused severe problems, but tramway engineers constructed a crossover, so trams could terminate outside our house, then return to the city centre via London Road.'

12.08am: HEs fell on the hosiery factory of James Hearth & Co Ltd, at 6 **Newarke Street**, destroying it and the adjoining Providence Baptist chapel. The Downing Building opposite was damaged but an electricity sub-station was saved. Considerable damage also done to the bottling plant of R.C. Allen & Co, in **Oxford Street**.

Bill Williamson, stationed at RAF Debden, Essex, was on leave and, of all days, had got married at Leicester Cathedral at lunchtime: 'The wedding party celebrated at my bride's parents' house on York Road. Bombs dropped on the powerhouse there, blowing our windows out. It was terrifying. The police cleared us out. We grabbed the cake and a few bottles and ran into a shelter in Lower Brown Street, where we carried on the reception with neighbours until 6.30am. It was so cramped, it wasn't very nice, but we did our best.'

At first, the Providence Baptist chapel trustees planned to rebuild the church in Buckminster Road, but the War Damage Commission withdrew the license and the compensation money was passed on to build a new church in Limes Avenue, Aylesbury, in 1957.

12.09am: An HE fell on **Welford Road** Recreation Ground [Nelson Mandela Park]. No damage.

12.10am: A stick of HEs fell across **Spinney Hill Park**, where a UXHE just missed a packed trench shelter, averting a disaster.

People were cowering in the underground shelter as four bombs fell on the cricket pitch. Norman Hastings recalled: 'As the bombs landed, water poured through joins in the concrete walls. We were really wet. It was terrifying to hear the bombs coming closer. One man was kissing his girlfriend, as he thought it was the last time he was going to see her.'

Graham Francis, then nine: 'When we arrived at the shelter, several neighbours were already down there with their pets: cats, dogs, rabbits and a parrot in a cage. Everyone was wrapped up and reasonably cheerful. Some of the men swapped jokes. It was dank and cold under the cricket pitch and the concrete walls dripped down one's neck. After an hour, it became quite airless in this concrete tomb, so someone suggested the ventilator be opened. To do this, one man climbed the stairs and went outside, walking over the ground above. We never saw him again, because at that moment, a bomb hit the cricket pitch. Everyone screamed as the concrete walls caved in. Water poured down and there was total darkness. The whole thing happened in a split second, for just as quickly, the walls reverted to their normal shape and it stopped "raining". Shortly after, we made our way back to the surface.' Ruby Baldwin was also in the shelter: 'The blast buckled the metal door so it could not be opened; we all sat on the benches hardly daring to breath. Then someone, crying, said "we'll never get out and probably die down here". However, a warden came and we all were soon out in the fresh air. My God, that was a relief.'

On November 24, 1940, No.42 BDS commenced work on the UXHE with AMPC and Leicestershire Regiment personnel. On December 3, Lt Lee and Sgt Samways attempted to defuze the 50kg UXHE, but the fuze could not be removed and so the bomb was detonated on site.

An HE fell in the road at the lower end of **Park Vale Road**. It broke but did not ignite the gas mains, closed the road and blasted houses.

A medium HE fell on the pavement in **Bradbourne Road**, near Rowsley Avenue, blocking the road and causing considerable damage to houses. A gas main burst. Arthur Gardner recalled: 'My sister Winnie was on duty in the ARP M/C. When bombs fell, the cooks had hysterics. My sister had to revive them with smelling salts. During the night, plotting officers nipped into the kitchen to grab snacks. They informed my sister of the latest incidents: "Incendiaries on Holy Cross church," then "Freeman Hardy's on fire". Later, "a bomb on Bradbourne Road". For the rest of the night, my sister was on edge, wondering whereabouts it had landed on her road.'

A medium HE hit 4 and 6 **Bannerman Road**, which collapsed, trapping several people. Water and gas mains were damaged. Rescue parties worked for 14 hours to free casualties. At 06.18am, one child was reported still trapped and a body was recovered at 2.45pm next day. One trapped taken to hospital, five injured. Yolande Townley, 31, was killed at number 4 and Cecilia Standen, 47, at number 6.

William Horner, then an ARP Ambulance driver, found a woman in an entry buried up to her shoulders. The Rescue squad hastily built a tunnel over her to protect her from falling debris: "Where the next house stood was a crater and we could hear moaning. Scrambling down, we found the body of a young woman [probably Yolande Townley] and an injured man.' Another explosion threw Mr Horner and his colleagues into a heap: 'I would like to pay tribute to my ambulance attendant, Miss Kathy Holland. She was very young and I will always admire the way she stood up to the horrors of that night.' Audrey Willmott, née Day, was devastated to find number four, her home, completely demolished. For days after, Audrey got used to the greeting: 'Good heavens, I thought you were dead.' People thought she had been killed as her name appeared on a list of victims. Ironically, while neither she nor her mother were injured, a female lodger [Yolande Townley] who had come to get away from the bombing in Coventry and had taken refuge under the stairs, was killed. 'My mother and I were left homeless, with two businesses run from the house, a hairdressing salon and a drapers, destroyed. Mother's little haberdashery shop at the front had disappeared, with lingerie strewn over the road. We were left with only the clothes we were wearing.'

An HE hit John Bull Rubber Co. Ltd, on **Evington Valley Road**. It is believed MoHS scientists recorded this incident as: 'HE plus IBs: Armament sub-contractors. Single-storey steel frame building, one beam cut through by HE. Completely gutted by fire. Machine tools all damaged. All production stopped.'

A UXHE was found at **Evington Valley Road**, near Mervyn Road, probably from the same stick. It would appear the above HEs were aimed at industrial targets along the Evington Valley Road area marked on Luftwaffe target maps.

12.14am: Needlemakers T.S. Grieve and Co. Ltd, in **Queen Street**, with nearby T. Venables & Co (Paragon Works) factory in **Southampton Street**, were on fire from earlier IBs, when Grieve's took a second hit. Eight fire appliances were sent, including two from Peterborough and Northampton AFS. At 01.32am, the Police IO reported the premises gutted. The HO report noted: 'Damage to Factory Engaged on Work of National Importance: T. Grieve & Co. Ltd: Engaged on sub-contracts to Bentley Engineering Co., covering presses, Bofors gun parts and bullet-making machinery. Factory gutted and machinery requires overhauling.'

A serious near-miss occurred. The MoHS scientists reported: 'HE: Underground commercial shelter: 1-2ft from 13" brickwork wall of reinforced concrete roofed entry staircase to 5-bay shelter. Explosion demolished staircase head and part of shelter. Also, two brick surface shelters on roadway. Bomb burst 8ft from back end of nearer surface shelter. No occupants.'

Fortunately, it was only a 50kg HE and had hit the entrance, rather than directly on the shelter. It was reported 'five [sic] people were killed and 14 injured when a bomb fell on the shelter. The factory above was on fire and an urgent message was received at M/C asking for "as much help as possible." Dozens were trapped and all available resources were rushed to the incident as a dramatic race between the fire and rescue took place. Many were saved in the nick of time.'

ARP Ambulance Officer Leonard Lee, of 199 Wicklow Drive, later received a commendation for brave conduct at this incident: 'Mr Lee was stationed at M/C. As Casualty Services IO, he proceeded to where a particularly dangerous situation was developing. His accurate and prompt reports enabled M/C to despatch adequate assistance. During this time, bombs were falling.' On January 31, 1941, the Duchess of Gloucester presented the Special Award of St John to Mr Lee 'for devotion to duty.'

Six-year-old Derek Alexander's father, Walter, 32, was the sole fatality. Derek remembers the shelter's roof caving in and the rest of his family being pulled to safety through a manhole. Ironically, apart from broken windows, Derek's family home in nearby Samuel Street was unscathed: 'If we'd have stayed at home, we'd have been all right.'

Perhaps the closest escape was Mary Dowsing, then 14: "I met my cousin, Molly, and we went to the Odeon to see, ironically, *The Case of the Frightened Lady*. About 8pm, an announcement came on the screen saying the siren had gone. We decided to stay. However, cinema staff decided to evacuate us all. We tried to make our way home. I've never been good at finding my way round Leicester, so we went up Queen Street. The streets were very dark and it was cold. On the way, we were pulled into a shelter at Grieve's factory by a warden. The shelter was packed. We went down some steps and it divided into shelters, each holding about 40 people, sitting in lines. We sat near the entrance, hoping to make a quick exit if there was a lull. We were frightened. We moved further in, because the toilet started to overflow and was very smelly. About 12.30am, the bomb fell, landing at the shelter entrance – where we'd been sitting. We were buried to our necks in bricks. The light in our part of the shelter stayed on. There was lots of dust. We didn't hear the bomb: It felt like I'd dived into a pool and the water had hit my ears with a bang. A little lad kept shouting: "get these bricks off me." We couldn't undo the emergency exit, because we couldn't move. We were there for what seemed like half the night. I remember smelling and feeling petrol spilling from a nearby lorry and saw flames filtering through the shelter and bricks. I believe wardens dug us out. I left my cousin there: I had no choice, as the wardens moved us on. I lost my glasses and new blue court shoes my mother had bought, but otherwise, was only bruised. I walked the streets. The wardens found me some men's shoes, miles too big. We were taken to some big arches, apparently the LMS Granary. I got home about 7am. Mother made me a cup of tea. My cousin's head was spilt open and she went to hospital.'

Nellie Bentley, then 13, and her four brothers and mother were evacuated to Samuel Street from London after their home was bombed. But within a week of moving in, the sirens sounded. A neighbour started panicking, so the family took her to Grieve's shelter: 'The shelter collapsed and we had to be dug out. There was panic and screaming when the bomb struck. I think I was knocked out because I don't know how long I was trapped. I was pulled out by my hair. Mother was under the rubble and was in the LRI for two months. The panic is still with me.'

Later, the fire spread to the LMS grain warehouse in **Samuel Street**, but was saved by five fire appliances, including two from Coalville and Hinckley. MoHS scientists recorded: 'HE plus two UXBs plus IBs. 5-storey grain warehouse. Bomb exploded on deep girder of 3rd floor, setting fire to surrounding goods. IB set fire to lift head on roof.'

Meanwhile, one of the UXBs proved particularly troublesome – even 50 years later. In 1987, engineers working on the new Central Relief Road approached the *LM* after hearing rumours a UXB was still present. Local, Reginald Ginns, warned: 'The story goes bomb disposal couldn't find the bomb because it hit a layer of running sand. The engineers working on the new road should proceed with caution.' Indeed, a wartime *LM* report recalled: 'Perhaps the most memorable UXB was in Queen Street. It had come to rest in a bed of moving sand. It moved from day to day, as fast as the BDS uncovered it.' Official ARP reports confirm there was a UXB at the LMS Goods Yard, on Queen Street, and BD records show that 'on November 24, 1940, No.42 BDS commenced work with 3 AMPC and 3 men Leicestershire Regiment.' However, the 1987 roadbuilders need not have worried: 'On December 28, 1940, the UXB was removed. It was the same type as removed from Mere Road – a PC 1400 "Fritz". Removal was supervised by Lt Lee and carried out by No.42 BDS.' The UXHE was taken away by Derby BDS in a truck, with police escort. Again, the big bomb was not defuzed before removal and was driven away live through the streets!

Post-war histories have recorded that five people were killed in Grieve's shelter. However, CWD records reveal only one person, Walter Alexander, 32, was killed there. They also reveal six people were killed at a neighbouring factory shelter – something overlooked since.

A 50kg HE struck the entrance to the packed factory basement shelter of T.S. Grieve and Co., in Queen Street, killing one man, Walter Alexander, 32. This was a near miss and many shelterers escaped with their lives. [Leicester Mercury]

Although only a tiny child, Sheila Arnold, née Hammond, remembers the bombs falling on Grieve's factory, directly opposite the Bakers Arms, where her father, the landlord, and his family sat under tables, until not a single window survived intact: 'My little friend, John Copson's family and the Grimmitt family were sheltering in Norman Jackson's factory at the back of our pub on **Peel Street**. The owner had given them the keys, because he thought they would feel safe there in a raid. The factory had a direct hit.'

P.W. James lived at 41 Peel Street: 'I was 11 and our neighbours were Mr and Mrs Grimmitt, a lovely couple. Mr Grimmitt played in the orchestra at Little Theatre. I was under the stairs with my parents. Mr and Mrs Grimmitt were in the factory opposite, Jackson's, on the corner of East Short Street. With them was their daughter Hilda and son-in-law, Sid Copson, their small son, John, and their visitor, Mrs Bramley. The factory received a direct hit and set fire to Sharp's woodyard opposite. Everyone in Jackson's was killed. Our front room was full of bricks, with the front door hanging from one hinge. I looked through the doorway and can still remember the loading door at Sharp's woodyard, red hot and ablaze, collapsing inwards.'

Missed in ARP records and largely unknown for 70 years, six people were killed sheltering in Norman Jackson's shoe mercers factory, on the corner of East Short Street and Peel Street. [ROLLR]

Marjorie Chaplin: 'My dear friend and neighbour, Mrs Bramley, went to the Grimmitts in Peel Street. I remember her saying, "Going out for tea, see you when I get back." My husband and I and our baby went with Mrs Bramley's daughter-in-law, who lived with her, into their Anderson shelter. After the all-clear, we waited for Mrs Bramley to return. After a while, my husband walked over Swain Street bridge to see if he could find her at the Grimmitts, but, he found the whole area wrecked. He was in an awful state when he returned, covered in smoke and grime. The look on his face told us everything.'

On November 26, 1940, the LEM reported: 'Simple Funeral of Air Raid Victims: The Bishop and heads of other denominations stood at the graveside when the funeral of ten people killed in an East Midlands city air raid took place. On the other side of the grave were families carrying wreathes and flowers. Said the Bishop: "We are united to declare that those who have fallen were in the front line. We say in our hearts as we sympathise with them, that though the enemy may harm the body and smash homes, he cannot touch the spirit or reach the soul of England." The coffins of these "citizen soldiers" were draped with the Union flag. The ceremony was attended by the Lord Mayor, Town Clerk, Chief Constable, chairman of the ARP Committee and ARP workers. In two graves were one family: Mr and Mrs George Grimmitt, their son-in-law and daughter, Mr and Mrs S. Copson, and their six-year-old grandchild, John Copson. They met their deaths together. On the grave of John Copson was a spray of white chrysanthemums bearing the words "From little playmate Roy."'

ARP records make no mention of this incident, which is surprising, because of the death toll. The nearest they mention is the neighbouring but wrong street: 'At 06.35hrs, police IO later reported several dead under debris at Carrington Street, one body recovered.' However, the CWD files correctly record Sidney Copson, 37, his wife, Alice, 36, and their son, John, six, all of 47 Peel Street, together with George Grimmitt, 69, and his wife Alice, 71, of 43 Peel Street, plus Mrs Florence Bramley, 57, of 2 Darley Street, all died at 'Jackson's shoe mercers shelter'. It would appear that in the night's confusion, these fatalities were attributed to the Grieve's factory incident: a confusion that has remained, until now.

12.15am: An HE destroyed the Ice Cold Storage Company factory, in **East Street**, causing damage to houses fronting London Road. Firemen tackling the fire were faced with a shortage of water. MoHS scientists seemed particularly interested in this incident, recording it in some detail, probably because of the unusual circumstances: 'HE, [believed 50kg], food cold storage warehouse. 2-storey steel frame building, 30ft high. Bomb struck parapet wall, made 2ft hole in flat roof (3-inch gravel, 1¼-inch asphalt, 6-inch insulating cork, 10-inch reinforced concrete beams). After passing through meat, butter etc stacked on first floor, bomb exploded in six-foot of ice stacked on ground floor, making crater 8ft x 2ft. Explosion blew down brick pier, badly cracked others. The supported wood floor collapsed with its load of meat etc into crater.'

12.16am: Several people were trapped when several small HEs fell on houses in **Woodland**

Avenue, causing widespread damage. Gas and PO cables damaged. At 12.45am, fire broke out and Stoneygate Terminus AFS sent. RPs freed trapped, two injured.

12.35am: An HE fell at the rear of 'working class houses' in **Richard Street**, causing considerable damage and injured seven people.

Miraculously, only two people were injured when a large HE fell on the north-west corner of **Cobden Street and Willow Street**, demolishing at least 10 houses and leaving a huge, brick-lined crater. Surface shelters were covered with debris, but shelterers were rescued unhurt.

Edward Hubbard, then 16, lived at 95 Cobden Street: 'My family had adjourned to our brick shelter. Fitted with bunks, it was home from home. The only drawback however, the concrete ceiling "sweated" and dripped over those on the top bunks. I watched the searchlights in the distance trying to pick out enemy aircraft. We spotted the odd plane's guns by their tracer bullets. I had a hot drink and retired to my bunk. We listened to the planes going over and the occasional "crump" of bombs landing. Then came the "whoss" of a bomb coming down. Pop exclaimed: "this one's close!" There was a tremendous explosion and we were thrown about on our bunks. The shelter rocked as if it was about to collapse, then silence, followed by the clatter of debris raining on the shelter roof, then silence again.

'On opening the shelter door to a pucker "bombers' moon", it was like daylight. "Not too bad", I thought – then looking right, it was unbelievable: everything had disappeared and there was a crater 25-30ft diameter and 12ft deep, 20yds from our house. The off-licence and store, run by the Freestones, plus four terraced houses in Willow Street and three more adjoining had disappeared. Two houses were declared unsafe and demolished. Inspection of the opposite side of Willow Street revealed the side of the house and chippy laying in the road. My thoughts were: "Those goose-stepping swines had destroyed not only our offy, but the chippy as well!"

The huge crater caused by a large HE bomb that hit the corner of Cobden Street and Willow Street, destroying ten houses in the vicinity. Beer crates from Freestone's off license, which stood on the corner, lie in the foreground.
[Leicester Mercury]

'Next morning, a policeman was posted at our gateway to stop looting: There were bottles of beer and cigarettes everywhere. Workmen covering the roofs with tarpaulins found a settee on our roof ridge. The shop's contents were scattered over the houses and the backyards. A hole was spotted in the railway embankment. The bomb squad was called and a UXB suspected. Sappers took the upper part of a coal truck off its wheels, filled it with sandbags and dragged it over hole until they were available to sort it out. But, a day later, Mr Freestone came looking for his safe that had been in the shop cellar. It puzzled him, as it was very heavy and would take three people to move it. But when the BDS dug a few feet down, they found the suspected UXB to be Mr Freestone's safe! He arrived with the key to see if it would open – it did! Pretty amazing, as it was thrown 100yds, clearing a three-storey factory before burying itself in the embankment. Mr Freestone collected his takings and went away smiling.'

12.40am: Four people were injured when The Lodge, in **Elmfield Avenue**, was destroyed by an HE, trapping people in the debris. At 12.44am, a County RP from Granby Halls depot was sent. At 01.01am, Inspector Ecob reported the Gas Department were urgently required, as gas was leaking into the wreckage where one person had still not been released.

Mary Jebbett, then 16, was playing the piano in her lounge in **Kimberley Road**, when a 50kg HE landed in the garden, blowing out the lounge window: 'I felt my head and thought it had been raining. But it was blood – my head had been split open. I was taken to St Philip's FAP, where I had stitches.'

A 50kg HE fell in the yard of a printing firm in **Samuel Street**, causing little damage, although one person was injured.

12.45pm: A 50kg HE fell at the bottom of the ramp leading to **Swain Street** bridge. A gas main was damaged.

01.05am: A medium-sized HE caused a crater partially blocking **Knighton Park Road**, between St Mary's Road and Victoria Park Road. A car ran into the crater, injuring two occupants. A UXHE was found at Lyndhurst School, **Knighton Park Road**.

In adjoining **St Mary's Road**, a 50kg HE hit the centre of Springfield, a large house, causing considerable damage but fortunately, all occupants escaped injury.

A small HE fell between 12 and 14 **Bolsover Street**, causing slight damage to several houses, the sewers, gas and water mains. No casualties.

01.15am: A 'very heavy bomb' – possibly one of a pair of PMs (the other PM fell on Knighton Road) – fell in **Shirley Road**, near Elms Road, causing a large crater in the road. Many houses were damaged by blast and several people trapped in the wreckage. Tragically, Janet Wates, 42, was killed at her home, 48 Shirley Road. A member of the WVS, she had just returned from helping feed the bombed-out in Coventry. Her name is listed on the National WVS Roll of Honour at their London headquarters. Five others were injured.

A medium HE demolished 17 and 19 **Saville Street**, killing Frederick Garratt, 55, and his wife, Hetty, 58, at number 17. Husband and wife were buried together. In Rufford Street, Ray Simpson, then seven, recalls: 'Mother was very frightened as we couldn't go in the Anderson shelter, as it was flooded, so we went under the stairs and Mother held a cushion over my head: goodness knows what use it would have been! The bombs got closer and Dad decided we were going in the shelter, saying it was better to get wet than killed. The bunks were just above water level. Somehow, we managed to stay dry – until our two lodgers came home and wanted to get in the shelter. Just then, a stick of bombs fell from Kitchener Road, across Boswell Street, finishing on Wadkins. The blast blew one of the lodgers into the shelter, knocking us off our bunks: we were all soaked, but safe! We laughed, but wet or not, there was no way we were going to leave the shelter. Next day, we couldn't go down Sidwell Street, as a house in Saville Street had been hit. The smell of gas was terrible. We found out two people had been killed sheltering under the stairs. Mother said there was no way we would ever shelter under the stairs again.'

A 50kg HE fell in the footway of **Green Lane Road**, opposite Wadkin Ltd, causing damage to gas, water and electricity mains. Other 50kg bombs fell in the drive, cratering the approach to Wadkin's.

01.16am: A large PM fell at the corner of **Knighton Road and Newstead Road**, causing another heavy casualty toll. Three large houses were flattened, as though the site had been cleared. Not even a single course of bricks was left. At 26 Knighton Road, Mrs Janet Lankester, 33, and her son, Robert, four, were killed. Little Robert's body was found at 54 Knighton Road, still in his pink and green pyjamas. His father, Dr J. H. Lankester identified his body. Mother and son's ashes were scattered at Leicester City Crematorium's Garden of Remembrance. Mrs Lankester's sister, Mrs Ruth James, 31 and her son, Bryan, three, were also killed. Both were also buried together. At number 28, the home of Dr Leonard Porteous, who was busy dealing with incidents in Highfields, Mrs Jennie Falber, 33, of Golders Green, Middlesex, and Mrs Leah Falber, 55, of Finchley, Middlesex, were killed. At 70 Knighton Drive, James Bibby, 66 and Miss Connie Newman, 19, the domestic servant, were killed.

Houses near Carisbrooke Road were also demolished and damage was done to property over a wide area. Every house in Elms Road, as far as Sidney Road, was damaged as well as Southernhay Road. An RSJ beam from one of the houses was bent around a tree on Knighton Road by the tremendous explosion. It is said small pieces of metal can still be seen embedded in the top of the stump.

Many casualties were reported trapped. Rescue work continued through the following day and night. Leicestershire's highest award for civilian gallantry was attained at this incident. The following day, the *LEM* reported: 'Somewhere in the town is an unknown hero. He saw an incendiary hit a house, broke into it, seized the bomb and rushed with it into the street. He dashed back again and brought two children out before having his burns dressed. The man was taken to hospital for further treatment without his identity being discovered.'

The unknown and unlikely hero was 'Beaming, likeable, 54-year-old William John Higgott, of 18 Knighton Drive, an Inland Revenue inspector, of rotund figure, ready open countenance and a bespectacled smile.' The *London Gazette* recorded: 'Warden Higgott arrived at an incident immediately after a bomb had exploded. Without regard for his own safety, he

The only known photograph of Warden William Higgott, who received the George Medal for 'courage and efficiency' at the Knighton Road incident. [Leicester Mercury]

entered a building which was a mass of ruins and in an unsafe condition. He came out with two children, one under each arm. He then returned and put out a fire in the upper part of the premises. He next went to a neighbouring building and extinguished a fire there. Subsequently, he did extraordinarily good work and extinguished another fire where a large bomb had exploded at the corner of two roads [Knighton Lane and Knighton Drive]. He showed a very high degree of courage and efficiency.' Mrs Higgott told the press: 'People said he did good work, but when I mentioned it, he just replied "nonsense".' Modest Mr Higgott would not accept he deserved the honour: 'Hundreds did more than I that night.'

It may have been at this incident that John Garner, of 6 Monsell Drive, Divisional Warden for 'F' (South Leicester) Division, won his commendation for brave conduct and devotion to duty, as stated in the *London Gazette*: 'Garner was assiduous in the organisation of wardens and rescue work, in which he took part. He was blown off his feet whilst working, but resumed and showed efficiency and good leadership.'

Another Warden, Kyle Dawson, of 1 Stoneygate Avenue, also received the same honour: 'Dawson worked through the night, carrying out his duties. He made several rescues, and in spite of bombing, went to the assistance of people who had been bombed out. He also went twice to a spot where a UXB lay [possibly one of the London Road area UXBs] to examine it. He was a great inspiration.'

Three large Victorian homes on Knighton Road were flattened 'so not even a course of bricks was left' by a 1,000kg Luftmine B parachute mine, which killed eight residents. Note the steel RSJ beam bent round the top of the tree on the right by the PM's fearsome blast. [Via Terence Burford]

ARP Rescue workers frantically clear the rubble at 28 Knighton Road, where Mrs Leah Falber, 55 and Mrs Jennie Falber, 33, of Golders Green, London, were killed. [Via Terence Burford]

01.18am: A large HE fell behind Hadfield's chemist's, at 26 **Allandale Road**, killing John Stansfield, 28, and injuring three. The shop and two adjoining houses were halved. The backs of the houses collapsed on several residents and it was some time before rescue workers could reach them. Escaping gas provided an additional peril.

Joan Farmer says: 'My mother, Freda Waterfield, née Hammond, lived at 28 Allandale Road. Then 18, she was attending secretarial college on London Road. As she walked home, incendiaries fell on houses in Stoughton Road and she saw people brushing them off their bay windows. She took refuge with her family in the cellar of 28

Allandale Road. Although the bomb fell nextdoor, fortunately, our mother and family were safe. The front of the house survived, the remaining part was demolished. Most of the family silver was looted.' Noel Rudkin recalls: 'The piles of rubble and debris-strewn garden became a playground for local children, called "The Damoes", short for "damaged buildings".'

Dora Greaves was a nursing officer at the St John's FAP in Clarendon Park: 'I lived at 350 London Road. I put on my tin hat and rushed off to the unit. On the way, a whizzbang fell in Allandale Road and I was thrown to the ground. When I got to the unit, I attended to a couple of soldiers who had been injured. It wasn't until hours later, I realised I had no knees left in my stockings!' That night, the Clarendon Park FAP dealt with 84 casualties, several of whom died. 'Mrs Greaves received the Defence Medal and is prouder of that than later founding a maternity home in Sheffield.'

The rear of 26 and 28 Allandale Road, where John Stansfield, aged 28, was killed. The large crater, centre, was probably made by an SC 250kg HE bomb. [Leicester Mercury]

01.22am: An HE fell at the rear of **Kitchener Road**, at Bolsover Street, destroying a house and trapping occupants, but no serious casualties.

02.18am: The final incident of the night was in **Birkdale Avenue**, at Knighton Road, where five people were injured when 'five residential houses of the best type' were damaged by HE and blast. Damage to gas mains.

Also, during the night, Mrs Susan Martin, 60, of 27 Sylvan Street, died of heart failure at the Ingle Street School shelter. But not all victims died that night. In January 1942, the *LM* reported: 'Related to the Loughborough coroner during an inquest on Miss Dora Lewis, aged about 53, of 176 London Road, Leicester, found drowned in the canal at Cossington, her friend, Miss Emma Barrow, said since Miss Lewis's bombing ordeal, she was concerned she had lost her grip. Times she heard the siren, she was very "strung up". She once suggested suicide. The coroner returned a verdict of suicide while of unsound mind.'

Eight hours and 17 minutes after the alert, the all-clear sounded at 04.04am. It was dark, but fires still flared. People staggered out from underground, dazed with lack of sleep and the concussion of an all-out air attack. Eve Holden put her arm around her mother and said: 'Don't worry, it's all quiet now.' 'Yes,' said her mother, 'perhaps the Jerries have gone home.'

Arthur Gardner recalled: 'After the all-clear, my sister walked home. Hurrying down Hastings Street, she was frightened by a herd of stampeding dray horses. Wide-eyed with terror, they galloped by from the Midland station.'

The first immediate post-raid ARP report, written just hours afterwards, said: 'From approximately 20.00hrs until 02.00hrs, HE bombs of all calibres fell on the City. The exact number is not known, but 150 is a fair estimate. Extensive damage, estimated at £1 million [£42.6 million] to business and private property.' In 1965, the *LM* noted: '2,000 were put out of work for one to two months.'

In 1944, the ILC reported: 'Approximately 150 HEs, 400-500 IBs and four para-mines descended upon Leicester. In this raid and in a one-plane attack on the following night, the destruction in the city was reported as: seriously-damaged houses: 550; slight damage and breakage of glass: 4,200 houses. Industrial damage: 11 properties destroyed, 72 others seriously damaged. Casualties: 108 people killed, 208 injured.'

However, a 2014 bomb count of ARP records shows that approximately 89 HE, 12 UXHE, 4 PM and 2 OB fell on Leicester that night, totalling 105 HE weapons, varying from 50kg to 1,400kg types. Fortunately for Leicester, the majority of the HEs were the smaller 50kg type.

Surviving ARP records are generally unspecific about the weight or even the number of bombs at each incident. However, even if we conservatively count the unspecified HEs as 50kg, around 17,100kg/17.1 tonnes of HEs were dropped that night. Estimates of IBs vary from '400-500' to 'thousands'. If we approximate about 1,500 IBs, then with the two OBs, that's about 2,000kg/2 tonnes of incendiary weapons, making a total weight of ordnance dropped about 20 tonnes. The Luftwaffe definition of a 'major' attack was over 100 tonnes, whilst a 'significant' attack was over 50 tonnes, so in Luftwaffe terms, Leicester's Blitz Night was a 'minor' attack.

Soon afterwards, North Midland Region compiled a report on the raid marked 'Secret', largely based on Leicester ARP Committee's own post-raid report. They sent their report to the MoHS in London. Its contents were not for public dissemination, so it can be taken as largely accurate. Its general conclusion was 'All ARP and AFS services worked well and ARP machinery operated in a very satisfactory manner.' Its more specific conclusions included:

'Reporting by wardens was uniformly good and the Control Centre [M/C] functioned well. The Controller was practically first in the City to notice IBs falling and immediately appreciated what was happening. A large part of the south of the City was cut off from the telephone exchange and an improvised messenger service filled the gap. The Messenger Service worked excellently.

'The proportion of killed to seriously wounded was unusually high and appears to be accounted for by the large number of residential houses demolished, approximately 170. 450 houses were seriously damaged and 2,760 required repairs. 18 industrial buildings were destroyed, 22 seriously damaged and 193 slightly.

'There were not a large number of persons injured. Consequently, no great strain was thrown on this service. In fact, only half the city's casualty services were in operation. FAPys

The sight that greeted ARP officials the morning after Leicester's Blitz Night: sunlight streams through the dust at the corner of Highfield Street and Severn Street. Note the wrecked ARP ambulance towing car, left. [Leicester Mercury]

functioned efficiently and the Ambulance Services – although initially there was shortage of ambulances owing to volunteer personnel not turning out – earned high praise for their evacuation of wounded under heavy bombing. The MOH says that he has nothing but the highest praise for the skill and courage displayed by all the Casualty Services.

'At 13 larger incidents, doctors directed FAPys, diagnosing injuries. The MOH reports rather a high proportion of seriously injured were sent to FAPs instead of direct to hospital.' This reveals a high-level of mis-diagnosis. However, the city ARP report tends to contradict the Regional report: 'The numbers of casualties admitted to hospital were: LRI: 41, General: 35. The system, recently adopted in Leicester, of attaching one or more MOs to each FAP worked very well. These MOs accompanied FAPys to incidents, gave such treatment as possible and directed cases to hospital or FAP. Most corpses were very badly damaged. Seven corpses remain unidentified. These were picked up on roads and are not associated with any particular incident. One trailer ambulance, three vans and five cars belonging to the Casualty Service were destroyed or badly damaged, besides the MFAU, which was a total loss.

FAP	Treated	Transferred to LRI/CGH
Bond Street (Fixed)	26	3
Broughton Road	0	0
Cort Crescent	2	0
Cossington Street	26	2
Granby Halls	36	9
Holy Apostles	1	0
St John's	34	16
St Philip's	38	21
Spence Street	11	3
Swain Street	31	7
Evington Point	0	0
Bond Street (Mobile)	5	3
City General Hospital (Mobile)	0	0
Total:	210	64

'The Ambulance Service trailers proved quite adaptable to raid conditions, being very mobile where streets were blocked. One trailer was loaded with casualties when masonry crashed on it, further injuring two of its patients and seriously damaging the trailer. The casualties were transferred to another ambulance and taken to hospital, the damaged trailer since repaired. Had the same thing happened to a converted car type ambulance, it would have been a total loss.

'Rescue Parties arrived promptly, but in major incidents, there appeared some lack of control. RPs were doing unskilled work of clearing streets when they should have been getting out people trapped under debris, meaning some corpses were extricated days after they had been trapped.

'The 200 soldiers used to help RPs quickened matters considerably. There was some difficulty getting labour to clear streets, owing to unskilled labour being drafted into Coventry. It is clear tunnelling, as opposed to removal of debris, is well-founded. We hope to secure unemployed miners from South Wales to form a tunnelling section. We already have the offer of 50 miners from Notts and Derby Coal Owners Association.

'At 22.59hrs, the County Controller rang the City Controller offering assistance. The City Controller accepted the offer and asked for 10 RPs to be sent to Granby Halls Depot: three parties from Loughborough, Market Harborough, Thurnby, Kibworth and Hinckley. All these parties were in action during the night and rendered very valuable assistance. Afterwards, the WVS fed them 100 breakfasts. These parties were released and replaced by fresh parties from Lutterworth, Shepshed, Mountsorrel and Anstey.'

On the yellow alert, fire appliances and ambulances were dispersed to various locations to prevent them being destroyed together in their station by a single bomb. In 1940, Leicester FB only had two TL appliances, a third added in 1941. Additional TLs were sent from Derby and Nottingham.

'The FB Inspector reports the Fire Services functioned well. The fires were all promptly dealt with. Non-interference with the water supply was of great assistance. This probably averted a major raid developing. The fire situation was complicated by the fact that Birmingham was being heavily attacked and at 21.18hrs, before any help was sent to Leicester, the Regional Third Stage move had been made to help Birmingham. At 22.30hrs, the District Officer in Leicester put into operation first and second stage moves, which brought in help from seven authorities in his district, and four from outside. The Regional Scheme worked smoothly and the supporting brigades were prompt and their work a high order.'

Chief Fire Officer Winteringham noted: 'The majority of fire calls were sent to Brigade HQ, from where they were passed to the Divisions. 103 fire pumps were in action with over 11 miles of hose. Some fires burned for three days. Apart from a few minor injuries, we suffered no casualties, but one or two men were treated for severe shock. It is very gratifying to know both the Regular Brigade and AFS were equal to the occasion, and although it was a stupendous task, they were quite the masters of the situation.'

Perhaps the severity of the raid caught some out, but although the siren did not sound until 10 minutes after the first flares fell, there was still 25 minutes to get to the shelters before the first HEs fell. It appears many remained in their homes. For those sheltering in the cellars of the large three-storey Victorian terraces in Highfields, it proved the worst refuge. With their slight delay fuzes, the HE bombs penetrated then exploded at first or ground floor level, or even in the cellars, bringing the above storeys down on those sheltering. No wonder the ARP reports state corpses were 'badly damaged'.

No. 42 BDS war diary recorded: 'Numerous reports received from Police HQ of UXBs in dangerous positions. Section Officer Lt R.C.A. Lee, Sgt Samways and L/Sgt Rowlands escorted in Police car to UXBs. Bombing was constant during this tour. Police car nearly wrecked when it ran into unreported crater.'

'Many people rendered homeless by destruction or damage to their property, and a much larger number – 900 – because of UXBs in their neighbourhood.' There were 19 UX or DA bombs [above the standard 10% average of bombload]. Impact on industry, which could not operate until UXBs had been removed was incalculable. Some 32 UXBs were reported during the raid: but after investigation, 13 proved to be portions of HE bombs, parachute flare casings etc. 120 BD personnel dealt with UXBs. By November 24, 15 UXBs had either been defuzed or exploded spontaneously.

'The work of dealing with the homeless was done by the Welfare Department under Mr Shilton, the WVS under Mrs Bates and Welfare IOs under Mr T. Wilkie. At 03.00hrs, Mrs Bates sent messages to WVS Leaders to report to the seven Rest Centres at:

1) Conservative Club, Queen's Road
2) Railwayman's Club, East Park Road
3) Medway Street School
4) Manchester WMC
5) Belgrave Liberal Club, Melton Road
6) Bond Street WMC, Bond Street
7) Braunstone Estate Community Centre

'At 03.35hrs, Mr Shilton (Public Assistance Officer) instructed Mr Ramsay, Master of Swain Street Institution, to send 500 blankets to the Railwayman's Club on East Park Road, for the evacuated. At 05.30hrs, Mr Shilton messaged Mr Ramsay to supply bread, butter/margarine and tinned meat to provide breakfast for 1,000 people: the rations to be distributed as follows:

Railwayman's Club, East Park Road	500
Conservative Club, Queen's Road	200
Manchester WMC	160
Liberal Club, Melton Road	95
Bond Street WMC	30
	985 people

'Throughout the night, excellent work was done by the Canteen Section under Mrs Ogle and Mr Pinder. The three mobile canteens, with two others from Melton and Uppingham, visited various incidents, supplying ARP, fire and police services with tea and sandwiches. Over 4,000 rations of refreshments were served by the MCs.

'The following figures give an idea of the food used at the RCs: 841 tins of milk; 432 quarts of fresh milk; 442 lbs of tea; 135 lbs of sugar; 262 tins of biscuits; 20 tins of Oxo; 46 tins of cheese; 335 tins of soup; 134 tins of baked beans; 420 tins of corned beef hash; 372 tins of stewed steak; 251 tins of Irish Stew; 112 lbs of margarine; 134 slabs of cake; 1,008 lbs of bread; 86 tins of salmon; 134 tins of stewed meat; 30 tins of sardines; 72 camp pies; 56 tins of baked beans; 249 tins of soup, all costing £345 12s 3d [£14,700], an average cost of just over 5d [£1] per meal.'

The WVS reported: 'During the fortnight November 17-30, we served 268,800 cups of tea, using over 6 cwt tea, 15 cwt sugar, 270 lbs margarine, 351 x 3lb slabs of cake, 300 loaves.'

The *LM* reported the next day: 'Fires Guide Midland Raiders: Firemen's Heroic Work as Bombs Fall: A number of casualties are feared in the most ferocious attack made on one town. Serious fires were started, the German airmen using these as guides, rained bombs upon the town relentlessly. Considering the weight of the attack, the damage done was less than many feared.' A day later, the *LM* reported: 'The fires were fought manfully by the firemen. The work of the AFS and regular firemen during the hours of darkness, while buildings showed like bonfires to the enemy, was magnificent. Today, many of them had scorched and blackened faces. They did not want fulsome praise. When I tried to persuade one officer to make the heroic statements that we like to read, all he would say was, "We did our job."'

The *LEM* reported, more dramatically: 'A.R.P. Heroes of Midland Town's Biggest Raid: Death came hurtling from the skies… [but] AFS, rescue squads and other ARP services, put to a drastic test, came through with flying colours. The town was in the front line and amid the toil, sweat, blood and agony, were performed deeds of heroism. The town's ARP services were described as "100% efficient". This tribute was paid to the ARP workers who had spent weary months of boredom, waiting and training, for their test, by a senior ARP official.'

Since the war, several people have claimed Nazi radio propagandist William Joyce, aka Lord Haw-Haw, broadcast *before* the raid that Leicester was going to be bombed. One man wrote to the *LM* in 1982 going as far to claim he heard Lord Haw-Haw announce: 'I know where Leicester is. I know Mellor Bromleys, Steels and Busks, Wadkins, British United… I know them all and we're coming to get you', actually giving the date of November 19 that Leicester was to be bombed. The man allegedly marked it on his calendar and before the raid apparently warned his workmates. Ingles also noted it was said Lord Haw-Haw called Leicester 'That place of fish and chips', but later wrote: 'Many people would have us know Lord Haw-Haw announced that on such and such a night, Leicester was to be raided. If any list of war criminals ought to be compiled, it is these foolish people who seemed to delight in spreading the rumour TONIGHT WE SHALL GET IT.' Even recently, some still claim to have heard Lord Haw-Haw talk about the raid on Leicester. Memory can play funny tricks after several decades. But the tale Lord Haw-Haw foretold the raid is incorrect. Firstly, although the Luftwaffe had night air superiority, they were not invincible enough to tip off British AA defences and RAF nightfighters their targets, let alone the exact date. Secondly, as Joyce's biographer Cole wrote: 'So widespread was the belief Haw-Haw announced certain areas were to be bombed on specific dates, after monitoring all his broadcasts, the Ministry of Information issued a statement: "It cannot be too often repeated Haw-Haw has made no such threats."'

An 'Accidental Blitz'?

From that night until the present, many still ask: was the Luftwaffe's attack on Leicester a mistake? During the war, a *LM* reporter noted: 'A month after the raid, Mr Ledbury, Chief Regional CD Officer, said 100 planes were used and it was the official belief the raid was a mistake! Two months after, every other man could tell you how the raid started: one story was a 'bus caught fire in Humberstone Gate and "gave the show away".' In 1944, when censorship was relaxed slightly, the *LM* asked: 'It was, even in official circles, thought the raid on Leicester was a mistake. German radio communiqués made no mention of the attack and it was Birmingham's heaviest raid and a night when Coventry was attacked.'

In 1960, the *LM* reported: 'Talking about that black night with Chief Casualty Officer Len Lee, Records Officer W. Dale and Deputy Group Warden Edward Doughty, a big question mark forms above the ruins: Was it all an accident? Even today, it's a controversy. It looks as if it always will be.' And, in their 1990 nationwide study of the Blitz, Webb and Duncan's chapter on the Leicester Blitz is entitled: 'Leicester – the Luftwaffe's error?' They asked: 'As Leicester did not appear to be a major target in the Luftwaffe's pattern of raids, it seemed as if the devastating raid was an aberration. Had it been made in error? No definite answer appears to be possible.'

Another rumour started straight away that an accidental fire at Lulham's shoe warehouse, in Northampton Street, had attracted the bombers to Leicester. The fire had indeed been started by IBs. As early as March 1941, the *LM*'s 'Mr Leicester' attempted to hint as the truth, as far as the censor would allow: 'Scotching a Rumour: There has been a particular rumour concerning an air raid on a Midland city. "They" say the raid was caused through an outbreak of fire in a warehouse.' Later, in 1944, the *LM* were able to give a bit more detail: 'The incident at Lulham and Co was never officially reported to M/C. It was thus not timed, but was known to be one of the earlier fires.' But the rumour persisted after the war and in 1960, Lulham's MD, R.N. Hill, wrote to finally set the record: 'There was a terrific blaze at the adjoining Boston Blacking Co. before our warehouse caught fire. I saw the incendiaries. What's more, we were compensated later as a war-damaged concern.' The MoHS scientists' report officially settles the matter: 'Oil Bomb and 18+ IBs. Shoe and leather warehouses (one block). 4-storey warehouses, one completely gutted.'

So, was Leicester deliberately targeted? It's clear Birmingham was the Luftwaffe's main objective, but not their only target: as well as Leicester, minor incidents occurred at Northampton, Coventry, Grantham and elsewhere. The following day, the *LM* reported German claims that other towns were also *deliberately* bombed: 'The Germans say… in addition, targets of military importance were attacked in a number of other towns. Today's German High Command communiqué describes the attack on Birmingham as a reprisal for British raids on residential districts in Hamburg, Bremen and Kiel.' Although Birmingham was mentioned, Leicester was not.

At the war's end, many Luftwaffe records were destroyed by the Germans in case they provided evidence for Allied war crimes trials. Luftflotte 2's records were destroyed, but some Luftflotte 3 records survived, now residing at the Bundesarchiv, Germany, including a list of sorties that night. Crucially, this document states: 'Als Ausweichziele wurden angegriffen' ['Secondary targets were attacked'] – and Leicester is listed, indicating the city was a deliberate Luftwaffe target.

Most bombers that attacked Leicester dropped fewer than five bombs. Clearly, bombers do not fly all that way with just a handful of 50kg bombs, so they may have been passing on their way to or returning from Birmingham and stoking a diversion in Leicester. Alternatively, there is the possibility bombers dropped a few HEs on Leicester, then dropped the rest on the surrounding countryside, which was also heavily bombed that night. If this was the case, then Leicester was the main target for these bombers.

The Luftwaffe document lists the following attacks on Leicester: 'Flieger Korps IV: Leicester: I/LG 1: durch 1 Ju 88 um 22.00 Uhr mit 1 SC 500, 1 SC 250 und LZZ 250. Wirkung nicht beobacht,' which translates as 'Flying Corps 4: Leicester: 1/LG1: by 1 Ju88 at 22.00 hrs with 1 SC 500 [HE], 1 SC 250 [HE] and LZZ 250 [delayed action HE]. Effect not observable.' Cartwright suggests this aircraft bombed the junction of Highfield Street/Upper Tichborne Street, killing 45 people. The time and number of bombs approximately correspond, yet the bombload doesn't: one of the bombs was a delayed action, yet all the HEs detonated instantly at this incident. The bombload corresponds more accurately to the 10.44pm incident at the Highfield Street/Severn Street junction, where a DA was discovered in the road. The timing is different by 44 minutes, but they often are in these records.

Recalling the night, Arthur Gardner said: 'Not one of us knew the grim reaper had commenced his back swing.' He didn't know his metaphor was more literal than he imagined, as the document reveals Leicester was also attacked by a bomber of 1/KG54, whose emblem was the Totenkopf or 'death's head': 'Flieger Korps V: Leicester: I/KG 54: durch 1 Ju 88 um 00.50 Uhr mit 1 SC 500, 5 SC 50 und 5 SD 50. Brande verursacht,' which translates as: 'Flying Corps 5: Leicester: 1/KG54: by 1 Ju88 at 00.50 hrs with 1 SC 500 [HE], 5 SC 50 [HE] and 5 SD 50 [HE]. Fires caused.' Interestingly, Goss records: '10-14 aircraft of I/KG54 from Evreux, were to bomb the industrial area north of Birmingham. They had no more exact target than this,' which suggests they may have joined the attack on Leicester.

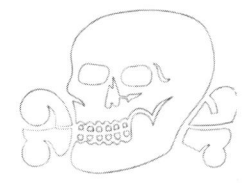

The totenkopf (Death's head skull) emblem of KG54. [Wikimedia]

The document also records: 'Amount of bombs dropped: On Leicester, 2 aircraft dropped 2 tons.' However, clearly, far more bombs were dropped than that. A 2014 count reveals around 89 HEs and 4 PMs (plus hundreds, if not thousands of IBs), totalling around 20 tons of bombs, over six hours, so therefore, it is apparent far more bombers were involved. Webb and Duncan stated 'more than 100 German bombers attacked Leicester that night'. However, the authors don't reveal how they reached that figure. The MoHS scientists stated they did not know the exact figure, but identified 20 bombers: 'one at 2,000ft, four at 5,000ft, four at 6,000ft, two at 9,000ft, six at 10,000ft, two at 12,000ft, one at 20,000ft. None picked by searchlights lower than 2,000ft.' The bomb count, distribution and times, indicate probably no more than 30 bombers attacked Leicester that night.

However, even if the above documentary proof had not survived, it is clear from the raiders' methodology, the attack on Leicester was deliberate, planned and targeted.

The bombing was preceded at 7.40pm by illuminator aircraft who identified the target with parachute flares for the following bombers. Next, at 7.45pm, firelighter aircraft used the flares as an aid to lay 'fire-ribbons' across the target area causing a Brandbombfeld ('fire-bomb field'), setting fire to buildings and providing better marking for the following HE bombers. It was common to select 50m spacing between the BSK 36s IB containers, producing a firebomb ribbon about 1,600m (1 mile) in length. This was about the size of the fire-bomb field next to Leicester LMS station. As Ramsey explains: 'For target marking, the firelighters laid a line of IB ('Ablauflinie') on the approach to the target at right angles to the approach track.' The MoHS scientists noted there were '55 fires (1 major, 5 serious).' They also suggested the 'glow from railway loco fires' may have attracted the bombers. This initial IB attack fell between Leicester LMS station and Welford Road, clearly highlighting the station area, rather than the city centre near the Clock Tower. The first main wave of HE bombers arrived over Leicester soon after 8pm and the first HE fell on the city at 8.14pm. Although both M/C and MoHS scientists identified the bombing in 'three main waves' of c.8pm onwards, c.9.40pm onwards and finally c.1am onwards, the staggered nature of the bombing was such that the last two waves are almost indistinguishable.

As Taylor states: 'Tactics were by now tried and tested. Instead of the bomber 'stream' favoured later by the RAF, German formations employed a multi-directional approach in order to confuse the defences, calling it the 'all points of the compass' approach. This required the attacking force to be divided into three or four waves, each timed to arrive over the target from different directions and different times to avoid collisions.'

Those on the ground attest to the staggered nature of the bombing. The following day, the *LEM* published: 'Raiders dive-bombed the town,' a warden said. 'They appeared to come singly, at intervals,' whilst Cartwright later recalled: '9pm: We heard German aircraft. They appeared to arrive at 20-30 minute intervals, so we took advantage of this to mash tea and visit the toilet, etc.' Mr H. Jarvis, a warden outside Leicester General Hospital, wrote: 'We observed the German planes seemed to set a course for the hospital chimney, then separate in different directions for their targets. The chimney seemed a good landmark and was used as such'.

Each of the HE bombing waves was preceded by IB fire-lighting bombers approximately 15 minutes before. The Luftflotte 2 bombers who flew up the River Soar from the south, target marking with IBs at right angles to the HE attackers. However, the last two waves could probably have navigated and bombed visually, using the fires started by previous bombers. Moonlight reflected on the Soar may also have acted as a navigational aid.

It is clear the primary target was London Road LMS station. This is not only obvious from the bombing pattern, but MoHS scientists also noted: 'Assumed target: LMS station and city in general. IBs dropped across centre of city on a South to North line, HE along 1½ mile line West to East.' Wood and Dempster also note railway stations were often the main secondary target.

Ironically, the railway and station seem to have largely escaped the worst of the Luftwaffe's attentions, whilst the surrounding streets, particularly in Highfields, receiving far worse damage. In 2006, a speaker at Ratby Local History Group suggested Highfields was bombed because Taylor Hobson's important lens factory, in Stoughton Street, made military binoculars. Yet the company, in existence since 1886, did not feature on the Luftwaffe's target map. A couple of bombs did fall near Stoughton Street, but the majority fell between London Road and Sparkenhoe Street, where there are no factories, purely residential properties of no industrial or military value. Some RAPC troops were billeted in shared civilian billets, but it's unlikely the Luftwaffe knew that. Highfields became the most heavily bombed part of the city – why?

The most likely answer is the phenomenon of bombing 'creep'. This is the tendency of bomber aircraft to prematurely release their ordnance, leading to a gradual spread of bombing away from the target. Taylor notes this phenomenon in the Luftwaffe attack on Clydebank, Scotland, in 1941. It was particularly noted later by the RAF during Bomber Command's night attacks on Europe. Middlebrook noted the crew's most vulnerable time was during the bombing run to the target. The pilot was required to keep the aircraft level in the face of air defences. The temptation was strong for the crew to release their bombs slightly before reaching the aiming point. The fires started by bombs fallen short tended to be used as an aiming point by subsequent crews, who in turn, also dropped their bombloads short. The result was 'the bombing inevitably crept back along the line of the bomb run.' Although ARP records state the bombers bombed Leicester 'from west to east', it is clear from eyewitnesses that once over the city, bombers circled, chose targets and bombed from different directions: so, it's fair to say, Highfields was likely a victim of bomb creep. It seems that it was the fires started by the first bomber to hit Highfields at 9.55pm, which proved the catalyst that started the creep of bombing away from the station. Afterwards, in a 20 minute period, six different incidents occurred in Highfields, over the space of just several streets, suggesting the ensuing bombing was relatively concentrated.

The first wave of bombers were relatively accurate, with much of their bombload accurately falling around the station. The smoke from their fires may have obscured the visual bombing of later waves, making them less accurate. This bomb 'creep' phenomenon may also explain the later bombings of Stoneygate, again, a chiefly residential area.

However, it is interesting and must be more than coincidence that the bombing pattern largely follows the Luftwaffe target maps: the targets marked all have bombs on/near them, whereas unmarked targets appear largely unscathed. Several eyewitnesses claim that due to the lack of AA opposition, the bombers flew low, picking out targets. This was a typical Luftwaffe tactic, which formed the criss-cross bombing pattern. Margaret Hatton was working in an AFS Divisional HQ: 'We looked up and saw a German bomber fly down the length of Great Holme Street: it was low enough, I could see the form of a German airman in it.'

KG26 pilot Horst Juventus recalled the sort of bombing Leicester endured, including bombing creep: 'In some [attacks] it was possible to see people fleeing from the flames, for we often flew lower in these night attacks. This was quite distressing, as it brought home the reality of the air war. The fires were like magnets to aircrews and they tended to drop their loads on them rather than search for "legitimate" targets. We could see firemen doing their best to put out conflagrations, while bombs continued to fall. We admired their courage.'

The Luftwaffe used electronic navigation beams to target Birmingham that night. Cartwright surmises whether they used the beams to bomb Leicester. After flying several hundred miles in the dark, the firelighter first wave did pinpoint Leicester station quite accurately, so, were beams used? The answer lies in the National Archives, Kew. The 'top secret' Ultra decrypts of the Luftwaffe's Enigma Brown codes, released in 1995, reveal German transmitters were ordered that night: 'All stations: Target 52: Birmingham,' indicating no beams were aimed at Leicester. But how did the bombers target Leicester so accurately?

From November 1940, Beleuchtergruppen KGr100 and II/KG55 used parachute flares to illuminate targets. Although not equipped with any special form of radio aid, the latter unit, Luftflotte 3's II/KG55, had considerable nocturnal operational experience and displayed particular skill at locating and illuminating targets at night. LC50 parachute flares were dropped by II/KG55 He111 at the commencement of major attacks. The other two Beleuchtergruppen, KGr100 and III/KG26, normally relied on X and Y Verfahren [beams]. Interestingly, 13 He111s of II/KG55 opened the attack on Birmingham, illuminating the target with flares between 19.12-20.10hrs, just before Leicester was illuminated. It is feasible other He111s of II/KG55 dropped marker flares on Leicester.

The Luftwaffe's Missed Opportunity

In their book, Webb and Duncan state 'the Germans were well aware that Leicester's industries were making a big contribution to Britain's war effort' – but were they? The fact that

A 1942 German military map of Leicester, with targets bordered. The overprinted bomb incidents and areas of incendiary attack show the concentration on factories in the Evington Valley area and London Road LMS station. Note the 'bomb creep' away from the station into Highfields. [Ian Franklin/Author]

Leicester's heaviest raid occurred when it was chosen as a secondary target and the net damage was relatively limited and recoverable, plus the city's few remaining raids proved even lighter, suggest the Luftwaffe did not regard Leicester as a priority target. Other similar-sized neighbouring cities suffered heavier bombloads.

In 1936, the League of Nations declared Leicester was Europe's second wealthiest city, mainly due to its industrial production. Most companies produced and distributed trade brochures, so intelligence was freely available. Yet, the few factories marked on the Luftwaffe's target maps, even in the 1942 edition, indicate German intelligence on Leicester was limited: they did not know to what extent Leicester was engaged on war production. Perhaps if they had, Leicester would have been raided more heavily.

In 1941, Leicester had 58 Vulnerable Points, vital to the war effort, including Ministry of Aircraft Production, Ministry of Supply and Admiralty contracts [see Appendix F]. These were important targets. Not only that, several companies were often conglomerated at one site, making even more of a high-yield target. One example, which, despite its size, was also missed off the Luftwaffe target maps and received no bombs, was Corah's St Margaret's Works: 'The four-acre works produced an astonishing tally of 26 million articles – 17.5 million men's socks and stockings included, along with cap comforters and anti-flash helmets. As for gun parts, 80,000 and parts for tank landing craft came from the factory's engineering department. Under the government's Concentration of Industry scheme were also the bombed-out industries of the Admiralty Victualling Stores, Standard Telephone and Cables Ltd and three hosiery firms. The Hosiery Rationing Committee of England, Wales and Northern Ireland also occupied 105,000 square feet.'

There can be no doubt Leicester was rich in important targets, but it appears the Luftwaffe were unaware to what extent.

WEDNESDAY, NOVEMBER 20/ THURSDAY, NOVEMBER 21, 1940

Ingles recalled: 'Wednesday morning was bright and sunny. Crowds thronged the streets, trampling through mud, water and glass to see what damage had been done. Many fantastic tales swept through the city about the damage: hundreds, some said thousands, had been killed. But business carried on as usual. The only folks who seemed concerned were those who thought Leicester was a "safe" place, and could be seen carrying suitcases towards the station.' George Morley remembers: 'From Highfields came the worst stories of bodies in cellars…'

Leicester must have wondered if the Luftwaffe would return again for round two. That night, it rained. The Luftwaffe repeated their attack on Birmingham, but with fewer bombers and fewer civilians died. Doreen Boulter was in Wigston: 'Father sat reading his *Mercury*, when the sirens wailed again. "Good garden stuff," exclaimed Father, "not another dose after last night."'

Leicester's sirens sounded at 7.55pm. The first significant report to M/C was that an IB had fallen in **Christow Street** at 8.17pm. Fire services reported it was a domestic chimney fire but within minutes, other IBs fell on parts of the city. All were dealt with by wardens and fire services. However, there seems to be scant details of these incidents.

Bombers continued to pass over to Birmingham, until a lull of several hours. Then, at 02.50am, a lone bomber released two PMs over Leicester. There is some dispute over where the first PM fell: Beazley says on Steels and Busks factory and the second on Victoria Park pavilion: ARP records suggest vice-versa.

MoHS scientists state: 'Mine 1) Crater 40ft x 20ft, demolishing gable end of 2-storey Victorian sports pavilion.' The shattering noise as the **Victoria Park** PM detonated provoked an initial report an aircraft had crashed there. Percy Barrow, the park keeper, 'saw the mine floating down, just missing his Lodge House as the wind changed direction', proving lucky for those inside. The PM fell on the gravel road in front of the pavilion, forming a large crater, blasting out most windows and damaging roofs overlooking the park. Five young women in the YWCA hostel opposite, in Granville Road, were injured by flying glass, though 85 others escaped injury. £11,192.10.6 [£477,000] damage was caused to the pavilion.

The abnormalities of blast are well-known. Although the PM detonated within yards of the pavilion, only the corner nearest the crater was demolished. Normally, PMs created shallow craters as they did not penetrate the ground, causing the powerful blast to radiate outwards. From the large crater and slight damage to the pavilion, it appears the ground absorbed most of the explosion and the crater funnelled the blast upwards and outwards, thus explaining distant damage down Regent Road. Later, the crater was converted into a concrete-lined NFS static water basin.

Originally a grandstand, it became a pavilion in 1883, when the racecourse was transferred to Oadby. Sadly, the pavilion's cast-ironwork, ornate brickwork and architectural detail were lost on some. Ingles remarked: 'The PM gladdened the hearts of many when it demolished the monstrous pavilion.' In 1941, a hut was built to provide temporary changing accommodation. The War Damage Commission paid towards a new neighbouring modern replacement pavilion, not completed until 1958. The surviving part of the pavilion, its toilet block, was finally demolished in 2006.

The *LM* reported: 'While firemen were tackling the fire, a plane could be heard machine-gunning. It is thought a British fighter was chasing the bomber.' Interestingly, RAF nightfighter ace Bob Braham chased an enemy aircraft in a Beaufighter, 'south-east of Leicester' – the approximate position of Victoria Park – but was unable to catch it.

Angela Winford-Ryder, then six, lived in one of the lodges at the entrance to the park: 'My father, a warden, was in the park when the mine landed. Mother panicked and took me outside to London Road. There was a red glow, with burnt paper flying around. I walked on crushed glass. When we returned, we found three wardens hiding under our kitchen sink!' ARP messenger Henry Matthews was cycling past when the mine exploded. He was blown off his bike and shaken but after a few minutes, continued on his duties. Afterwards, he returned and picked up a piece of the mine, which 60 years on, he still used as a paperweight.

Whilst the Victoria Park PM caused no damage vital to the war effort, the second PM scored a direct hit on an important industrial concern. The MoHS scientists reported:

'Mine 2) Messrs Steels and Busks Ltd, **St Saviour's Road:** Crater: 24ft x 10ft, in private 18ft-roadway between two factory blocks. Damage: Very severe, due to blast and fire.

'Main Block: 2-storey frontage, basement undamaged. Ground floor: bad cracks in staircase well. First floor: back wall nearest explosion demolished, all inside partitions distorted, gutted by fire. Roof lifted and scorched. Two workshops: major portion of roof trusses down, building irreparable, but machine tools mostly undamaged; blast thrust stanchions six-inches out, likewise roof

The crater left by a 500kg Luftmine A parachute mine which landed between two factory blocks at Steels and Busks Ltd, St Saviour's Road. The blast warped the factory's RSJ beams supports and blew out windows and walls. [Leicester Mercury]

A policeman and officials examine the damage to the ornate Victoria Park pavilion, the north-eastern corner of which was damaged by a 500kg Luftmine A parachute mine. In the background can be seen De Montfort Hall. [Via Terence Burford]

girders forced into far wall, displacing it one-inch. Tool safe: (equivalent to brick surface shelter) 18-inch brick walls, 9-inch reinforced concrete roof, fitted with armoured doors, 21-ft from crater: although severely damaged, preserved press tools therein.

'Side Block: 3-storey building, all but front section so seriously damaged by blast and fire as to require rebuilding; barrier wall 55ft from crater saved valuable equipment stored. Two outbuildings demolished, motor from top of lift shaft, 30ft from crater centre, found in crater. Salved machine tools being remounted in undamaged section to resume production. High tension electrical gear shattered, low tension workable.'

The HO report noted: 'Steels and Busks changed from making women's corset parts to parts for Spitfires. Fortunately, machine tools were undamaged and have since been moved to another factory. Damage to Factories Engaged on Work of National Importance: S & D Rivet Co Ltd, Ariel Works, Temple Road: Completely incapacitated. Serious, as they are engaged upon rivets, buckles etc and assembly of chin straps for steel helmets.' Damage to business and private property was estimated at £118,000 [£5.02 million].

Winifred Townsend, née Dormer, then an 18-year-old lathe turner on a night shift at nearby Mellor Bromley's factory, thought she was going to die: 'The bang from hell blew all the windows and glass roof panels over us. We got down on our hands and knees and crawled to our underground shelter. Everyone was shocked – but alive.'

This was a lucky strike on the bomber's part, because PMs were difficult to aim as they were highly susceptible to wind direction. The PM also damaged doors, windows and roofs in surrounding streets. The PM's parachute cap was found in Staveley Road. Thirty-five were injured, with four hospitalised.

Although the raid did not have the ferocity of the previous night, the ARP were taking no chances and this was the night of Leicester's longest alert, from 7.42pm to 06.17am: 10 hours and 35 minutes.

The Great Anti-Aircraft Scandal

In the two nights' raids, destruction in the city was reported as: seriously damaged houses: 550; slight damage: 4,200 houses. Industrial damage: 11 properties destroyed and 72 seriously damaged. Some noted the ease with which the Luftwaffe blitzed Leicester. Fifteen-year-old R. Sperry, sheltering opposite St Philip's church, Evington Road, wrote in his diary: 'Many bombs dropped. No ack-ack fire – why not?' DC Jock Joiner, badly injured on Blitz Night, noted: 'There was no ack-ack, so the pilots came in as low as they liked. The Germans caught us with our trousers down. We took a hell of a beating.' Dr Duncan Porteous, Senior ARP Medical Officer, said: 'We hadn't a gun. We hadn't any defence at all. No British plane. German planes were just coming over, whistling these things down.'

Indeed, CD Committee minutes record: 'The Committee express their concern at the fact that 1) a considerable bombing attack on the City had developed before the sounding of the sirens and 2) there was small evidence of defensive action.'

Tucked away in the National Archives is an astonishing and desperate type-written letter sent by Leicester and County Chamber of Commerce, begging the Prime Minister to act:

'The Rt. Hon. Winston S. Churchill C.H. M.P,
Prime Minister,
London S.W.1.

21st November 1940

Sir,

Leicester & County Chamber of Commerce in association with the Lord Mayor of Leicester urgently request protection against the dive-bombing of their people and industrial premises. Morale of people is high and can best be maintained by instant retaliation. At least give us a chance to hit back.

The quite impartial and unanimous opinion of the meeting was that a considerable amount of serious damage had been done, with loss to industri-

alists and their workpeople, in the recent raids here and there was no evidence of defensive or retaliatory measures having been taken.

In the City and County are many firms producing munitions, components, equipment, clothing and boots for the services. Many firms have enormously increased their plant and their output. Several firms have transferred their businesses from London, others seek to do so. In addition, Leicester and the County – being reputedly a safe area – have received thousands of evacuees from London and the Coast Towns. Recent events have shown that we are almost unprotected against attack from the air.

German aircraft have visited the City and many places in the County, caused great fires and by the light of these fires, been able to dive unhindered to destroy industrial and residential properties.

The morale of the people is high. Their attendance at work is good. All of them want to work, especially those who are doing work in furtherance of the waging of war, but a feeling of impotence induced by a complete absence of reply to the German attack is likely to have an adverse effect upon morale and upon production for war purposes.

Hardship and danger can be endured if there is the satisfaction that at least some reply is being made to the enemy's attack, but the feeling in general is that there should be immediately adequate means of protection for the people, their homes and the factories. It is a lack, which in our considered opinion, should be remedied without delay.

The people of this City and the County "can take it" but they long to hit back.

On behalf of the Chamber, I beg you to use your great influence to provide this City and County with adequate means of defence and retaliation.

We wish you God-speed in your work for the nation, the British Commonwealth and the world. I am Sir, Your obedient servant,

*H.F. Henderson,
President.'*

Leicester and County Chamber of Commerce's president, H.F. Henderson, wrote a desperate letter to the Prime Minister Churchill begging for air and ground defences for Leicester. [Author]

It would have been little consolation for Leicester's citizens to know that in 1940/41, AA defences made little difference to the Luftwaffe. Nonetheless, their demand for AA defences proved their morale value, if little else. Even though few AA guns were available, not providing any was a tremendous risk, leaving Leicester at the Luftwaffe's mercy.

Whether Leicester and County Chamber of Commerce's letter ever reached as high as Churchill is not known. However, it must have reached some upper level in the military, as just six weeks later, 32nd AA Brigade ordered the deployment of HAA guns around Leicester.

One little-known result was 'trekking'. McDougall wrote: 'Large numbers of persons from Leicester trekked into the County each night, fearing another visitation, seeking what shelter and accommodation they could find. This nightly exodus went on for many weeks, gradually diminishing as the winter passed.'

It would be almost five months till the next bombs fell on Leicester. But people remained jittery. At 11.35pm, on November 24, Mrs Aldridge, 64, of 126 Clarendon Park Road, suffered a fracture and shock on the sound of the siren and was taken to the LRI. On December 20, at the sound of the siren, Mrs Susan Bocking, 79, of 16 Hazelwood Road, collapsed and Special Constable No.222 H. Goode, of 107 Nansen Road, suffered a cut to his left eye and right shin. Both were treated at St Philip's FAP.

On December 22, **Manchester** was heavily bombed. Leicester FB sent assistance. A month later, the Lord Mayor of Leicester received the following letter: 'Town Hall, Manchester, 23rd January 1941: Dear Lord Mayor, the Director of our FB has written to the Chief Officer of your FB to express his personal thanks to the officers and men who worked so magnificently here after the recent heavy air raids. May I now, through you, express the thanks of the city to your Authority for this invaluable assistance? You will be pleased to know the Chief Constable has reported that every aiding unit, whether Regular or AFS, showed it had been excellently trained in fire-fighting and worked with enthusiasm and bravery. If you will convey the thanks of the citizens of Manchester to the officers and men who came here to help us, I shall be personally grateful to you. Yours sincerely, R. G. Edwards, Lord Mayor.'

In November 1941, the *LM* reported: 'Honoured at an investiture by the King at Buckingham Palace was Mr D. Sargent, former Third Officer of Leicester FB, who received the BEM (Civil Division) for gallantry and exemplary conduct during severe air raids on Manchester. The notification paid tribute to Sargent's skill and organisation, which was instrumental in saving much valuable property. A contingent from Leicester was among the men he directed during many hours fire-fighting in Manchester dock area. Mr Sargent was twice caught by bomb blast and personally dealt with many incendiary bombs. Soon after receiving notice of the award, Mr Sargent left Leicester to take appointment as Staff Officer at the Chief Regional Fire Officer's HQ at Nottingham. He played a big part organising Leicester's AFS.'

1941

Fortunately for Britain, many of the continental airfields were in a poor state through overuse and the severe winter weather. The bad weather continued, curtailing Luftwaffe sorties, providing respite for Britons.

Tragically, on January 11, two fire watchers were accidentally gassed whilst on duty at their factory. Frederick Hanley, 21, of Cambridge Street, was dead on admission to the LRI. His colleague, William Siddel, 22, of St Michael's Avenue, was hospitalised. They were found the next morning suffering gas poisoning, at Messrs Dallow, Lambert & Co., ventilating engineers, of Spalding Street. The inquest heard that 'the two fire-watchers went on duty for the first-time. In the messroom where they slept was a gas stove. The taps had been left on, but the meter controlling the taps in adjoining premises was off. The meter was turned on, the gas escaped from the stove and gassed the men. "A pure accident, for which no one was to blame," said the coroner.'

Fire watcher Frederick Hanley, aged 21, of Cambridge Street, who accidentally died from gas poisoning whilst fire watching at Messrs Dallow, Lambert & Co, Spalding Street, on January 11, 1941. [Leicester Mercury]

On January 31, an interesting case of looting was heard in Leicester: 'Sentence of five years penal servitude was passed at a Midland Assizes on a 32-year-old traveller, who admitted looting a house after it had been bombed. He admitted theft of a fur coat and cheques. He also pleaded guilty to breaking into and stealing from another house two watches and about 10s 3d [£22]. He was sentenced to three years on the housebreaking charge, the sentences to run concurrently. The stolen goods were valued at £100 [£4,260]. The defendant asked that 14 other offences be taken into consideration. Questioned by the judge why he reverted to crime, the defendant broke down, held up his hands, and said it was because he had no use in them. "This is a charge which the law authorises punishment of death," said the judge. "The housebreaking and stealing charge sunk into comparative insignificance beside the charge of looting. You are addicted to burglary and housebreaking." The traveller's case was one of several that went before Prime Minister Churchill in 1943, regarding the disparity of sentencing in looting cases: 'Case 838523: traveller, of Welford Road, Leicester: five years penal servitude for looting and three years for housebreaking and larceny, to run concurrent. Five previous convictions for larceny.' He was due for release in June 1944.

Tuesday, April 8/Wednesday, April 9, 1941

During the day, Herbert Morrison MP, Home Secretary and Minister of HS, visited Leicester. The *LM* reported: '"Men and women, I see you will be ready and stand firm if trouble comes. I want you to feel that you are doing an important job for your city and country." Thus, Mr Herbert Morrison addressed a parade of Leicester's ARP services lined up in Town Hall Square. It embraced a full 21 branches of CD. Mr Morrison spoke to many men and women. They were received at the Town Hall by Lord Mayor Cllr W.J. Cort, ARP Controller Cllr C.R. Keene and Town Clerk L. McEvoy. Speaking from the Town Hall steps, Mr Morrison said CD was an army of ordinary people, a united lot, coming from all walks of life. The defence forces were playing a great and worthy part in these cruel and wicked times. He congratulated the local authority on creating Leicester's unit of the CD army.' Little did those assembled know, just that night, Leicester's 'CD army' would be tested again…

During a full moon, the Luftwaffe returned to Coventry, with a heavy raid of 237 bombers, killing 281 civilians. In Leicester, Ingles recalled: 'We heard the sirens many times, but for several weeks, no bombs dropped. There was nothing but the incessant drone of enemy planes. To those of us in CD, the first three months of 1941 meant many hours of ceaseless vigil. When the dogs began to bark, I knew danger was imminent. Amid the dogs' howling, many thought it was just another "stand to". But those who believed in the omen of the dogs thought differently. They were right, for this time, the thud of bombs mingled with the roar of enemy aircraft.'

The sirens sounded at 10.39pm. Coventry's fires could be seen from the tower at Leicester's Central Fire Station. City firemen were standing by to go to Coventry's aid, when at 01.29am, it was reported flares were seen in the Aylestone direction. In 1964, reporter William Kidd noted: 'whichever plane dropped the flares must have changed its mind, because it was not until 3am that bombs were dropped.' Interestingly, the flares may have been dropped by a German bomber, attracting an RAF Hurricane nightfighter, piloted by Pilot Officer Richard Stevens, who shot it down at Peckleton, before it could drop any bombs on Leicester (See *Beneath Hitler's Highway* by Austin J. Ruddy).

The 2nd AA Division reported: 'Raid 100 entered Sector from east and dropped HE in Leicester at 03.10hrs.' Leicester ARP reported: '03.02am, Four HEs fell in a line from the Midland Station to **Ash Street**, off Humberstone Road, damaging 52 houses, leaving five unfit for habitation. Gas, water and sewers damaged.'

MoHS scientists recorded: 'Assumed target: railway or works. x4 HE (x2 500kg HE). 3 seriously injured, 2 lightly injured.

'Bombs 1) and 2): Believed 250kg HEs made craters 30ft x 5ft at ends of gardens in **Prestwold Road**.

'Bomb 3): 500kg HE: Direct hit on George Green & Sons boot factory, **Ash Street**. Bomb burst 8ft inside factory, making crater 35ft x 12ft. 60ft of wall blown down. Roof blown out 27ft x 62ft. 22ft from crater was partially-completed surface shelter without roof. About 6ft of its wall blown down and shelter moved 8". Five casualties and £4,500 [£183,000] damage.

A direct hit by an SC 500kg HE bomb on George Green & Sons boot factory, in Ash Street, left a 35ft x 12ft crater, as witnessed by a young AFS fireman, right, using a Coventry Climax light trailer pump to remove water from it. [Via Terence Burford]

'Bomb 4): Fell close to Co-operative Society grocery warehouse in **Ash Street**, leaving crater 48ft x 12ft. Two bays, measuring 22ft x 22ft, of each of the 6 floors, came down. Eight-storey brick staircase fractured from top to base. Basement with tons of precious food flooded 17" due to damaged pipes.' £10,000 [£406,000] damage. Interestingly, we know the 'Co-op Flour Mill, LMS, Leicester' was specified Luftwaffe target, GB 6 55. Adcock & Shipley tool factory, in **Forest Road**, received superficial damage.

The bombing damaged houses in **Beech Street** and destroyed 13 **Unity Avenue**, where people were trapped. No 11 also had to be demolished, whilst 5, 7 and 9 were seriously damaged. Injured arrived at Spence Street FAP, overseen by Dr M.S. Bryce. 25 homeless persons were sent to Green Lane Road RC.

The *LM* reported: 'Widower, 75-year-old James Walsh, living alone, was injured when his house collapsed. He was rescued after warden King and a night worker, Bob Weston, sawed through the roof. Warden King said: "Someone said: 'There's a man trapped here.'" I could

When an SC 250kg HE struck the Co-operative Society grocery warehouse in Ash Street, it brought down six concrete floors and destroyed tons of precious food. [Via Terence Burford]

see the house had shored itself up as it collapsed. Bob Weston and I managed to reach the man, saw through the roof joists, and, lifting it on our backs, pulled the man from his bed. We lowered him to the police, who were waiting below." Walsh, who is deaf, heard a bang and thought he had kicked his hot water bottle out of bed. Then a wooden partition fell across him and the roof collapsed on top. The partition probably saved his life.

'Mr and Mrs Hargreave found themselves trapped in their home and had to get out through the window. They were in bed at the time, fortunately, for their garden shelter was wrecked. Firewatcher William Jobling was standing next to foreman Jack Reid when a piece of pavement came through the roof and hit him on the head. PC Clement Adkin, 24, suffered a lacerated face and was hospitalised, as was Fred Atkins, 64, and William Coleman, 37, suffering scalp wounds and Mrs Florrie Forknall, 62, of 7 **Unity Avenue**, who suffered bruising.' Tommy Wright, 64, was also injured.'

The following day, Arthur Hassall, a 14-year-old ARP messenger at Erskine Street ARP depot, was sent to the incident. He returned to his depot to deliver a Rescue party situation report. He remembers feeling very proud sitting on the tram, with all the passengers staring at him, wearing his 'Messenger' armlet and helmet with the letter 'M'!

Over the month, Leicester's AFS was called to aid other cities. At 02.11am on April 11, Leicester AFS sent 10 pumps to **Birmingham**. The convoy returned at 3.54pm, except one regular appliance which returned on April 14. On April 24, at 01.15am, the Regional Fire Scheme was put into operation. At 2.33pm, five pumps and crews left Granby Halls AFS for **Bristol**, returning on April 26. Additionally, 30 AFS were sent to **London**.

On May 4, Leicestershire's FBs received a Regional Call for **Liverpool**. Second Fire Officer Cramp later recalled: 'I visited various places during the war, but the worst I attended was when I received instructions from the Regional Office at Nottingham. It was about 1.30pm and I had to take five towing vehicles with pumps, two motorcycles and one canteen with 25 firemen and proceed to Nottingham, Mansfield, Chesterfield and Sheffield. At all these places, I took the same number of vehicles and men, so now I had a large convoy of 25 vehicles with pumps from Loughborough, Swadlincote, Derby, Chesterfield, Mansfield, Worksop, Radford and Long Eaton, with a motorcyclist front and rear to stop cross traffic, plus 80 personnel. We went to our first destination, Stockport fire station, arriving about 8pm. The alert had sounded. I ordered a meal, but half way through this, another message arrived, telling me to proceed to the Deaf Institute in Liverpool. After filling up with oil and petrol, we were away to Manchester. While travelling along Lancashire Road, Jerry spotted us and dropped a stick of bombs in the fields alongside. Only one minor accident occurred when a driver took fright at a roundabout and hit a bollard, flattening his front wheels. He was left to clear the situation. We proceeded to Liverpool. It was like hell let loose. At 3am, fires burned everywhere. I have never seen so much broken glass and shrapnel and bombs coming down. Streets of houses being pushed over like a pack of cards.

'The all clear sounded at dawn and little children came out of holes in the bombed ground, crowding round the canteen van for a drink and biscuits, which my steward, Mrs Eva Hyde, provided. She had been with us all night whilst we fought the fires. At 11am, we managed to get breakfast and then, the whole squad, using their gas mask cases as pillows, lay down along the kerbside and slept for two hours. Then, another order asked me to take 15 trailer pumps, without towing vehicles, to the landing stage, where sailors loaded them on board a naval destroyer, opposite the Liver Building. The firemen went below for the crossing to Belfast. Their stay lasted for two weeks.' However, Cramp does not mention the conditions there. Fireman George Woods, based at Mansfield, Nottinghamshire, was part of the

Mrs Eva Hyde, right, serving food from her AFS mobile canteen at a domestic fire at Messr Spurway, Free School Lane, c. 1940. Next to her, enjoying a cup of tea, stands Second Officer Arthur Cramp. Mrs Hyde was mentioned in the London Gazette *for her gallant conduct when she operated her canteen during a raid on Liverpool in May 1941. [Via Malc Tovey]*

column and states the FB told the men's families they had been 'posted away', but refused to disclose where. Billeting conditions and food in Northern Ireland were basic. On June 5, 1941, Leicester AFS received a letter from Liverpool's Town Clerk, conveying the thanks of Liverpool Fire Authority.

At 02.35am, on May 9, 1941, three AFS pumps and crews left Granby Halls for **Nottingham**, which was receiving its Blitz Night.

On Sunday, May 11, tragedy struck Leicester's ARP Rescue service. The *LM* reported: 'Two Leicester ARP volunteers were fatally injured and seven others hurt, when the lorry they were travelling in overturned. The men were on their way to a CD Service at Leicester Cathedral. The dead are: William Jelly, 44, of Wigston Lane and Archibald Mayes, 52, of Conaglen Road. The injured are: William Gudger, of Heathcote Road; Harold Dimmock, of New Parks Road; William Abell, of Grace Road; Harold Smith, of Hawkesbury Road; Ernest Idale, of Middlesex Road; Frank Charlesworth, of Cavendish Road; William Henton, of Windley Road. Only one of the volunteers escaped injury. He was wearing his tin helmet and was thrown against a fence, the impact bending his helmet. Jelly died from multiple injuries compatible with being severely crushed. Mayes suffered from severe shock, following multiple injuries consistent with having been thrown out of a car.' Four days later, 'Controller C.R. Keene, Deputy-Controller Lt Commander M.A.C. Ritter and Depot Superintendent Mr Wykes attended both funerals. Interment of Archibald Mayes took place at Saffron Hill Cemetery. For the burial of William Jelly, there was a service at St Christopher's church.' On June 20, 'A 19-year-old, of Cavendish Road, was fined £5 [£195] for driving a lorry to the danger of the public. Prosecuting, Mr Cecil Bray described how the two lorries left Aylestone ARP depot, one with six men, the other with seven. Near the bend of Aylestone Road with Saffron Lane, the lorry driven by the defendant attempted to pass the other lorry. The defendant's lorry swerved, touched the back of the other lorry, went into the offside gutter, mounted the pavement and crashed into a tram standard. All the men were thrown out, one falling 10yds away at the feet of a cyclist, who was hiding behind a tree. The prosecutor left it to the magistrates to decide if the drivers were racing. The magistrates dismissed the charge of driving to the danger of the public, but convicted the defendant of driving without due care and attention.'

SATURDAY, MAY 17, 1941

On the night of May 10/11, 1941, London suffered its last heavy air raid, causing the most casualties in one night: 1,436 dead and 1,800 seriously injured. This marked the end of the eight month London Blitz, as Hitler turned his machinations towards Russia. However, for the Provinces, all was not done. Just six days later, once again, the Luftwaffe attacked Birmingham, dropping 160 tonnes of HEs and 2,000 IBs. The bombing was inaccurate, with Nuneaton accidentally attacked, killing 83, compared to 30 in Birmingham, supposedly the main target.

Leicester was in the line of the Nuneaton attack and her sirens sounded at 12.13am. Ingles wrote: 'Just after midnight, we heard the drone of planes. As the night was bright and starlit, many went out into the streets. Suddenly, as we watched, there was a roar and flash of flame, for bombs had fallen a few hundred yards away in **Braunstone**.'

Around 01.10am, a single bomber dropped bombs across the Corporation estate. An HE fell on **301 Gooding Avenue**, another fell at the rear of **11 Webster Road**, demolishing a semi-detached house and trapping two women under the debris. Casualty IO J.J. Dexter reported: 'I received a call from M/C at 02.00hrs to proceed to Webster Road – casualties reported trapped. I arrived at 02.05hrs and found five houses badly damaged, a bomb dropped in the back garden. Five casualties were found in 11 Webster Road: Mr Frank Johnson, 45, Mrs Beatrice Johnson, 44, and Derek Johnson, 11, had been rescued injured from the front bedroom. They were taken to Cort Crescent FAP. In the back bedroom, Miss Betty Johnson and her aunt, widow Mrs Frances Peake, 42, (Mrs Johnson's sister) were trapped. Miss Johnson was pinned by debris and lying on Mrs Peake, who was dead. The Mortuary Squad was ordered, but took 1½ hours: possibly due to damaged telephone communications. Miss Johnson was rescued after four hours. Dr MacDonald injected Morphia to ease any pain and to keep her quiet whilst rescued. She was examined by Dr MacDonald, who found no serious injury and ordered her removal to the LRI. She was kept in because of severe shock. A bright and plucky girl. It was due to the courage and care of the Rescue Party from the College of Art, under Leader P. Jarvis, that this girl did not receive serious injuries during her rescue. Her last words to me when I told her she was a brave girl, said "No, it's your men who are brave" and asked me to thank them. She even told the Ambulance Attendant on the way to the Infirmary that when she was better, she would go to their depot and learn first aid. My comments are:– A poor report sent to DRC by wardens. When I arrived at the incident, there was no RP or FAPy, so I sent my driver back to G2 [Trinity Methodist depot] for a FAPy and RP, as people were starting to do rescuing. I had the greatest difficulty stopping them and had to call the Police IO, because it would in have been fatal to the girl. The incident was closed at 05.00hrs.' Five others were injured in Webster Road. In total, 23 houses were damaged. Casualties were taken to Cort Crescent FAP, under Dr J.S. Mann.

An OB made a 5ft crater on the roadway in **Gooding Avenue**, igniting but without causing damage. It was extinguished by fire watchers. Winstanley Drive AFS also attended.

An HE fell outside **33 Cort Crescent**, injuring resident Thomas Marshall, 30, the crater blocking the road. It could still be seen in 1964, covered by an asphalt patch.

Two men, right, look into the crater caused by a 250kg HE bomb, which threw up tons of earth and demolished the rear of homes in Webster Road, Braunstone. The Anderson shelter, bottom right, though buckled, survived the near hit. [Via Terence Burford]

A UXHE fell beside the concrete road into **Braunstone Park** from Hinckley Road. Eleven houses were evacuated. The *LM* later reported: 'The earth quite literally moved for Mary Kimberley when she was with her boyfriend. The couple were enjoying a moonlit assignation in Braunstone Park. Mary explained: "All of a sudden, we heard this plane come over. Next minute, I was dazed, in the gutter. The bomb had dropped in Cort Crescent. I didn't know where my boyfriend was, as I ran straight home, as I thought Father would be after me. I didn't tell him – I just went straight to bed."' On May 22, 1941, No.42 BDS commenced work on the UXB. It was found to be a 250kg HE with a No.15 fuze and removed five days later.

The alert remained until 05.04am. Property costing £1,830 [£71,000], not including personal effects, was destroyed. The Salvage and Removals Service recovered six loads of furniture. Cleansing staff removed glass and oil from the road.

The Blitz may have been over, but ARP casualties continued. The *LM* reported: 'A verdict of accidental death was recorded at the Leicester inquest on William Lonslow, 53, a fire watcher who was found dead in the staffroom lavatory at Messrs Burton's shop, Gallowtree Gate, on June 1, 1941. Witness Kenneth Everitt said the room was warmed by a small gas radiator. The gas tap was partly turned on. As soon as witness touched it, the flexible tube came off. He understood Lonslow had no sense of smell. PC Spencer expressed that Lonslow was affected by the gas whilst asleep and collapsed on going to the lavatory.'

And, a month later: 'How a fire-watcher fell through a skylight of a dyeworks and was fatally injured was told at the inquest of Charles Goodby, 42, of Asylum Street. Goodby was fire-watching at Messrs J.E. Pickard & Sons, Grasmere Street, on July 8. Fellow fire-watcher Eric Kimberley said Goodby offered to show him the roof. They went up a crawling ladder. Goodby sat on the roof's apex. Witness saw Goodby sliding past him on the glass roof. There was a crash and witness found him on the floor, 24ft below. The glass was ¼-inch thick. Just before he started sliding, witness said to Goodby: "Are you sure it's safe, Charlie?" and he replied: "Yes, safe as houses." The Coroner recorded a verdict of accidental death. Mr Goodby served through the last war from its outset until 1918, having enlisted aged only 15.'

The Luftwaffe's presence over Britain rapidly thinned as Hitler moved the majority of the force eastwards in preparation for the invasion of Russia. This provided the ARP services with some respite after a year of night alerts. Ingles noted: 'What had happened to the Luftwaffe? During the last weeks, there had been an ominous lull in enemy aircraft activity. "Surely, this is the end of bombs for us," we said hopefully.'

Monday, July 14, 1941

Leicester's new HAA defences recorded: 'Low cloud all night and very dark. One enemy raider, Raid 614, made landfall at Sutton-on-Sea, Lincolnshire. At 01.26hrs, Grantham HAA fired two rounds at raider, which flew an erratic course to Leicester. Leicester's defences received permission to engage target at 01.22hrs, but this was withdrawn at 01.40hrs, as the aircraft was believed possibly friendly. Permission once again given to engage at 01.42hrs. The e/a was plotted by Syston HAA Site, who estimated it at 3,000ft-4,000ft. However, radar was unable to accurately obtain its height and the target passed almost over Syston HAA Site, as it headed for Leicester.'

Leicester's sirens sounded at 01.44am. This raid – the last on Leicester – is often reported as just having caused damage to Conduit Street, however, once again, Highfields received most of the bombload. At 01.50am, the lone raider flew over London Road LMS station, dropping a mixed bombload, extending eastwards, causing one death, seven injuries, plus much damage. MoHS scientists recorded: 'Assumed target: LMS station.'

Bomb 1): OB exploded on vacant land facing the YMCA **East Street/London Road**. No damage.

Bomb 2): 50kg HE fell on **LMS station** parcels office, causing fire. Damage not extensive.

Bomb 3): 50kg HE fell on **LMS railway embankment**, end of Andover Street. Unoccupied communal brick shelter in Andover Street badly fractured and will require demolishing and rebuilding.

Bomb 4): 50kg HE fell on **Slate Street/Conduit Street** corner, demolishing 62 and 64 Conduit Street. Landlady Miss Eliza Mott, 63, of number 62, was killed instantly in her

ARP Rescue personnel search the rubble for casualties at 62 and 64 Conduit Street, the day after it was bombed. Here, landlady, Miss Eliza Mott, 63, was killed. An ARP ambulance car and trailer waits further down the street. [Leicester Mercury]

Blitz hero of the night was Dennis Smith, 19, of Conduit Street, who despite an injured hand, repeatedly shinned up a drainpipe to rescue an injured soldier trapped on a burning roof. [Leicester Mercury]

kitchen, her broken remains were recovered from beneath the rubble. The *LEM* reported: 'Upstairs, Private Charles Peckham, her lodger, was blown from his bed on to the roof of the neighbouring house. He had seriously leg injuries and was hanging over the parapet, amid swirling clouds of dust and flames. Denis Smith, 19, [of 70 Conduit Street], heard Peckham call for help. Smith climbed a 25ft drainpipe, although he was suffering from a poisoned hand. Just as he reached the roof, his septic hand, which he had cut mending his bicycle, gave way and he fell. Neighbours were busy extinguishing the flames and others were searching for a ladder, but Smith didn't wait. Again, he climbed the pipe, this time, reaching the top. "I got Peckham on my shoulders," Smith said, "and tried to climb down the pipe with him, but he was pretty badly hurt and I wasn't sure he could keep his grip round my neck. A ladder at last arrived and I managed to scramble down it carrying Peckham: how, I don't know."' Smith injured his other hand and arm and was treated at the LRI. He was in the Army, but was returned to his work as an engineer. Miss Miriam Scott, 20, inspired neighbours to deal with the fire. She carried buckets of water, helped by her mother, from their kitchen tap. Rescue squads worked hard to free six trapped persons, but were handicapped by leaking gas. Rescue worker Frank Charles, 37, suffered gas poisoning and was taken to St Margaret's FAP, as was AFS fireman Jack Cassell. Houses in Andover Street and Upper Fox Street were also damaged.

Bomb 5): 50kg HE fell on pavement in **Lincoln Street**, damaging houses and roofs. Burning gas main in road quickly extinguished by AFS.

'Bomb 6): 50kg HE fell at Mr A Peer's motor garage on **West Goscote Street/Gartree Street**, damaging vehicles. Also damaged on Blitz Night.

Bomb 7): 50kg HE fell **between Guthlaxton Street and Stoughton Street**. Hill & Benson Hosiery, in Guthlaxton Street, suffered £1,000 [£39,000] damage. Three injured.

IBs fell on roofs in **Stoughton Street**: 'Men and women did excellent work extinguishing incendiaries. Joseph Holyoake, wearing only his pants, and Mr Keeling, dealt with one on **Guthlaxton Street** which was endangering property. Miss Ethel Smith extinguished another by piling a sandbag and 20 bricks on it.'

Bomb 8): 50kg HE made a large crater at rear of 9 **Worthington Street**. Betty Williamson recalled the strange sight that greeted her aunt: 'My aunt Emma Moore's home, at 9 Worthington Street, was half-demolished by the bomb. The previous day, there had been a severe rainstorm and the ground was still soft. Aunt Emma, a Dig for Victory enthusiast, had planted her garden with salad crops. The morning after, she was astonished to find a circle of spring onions, equally spaced six-inches apart, lying around the edge of the large crater and at the bottom of the hole – the outside toilet, complete with cistern.'

Bomb 9): 50kg HE fell in garden in 36 **Twycross Street**, at the entrance to an Anderson shelter containing Mr and Mrs Claude Poole, with daughters Pamela and Doreen. Although the blast almost lifted the shelter out the ground, apart from shock, all four were were uninjured, again showing the brilliance of the Anderson design. Two unoccupied brick shelters were damaged.

Bomb 10): A UXB was found at **2a Twycross Street** and 60 people had to be evacuated. On July 17, No.135 BDS located a 50kg UXHE with a No. 50 booby trap anti-disturbance fuze, which they defuzed and removed the following day.

At 01.59am, as the raider left the Sector, a further two HAA rounds were fired at it. The all-clear sounded in Leicester at 02.23am.

Mr and Mrs Claude Poole, with daughters Pamela and Doreen, had a miraculous escape when an SC 50kg HE bomb exploded immediately outside their Anderson shelter. Although the blast almost lifted the shelter out the ground, apart from shock, all four were were uninjured, again showing the brilliance of the Anderson shelter design. [Leicester Mercury]

The *LEM* reported: 'Hun Savagery in Midlands: Crater and wrecked houses after bombs dropped during the night. Fleeing [sic] Raider Unloads on E. Midlands Town: The bombs mostly fell on workers' houses.'

The assumed main target, the LMS station, suffered minor damage, but once again, a lone raider missed its target and civilians paid the price. Some 85 houses also suffered roof and chimney damage and 24 glass damage, costing £4,574 [£177,000]. Sixteen van loads of effects were cleared by the Salvage and Removal Service. Welfare service officers reported in the following days, 'a large number of the public [sightseers] had an adverse effect on local morale.'

On August 1, 1941, the *LM* reported an interesting follow-up: 'Two officers in charge of a building occupied by the military in a Midland town were fined for offences against blackout regulations today. They were 51-year-old and 40-year-old lieutenants. A police inspector stated one night, a stick of bombs was dropped, beginning in a line from the building where the light was shown, in a part solely used by officers. In the case against the younger lieutenant, it was stated a light was shown from the same part of the building at another date. When spoken to by a special constable, he said: "I'm frightfully sorry this has happened." Both lieutenants were fined £3 [£116]' This could relate to the raid on July 14, 1941 or, alternatively, April 9, 1941.

In September 1941, as part of an increased focus, the CD Duties (Compulsory Enrolment) Order 1941 decreed all men, between 18-60, would have to enrol for CD work. Also that month, the term 'ARP' was phased out, to be replaced by 'Civil Defence'.

November was a bad month for Leicester's CD. On November 5, 1941, the *LM* reported: 'Representatives of Leicester's CD Services attended the funeral at Knighton parish church today of 18-year-old David A.H. Mather, of 16 Northcote Road, a volunteer ambulance driver, who was killed when his motorcycle skidded in Granby Street, last Saturday. Squads from his depot, under Deputy Depot Officer H.A. Langley, formed a guard of honour at the graveside.' Volunteer Mather *may* have been rushing to report for duty following the siren. On November 15: 'William Penn, of Percy Street, was taken ill while fire-watching at the Town Hall and was taken to the LRI, where he died. A married man, he worked in the Treasurer's office and had been passed A1 for the Army, awaiting his call-up papers.'

1942

1942 started off where 1941 left off: on January 8, another Fire Guard, Herbert Wallis, 46, of Guthlaxton Street, collapsed and died whilst fire-watching at Leicester's Theatre Royal.

Such was Russia's drain on the Luftwaffe, between January and April 1942, III/KG2 were the only German bomber unit available for raids on Britain – and they were operating at a quarter strength. Ironically, it appears it was RAF Bomber Command's attacks in March and April 1942 that drew German attention back to Britain. As Rothnie reveals, 'The Luftwaffe was being put together to launch a renewed attack on Britain's industrial cities, such as Birmingham, when the raid on Lubeck forced an abrupt change of policy. As the units gathered, Hitler gave the instruction they should concentrate on historic cities with a series of terror raids against civilian populations. German bomber strength in the west increased over 50%, to over 200 serviceable aircraft.'

In late April, Exeter, Bath, Norwich, York and a month later, Canterbury, were bombed in sharp raids. But, not for the first time, Hitler thought with his heart than his head. Although Midlands cities, such as Leicester, were similar size as the Baedeker cities, they were not attacked, probably because they were believed not historic enough. However, with Hitler's limited Luftwaffe resources, rather than targeting Britain's heritage centres, the destruction of whose historic buildings would make little difference to Britain's war production, had lightly-defended industrially-rich cities, such as Leicester, been attacked, significant damage could have been caused to the war effort.

Although Leicester was not raided during the Baedeker Raids, its NFS saw service assisting targeted cities. NFS fireman Arnold Granger recalled: 'On 27th April 1942, NFS men and women were asleep in their bunks in Leicester's fire stations. Senior officers of No.9 Fire Force Control were aware a serious attack was taking place 120 miles away at **Norwich**, and at 2am, an order was received for fire appliances. Messages were sent by telephone to the Leicester stations for 20 regional pumps, with 100 men, motorcycle dispatch riders and a mobile canteen to assemble on Uppingham Road, near Trocadero Cinema. Within minutes, alarm bells sounded and 100 men donned their gear and loaded their kitbags with iron rations on to appliances. Through the night, the convoy moved in perfect order and entered the Reinforcement Base at Peterborough, one and a half hours later. The senior officer reported to the Control Room, emerging to tell us we must go to Kings Lynn. This caused consternation, but something big was on. At Kings Lynn, the convoy was ordered to Norwich. There was no doubt about it – this was a big one. The convoy sped through the sleepy town of Swaffham. Early risers in Great Fransham and Scarning looked in amazement at so many fire appliances. Wending their way through East Dereham, with bells clanging and on to North Tuddenham and Hockering, the vehicles sped until, above the dawn, a thick pall of smoke was seen. In the centre of Norwich, the scene chaotic. Our senior officers reported to Central Fire Station and we were directed to take over from exhausted local crews. Huge fires were still burning, but ARP services were getting to grips with the situation. The noble cathedral spire still stood defiantly against the sky – a symbol of courage against adversity. At 6pm, Leicester crews were ordered to a hospital on the outskirts, where Canadian Pioneer Corps had a field kitchen. The meal was rough and ready, but eagerly eaten by fire crews. About midnight, crews were ordered to appliances and assembled in convoy. So, 100 firemen returned to Leicester, awake and active for a day and a half, begrimed and exhausted, aiding a stricken city. As the men cycled or walked home, folk hardly gave them a smile. Ignorance is bliss: "Lucky Leicester again."'

Despite Leicester's escape, the CD Committee feared the Luftwaffe would return: 'Recent attacks suggest there is the possibility many more similar attacks will be made on towns of comparable size. It will be as well to take the opportunity of reviewing all CD precautions, as the attacks now being made seem to concentrate on towns which have so far escaped bombing of any serious nature and where ground defences are believed not particularly strong.' It wasn't just the authorities who were concerned: 'In 1942, Home Intelligence weekly reports picked up public rumours Lord Haw-Haw had supposedly promised Leicester would be bombed. This was probably because it had not been and public tittle-tattle led to rumours it would.'

But the lack of raids, combined with longer working hours, made compulsory CD duties an additional tiring chore. Similarly, an unusual case of disciplinary action occurred in April 1942, when the Controller reported that an ambulance driver, of the Crusaders Hall depot, refused to comply with instructions requiring personnel to 'march in an orderly manner between the depot and Town Hall for drawing weekly wages.' The CD Committee resolved proceedings be taken against the driver under the Defence Regulations, for failure to obey a lawful order.

Tragedy struck in the early hours of October 4, 1942, when 'Harry Booth, 28, of Coventry Street, was found dead at a wardens' post at 15 Leamington Street. Mr Booth, a voluntary CD worker, had reported on Saturday night for duty. When found in the morning, he was lying face downwards.' Eleven days later, the *LM* reported: 'It was practically a death-trap for anyone to sleep there and should never have been used as a wardens' post,' said Leicester Coroner, Mr E.G.B. Fowler. A verdict of accidental death through suffocation was returned, the Coroner saying it was a death that should never have taken place. PC Dolman said he was called to the post, situated in a small room, where a gas boiler used for central heating. There was no ventilation and a window was blocked. Chief Constable Cole expressed personal regret and that of the Wardens' Service. Mr Booth had been a very valuable and conscientious warden'. On June 30, 1944, Mrs Ellen Booth, at Nottingham Assizes, was awarded £2,300 [£78,575] damages against M.C. Turnor and Co. printers, in respect to the death of her husband.

Sunday, November 15, 1942, saw the first new 'CD Sunday' event, created by Winston Churchill, who described it as: 'A reminder of the great defensive effort. While we rejoice in the deeds of the Navy, Army and Air Force, we remember when Civil Defenders did so much to keep our will to victory invincible.' Across Britain, special church services were held and CD forces paraded. In London, King George VI took the salute, as 1,000 veterans of the Blitz marched past. CD contingents from all the bombed towns and cities 'commemorated the civilian victory over the Luftwaffe two years ago. Leicester's representatives in London included: Group Warden George Emmett MM; Sector Leader Cyril Edmunds; Warden John Higgott GM; Deputy Divisional Warden William Tanser; Rescue Party Leader F. Carter (Rushey Fields depot); Rescue Party members W. Searle (Woodlands) and D.J. McLeod (Uppingham Road); Rescue Party Leader J. Toon (Western Park); Casualty Party Supervisor O.B. Goodall (Western Park); Squad Leader S. Smith (Woodlands); Stretcher Bearer A. Bolton (Uppingham Road) and WVS County Borough Organiser, Mrs D.M. Bates, with Commanding Officer H. Neal MM (Woodlands).' Soon afterwards, on the second anniversary of the Leicester Blitz, 'The Committee and officers responsible for Leicester's CD in 1940 and the city's CD workers who took part in the National CD Day celebrations in London, held a reunion at one of the depots. It was arranged by Mrs Dorothy Bates, WVS County Borough Organiser, incidentally, the only woman from Leicester to attend the London parade. She explained that coaches met them on their arrival in the capital. Dinner was served in three large restaurants, where they were joined by many distinguished people. The visitors went on the Odeon Theatre, where they were also honoured by Admiral Evans and Mr Attlee, on behalf of the government. They also attended a ceremony at St Paul's Cathedral, where the King and Queen were present. The visitors were made to feel the national pride in their work.'

Meanwhile, in Leicester, 'About 3,000 CD workers took part in the CD Sunday parade on Victoria Park. Thousands witnessed the parade and the route to the park was lined with people. After the parade formed, Lord Mayor Alderman Taylor, the Bishop of Leicester Dr Smith and others led a short service. Afterwards, the Lord Mayor took the salute and the parade marched to Charles Street before dispersing.'

But yet again, the year ended badly for Leicester's CD. On December 15, 1942, a 'Leicester lad was killed fixing black-out: After having been whirled round a shafting and terribly injured at Messrs Willson's printing works, King Street, Alan Osborne, 17, of Melton Road, was able to tell how the accident happened. He died in the LRI next day. It was stated the lad was responsible for the black-out and a complaint had been made light was coming through an aperture in the wall. Osborne went up to cover the aperture with a sack, but the sack caught in the shafting and when he tried to free it, he was wound round with it. The shafting made 180 revolutions a minute. Harry Allsopp, an engineer at the works, said he saw Alan had been wound round the pulley shafting. Osborne was badly injured, but conscious. They had difficulty liberating him. Coroner Mr E. Fowler recorded a verdict of accidental death. It was most unfortunate a young lad of such promise lost his life this way. Sgt Fenney, the Coroner's Officer, said he had been asked by ARP personnel to say how greatly they deplored the death of the lad, who had been a most competent messenger.'

In 1942, although the Luftwaffe bomber force had shown it still had teeth with the Baedeker Blitz, those teeth were now gradually being punched out on the Russian Front. The Luftwaffe had not returned for an expected winter blitz and continued training and inertia tired the CD services. Both national and local government had to find a way to maintain efficiency, alertness and morale. On December 30, Lord Trent, Regional Commissioner, in a New Year message to all CD personnel, expressed thanks for the steadfast and loyal devotion to duty shown during the past year: 'We must not relax for one moment, but steel ourselves to be fully prepared for any futher onslaught that Hitler, in his desperation, may hurl at us.'

A Leicester CD FAPy leader, in the white helmet, about to tie a casualty label to a mock casualty on a stretcher, during an exercise in the Wharf Street area, c.1942. By now, the CD had proper battledress uniforms and equipment. [Leicester Mercury]

CD officials were concerned that the Baedeker Raids would spread to other cities and the Germans would use poison gas. Exercises took this into account: here we see a FAPy in full anti-gas gear from G2 Trinity Methodist depot attending to mock casualties in the Braunstone area in May 1942. [Leicester Mercury]

1943

Although no bombs had fallen on Leicester for over a year and a half, the city was still vulnerable. An example was reported on February 5, 1943: 'Fire Guards in Danger: Three fire-watchers on duty at Messrs Corts, Ltd, ironmongers, corner of Cheapside and Silver Street, when fire broke out, probably owe their lives to the prompt action of the police. When the alarm was raised, flames had reached a corridor, their only means of escape. Considerable damage was done. The fire, discovered by the War Reserve Policeman Bird, broke out on the first floor and spread to the workshop over several shops in Silver Street, where it was stopped by the NFS. The workshop had fallen in when the brigade arrived with five machines and two turntable ladders. Much stock was lost.'

CD personnel continued to die in the course of their duties. On March 28, 'A Leicester Special Constable died under tragic circumstances on his beat last night. He was William Levers, of Fosse Road South, and had just met another Special Constable, named Hastings, at the corner of Mountcastle and Narborough Roads, when he collapsed. He was taken to the LRI but was dead on arrival. Mr Levers was 56 and a railway company's inspector.' Likewise, on June 10, 'Ernest Mason, 51, of the CD Rescue Service at Rushey Fields depot, of Hill Rise, Birstall, fell at Melton Road, Leicester, whilst alighting from a lorry on duty and died at LRI. The Coroner expressed the lorry driver was not to blame.'

In June 1943, Grimsby, on the Lincolnshire coast, suffered saturation bombing by German SD2 anti-personnel butterfly bombs. On July 13, the Luftwaffe returned and bombed the town again. A regional assistance call went out to North Midland CDR. Some 70 Rescue workers reported from Nottingham, Leicester and Lincoln to Willingham House, to assist Grimsby. Leicester's CD Committee minutes record: 'Rescue Service Staff Officer, Mr Wragg and a Rescue Party Leader from Rushey Fields depot, Mr Phipps, gave an account of work performed by three Rescue Parties (one each from Rushey Fields, Aylestone and Humberstone depots, comprising 21 men) on July 15. They spent two days assisting the rescue of trapped people and carrying out shoring-up work.' On August 25, two Leicester rescue parties were sent to **Cleethorpes** to demolish dangerous buildings. Two new Leicester squads replaced them from August 30. Similarly, after the dropping of 700 butterfly bombs on **Hull** on August 17/18, 1943, 15 Leicester NFS motorcycle dispatch riders rode there to assist post-raid operations.

In an effort to reduce strain on the CD services, most of whom were also working long hours on war work, in August, it was announced: 'Mr Herbert Morrison's new instruction, discouraging unnecessary manning of wardens' posts by p/t personnel will not, it seems, necessitate any change in Leicester. The 70 CD Group Posts are manned at night by p/t personnel. Previously, these Group Posts were worked by f/t wardens, who have now been directed into industrial work.' But conditions in some CD premises were still not condusive to good health. A Group Warden wrote to the *LM* in October: 'Many brick posts are extremely damp. Under these conditions, the first thing wardens do is switch the electric fire on "full blast." Even in a dry post – if a thing exists – heat is necessary and precious fuel must be used. Many posts are manned nightly – how does this square with the "save fuel" campaign? A.V. Norman (Group Leader 779), 544 Aylestone Road.'

Still, CD fatalities continued. On November 11, almost two years to the day after a previous FG death at Leicester Town Hall, 'Fire watcher Mr Harry Hulls, of Leicester Road, Anstey, collapsed at the Town Hall, and at the LRI, was found to be dead. He was 61 and a clerk in the Electricity Department. Mr Hulls complained of feeling unwell. His chief fetched some brandy, but found Mr Hulls collapsed.'

Leicester CD Rescue personnel who took part in the CD Reserve operations to assist Grimsby, Lincolnshire, on July 15, 1943, following a heavy air raid: believed to have been taken outside the Rushey Fields CD depot. [Leicester Mercury]

1944

The year started as it had left off – badly: 'William Booth, 48, of Eaton Street, was found gassed after fire-watching duty on February 13/14, 1944, in a hut at Messrs Fergusson builder's yard, Campbell Street. At the inquest, Booth's daughter stated her father had impaired hearing and 'no sense of smell', through being wounded in the last war. He received a disability pension. George Tilliard, yard foreman, said he noticed a smell of gas and found Booth on the floor. The coroner recorded a verdict of accidental death. Similarly, in April 1944: 'A verdict of accidental death was recorded at the inquest on Ernest Bown, 70, of 85 Walton Street. [On April 3] whilst fire-watching at Messrs A. Kirkland & Co.'s works, Western Road, he knocked over an electric fire, having apparently dozed in a chair, overbalanced and sustained burns, which "would not have been serious in a younger man"'. A doctor said Bown, however, 'took no interest in recovery.' He died on April 18, 1944.

For the past four months, the Luftwaffe had resumed raiding on Southern England, with the 'Baby Blitz'. Perhaps concerned it would spread, in May 1944, Leicester CD Committee reprinted 10,000 copies of their 1940 leaflet *After The Raid*.

A final, mainly forgotten evacuation, as large as in 1939, perhaps larger, came to Leicester in summer 1944, when the Nazis launched their revolutionary V-weapon attacks against Southern England. On June 13, the first V-1 flying bomb hit London and soon, the government restarted its evacuation plans of 1939. Between July 7 and 17, 1944, Leicestershire received 30,000 evacuees. Leicester was already bulging at the seams with war workers, Pay Corps, ATS and other service units, but homes were found for all of them.

In: Sector Warden Harry Howard, right, with London evacuees at a Leicester wardens' post before being distributed to their billets, from Sir Jonathan North School, Knighton Lane, during the V1 attacks, still clutching their gas masks on July 11, 1944. [Leicester Mercury]

Although, for the moment, V-1s did not reach Leicestershire, local CD services provided valuable assistance to their war-weary comrades in Southern England, developing first-hand experience of V-weapon warfare. Warburton records: 'In spring 1944, when preparations for the Allied invasion of Europe were near completion, High Command had to consider the enemy resorting, as a counter-measure, to renewed heavy raiding of London. Therefore, the MoHS decided to strengthen CD services by bringing in Regional Reinforcements from the Midlands and the North. In March 1944, arrangements were made to receive at St Egbert's depot, Chingford, No.1 Unit of No.III Regional Column, to supplement existing services in London Region. The Column consisted of 43 officers and men, with Rescue vehicles and equipment, including ambulance, decontamination lorry and dispatch rider, organised in five parties. Operational control was by the Group Controller and Co-ordinating Officer, the Borough of **Chingford** responsible for billeting and feeding the men. The personnel, drawn chiefly from Nottingham, Leicester and Derby, arrived in Chingford on March 30, 1944, from their base at Willingham House, Lincolnshire, and were changed over monthly. Thus, each man did one month's duty. In the early part of their stay, little enemy air activity was experienced, but at the few incidents, notably on April 19, the Column gave very useful assistance, proving a most valuable addition to local services, particularly during the flying bomb period. They were frequently called to render assistance to adjoining authorities, more important incidents attended being: High Street, **Lewisham**, June 28; Dames Road, **Leyton**, July 27 and High Street, **Walthamstow**, August 16, 1944. The first mentioned was one of the worst flying bomb incidents within London Region. Late in August 1944, the flying bomb attacks ended, and on September 22, 1944, the Column returned to its Base.' Likewise, '28 f/t CD personnel were permanently transferred to Cambridge Region in April 1944 and 21 to the Kent County Mobile Reserve in May 1944. These personnel later returned.'

Soon, the strain on London's wardens became acute and a request came for volunteers to relieve them. The day after the first V-1 evacuees arrived in Leicestershire, county CD personnel went in the opposite direction, to the war zone: '137 Leicester wardens went to London. 24 wardens completed 72 weeks duty in **Greenwich** and 137 wardens completed 301 weeks in **Woolwich**. Two Leicester wardens were injured by V-weapons. Warden T.H. Powell was injured on July 31, 1944, at Greenwich and given a war injury allowance.'

A fascinating record has survived written by Highfields Group Warden George Emmett, entitled 'Diary of a Week's Duty in London':

'Saturday 26th August: Left Lei by coach at 08.10hrs: A glorious morning, everybody in high spirits and a lot of leg pulling. Reached Shrewsbury House [CD Control Centre, Shooters Hill] at 13.25hrs. A rather disturbing occurrence happened. Wardens causing a disturbance. Managed to smooth it, but reported it to ARP Office Leic. Met Mr Helwig

Out: On platform 4 of London Road LMS station in July 1944, Chief Constable and Chief Warden O.J.B. Cole, first right, sees off departing Leicester wardens who have volunteered to help their London counterparts facing V-1 flying bomb attack. Standing third from left: Highfields Group Warden George Emmett MM. [Leicester Mercury]

and he took us for a walk round the District and our duties were given us. We had food at Plumstead School.

'Saturday 27th August: 07.00hrs: Cup of tea brought to us in bed and hot water ready for shaving, as good as hotel service. 07.30hrs: Siren Alert. 07.45hrs: three Wardens with me, Peet, Pepper and Towers, had first view of D.B. [doodlebug] going over, very low, directly above us. They were quite thrilled. Went with D.W. [District Warden] to the club and we were made Honorary members for the week.

'Tuesday 29th August: An alert an hour. One D.B. dropped on District 8, against Eltham church. [3 dead, 50 injured]. Three alerts in an hour. One came over very low. A lovely sight with dozens of searchlights holding them in beams. For a time, everyone was on their toes for they were coming in from all directions, but it was our lucky night and they all went over.

'Wednesday 30th August: 08.00hrs: Breakfast forgotten, everybody under tables: coming down straight over us. A terrific whistling and thud. Then the school and ground seemed to move. Glass flew. Some breakfasts lost. Just missed us and dropped in Herbert Road. Lei Wardens were quickly on the job. Very extensive damage. Just been informed Warden Grenfell injured in incident at Eltham. Cut artery in foot. D. Morris, a Lei Warden, was blown from his cycle whilst taking a message and severely bruised his shoulder, but carried on and helped relieve trapped people. Went to Eltham church incident to see Leicester Wardens. All quite happy. Mr Harvey told me he was staying the three weeks. We met Lei Controller Mr Worthington & Mr Bailey D/FG Officer.'

In October, Wing-Commander Sir John Hodsoll, Inspector General of CD, visited Leicester for a short tour of CD establishments. Speaking to personnel at Aylestone depot, Sir John thanked them for their keenness and efficiency. He also expressed appreciation for what Leicester CD workers had done to help London during flying-bomb raids. He said they had been in a tough place and done a grand job. 'In the first batch was warden F.W. Hilliard, of 104 Curzon Street, a one-legged man, expert in first aid. He is a shoe repairer. He was only told the night before he was a member of the next day's party to London, so stayed up until 2am finishing his tradesman's work, so no customer would be disappointed. Leicester Rescue Service had 28 men permanently transferred to Essex and 21 to Kent. In addition, 47 were at Market Rasen reinforcement centre, from where squads were switched to wherever necessary. Two Leicester ambulances with two women drivers and two attendants operated to various incidents. Leicester Rescue Service also sent several City Surveyor's staff to **Crayford**, Kent, for their operational expertise. Leicester's Deputy Controller, Mr F.G. Bailey, was several times at **Acton**, working as Acting Controller, with his Assistant Mr S.J. Kent. Controller Worthington spent two days in London during considerable activity. Insp. F. Shelvey also visited during the raiding period.'

Leicester's citizens also helped the bomb-stricken South: 'Wardens canvassed householders for shelter bunks. An appeal was made by the MoHS for Morrison and Anderson shelters to send to Southern England. The result was very generous, considering the Luftwaffe was still capable of attacking Leicester. Some 831 Morrison shelters were sent, with 305 tons of Anderson shelter parts, equivalent to 762 shelters, plus 6,645 public shelter bunks and 80 Anderson bunks.'

Fortunately, the V-2 rocket attacks, which started to hit Southern England from September 1944, never reached Leicestershire. It became apparent Leicester's CD services were over-manned compared to the actual threat: no bombs had fallen on Leicester for over three years, so on September 6, the MoHS announced substantial reductions in CD. Stand-by duties for FGs were discontinued from September 12. Nightly duties by p/t CD personnel, with the exception of M/C, were discontinued from October 14. P/t personnel were only to report on the siren or enemy action. The *LM* announced: 'steps are to be taken for the progressive reduction of the organisation. F/t members selected for release are to be given a months' final notice on October 15.' From this date, 10 of the 13 FAPs were closed, as were the four DRCs, leaving all reports to be made directly to the M/C. From November 15, 100 out of 238 wardens' posts were shut, as were 10 of the 17 RCs. However, a letter in the *LM* highlighted a downside of this reduction: 'Mr Morrison has often spoken warmly of the fine work of the CD workers – who today are drifting, unprovided for, on to the labour market. These men, after five years' splendid service, are being directed into unskilled and poorly paid employment. Surely a truly grateful country could offer greater evidence of their apprecia-tion? George Nicholls, Chairman, Auxiliary Police Association, Leicester.'

However, Leicester's assault from the air was not quite over! On Tuesday, October 2, the

LM reported: 'A bomb fell in Leicester yesterday – and few people knew about it. It was a smoke bomb, dropped accidentally from a British aircraft. It fell half an hour after the sirens had sounded in the normal periodic test, and landed in Northampton Street, beside houses at the bottom of Swain Street bridge. Few people were about, but one or two threw themselves to the ground. There was no damage, just a lot of smoke. Inspector Fred Shelvey, from Police HQ, dealt with this "incident", which occurred within 100yds of his office. He carried what was left of the bomb back to the police station.' Perhaps some RAF bomb aimer passing high over Leicester couldn't resist squeezing his release button…

In the week before Christmas, Leicester's CD services continued their welfare duties bringing cheer to the V-weapon evacuees. The *LM* reported: 'Between 7,000-8,000 evacuee children will be entertained at Christmas parties, including a big party at De Montfort Hall and pantomimes. London County Council, Leicester Welfare Council and the Lord Mayor of London's Air Raid Distress Fund are helping financially.'

Ingles wrote: 'An alert sounded at 5.30am, on Christmas Eve, when flying-bombs were reported overhead and we heard gunfire.' That night, V-1s hit Manchester. As a morale booster, on Christmas Day, churches were allowed to light their stained glass windows.

1945

The government launched a scheme for towns and cities to send aid to areas still under attack. Co-ordinated by the Ministry of Supply, from February 1945, Leicester wardens and WVS collected clothing, bedding and furniture for **Fulham**, London, which had suffered considerable V-weapon damage. On March 26, the *LM* recorded: 'Some 250-300 loads of furniture were collected from Highfields, Stoneygate, Evington and Humberstone. Mr F. Briggs, collection committee chairman, said 1,000 wardens were removing and were all most elated at the householders' response. The weight of goods to be forwarded will be in hundreds of tons.' The scheme started to be wound down during April 1945. Mr Briggs described the public's response 'as one of the most astounding things that has happened in Leicester.' He had been told the result 'exceeded anywhere else in the country.'

Ingles wrote: 'On Sunday, March 4, the sirens sounded again, just as I was finishing duty at 1am. I waited with other SCs in Rushey Fields Report Centre until the all clear at 2.20am. Many of us thought we heard hostile planes, but there was no action over the city.' Ingles had witnessed Operation Gisela, when Luftwaffe intruders attacked RAF Bomber Command aircraft returning from Germany. Around 20 RAF aircraft were shot down, including two Lancasters in Rutland. However, Leicestershire would not escape just over two weeks later. Exactly seven weeks from VE Day, the Luftwaffe made another last desperate stab at RAF Bomber Command. Ingles recorded: 'Tuesday, March 20, 1945, has a special significance for Leicester, city and county. This was the night of the city's last air raid warning. The sirens sounded at 10.20pm and the all clear at 10.51pm and the last bombs to be dropped on Britain from a piloted enemy plane fell at Bottesford, Leicestershire.'

With peace approaching, ironically, on March 28, the *LM* reported: 'Leicester's most disastrous fire throughout the war years, except on the night of the Blitz, destroyed three large office and warehouse premises. An estimate of the loss is £180,000 [£6.3 million]. A total of 13 firms have suffered either complete gutting or considerable damage. The premises gutted are Messrs Davies & Co Ltd, leather merchants, of 17 Albion Street; Messrs Lindrea & Co Ltd, leather merchants, of 14 Albion Street and W.S. Whittow & Co Ltd, leather merchants, of 10 Albion Street. The outbreak was noticed at about 4am. With fire on two fronts and the high buildings creating a vacuum, the NFS were faced with great difficulty. For a time, the corner of the *Leicester Mercury* roof was alight. These flames were attacked from the roof by director secretary Mr A.W. Peake, Mr Baston and a fireman with a stirrup pump. The *LEM* courteously placed their departments at the *LM*'s disposal. Two firemen, Sydney Sharman and Arthur Holmes, were taken to the LRI. A look round shows what an excellent job the NFS did holding the worst of the fire to these buildings. Their fine efforts saved a block stretching up Belvoir Street.' It is interesting to note that the FG system of fire-spotters had been stood down eight months previously.

On May 2, 1945, three days before European victory was announced, orders were received for the CD services to disband. The *LM* reported: 'Today's stand down of the CD Services affects 8,000 p/t and f/t workers in Leicester, f/t members being a small number now. CD ceases as a war organisation, but there are still jobs to be done: to assist returning thousands of evacuees, the reception of ambulance trains, general clearing of service equipment and removal of air raid shelters in streets.'

On Tuesday, May 8, 1945, people in Leicester ran for shelter as rumbling and flashes came from the skies – this time, it was a natural phenomenon: thunder and rain disrupted VE Day street parties. Later, after nightfall, fires once again blazed in the streets: but this time, not due to German incendiaries, but celebratory bonfires. Less than two months after Leicester's last all clear, Leicester's war ended. As CD Medical Officer Dr Porteous said: 'The main feeling was relief: Thank God it's all over.'

Unlike elsewhere in Britain, Leicester CD Committee's victory celebrations were muted, to say the least: 'On the question of a commemorative service certificate for CD personnel, as issued to neighbouring counties,' on July 16, 1945, the committee resolved 'in view letters of thanks have been sent to personnel, the suggestion a further certificate of thanks be issued, be not entertained.' Likewise, 'subject to there being no further guidance from the Government, this Committee are of the opinion that no arrangements should be made for a final CD parade.'

However, Leicester's NFS and Police didn't take this approach. On Sunday, May 27, 1945, '1,000 members of 9th Area NFS marched from Central Fire Station to Leicester Cathedral for their stand down service. Every seat was taken and some heard the service in the churchyard. The Provost, Very Rev. H.A. Jones, a p/t NFS member, said they had gone through fire and water. They had done good work and what they had gone through, they would remember to their dying day. They had not a single fatality.'

The Police also marked the occasion. On June 6, 'Major General Sir Llewelyn Atcherley, Inspector of Constabulary, made a farewell inspection of Leicester Special Police. The parade on the Cattle Market was 200 strong. Attending were Lord Mayor and Mayoress, Alderman and Mrs John Minto, the Watch Committee, Chief Constable Cole, Deputy Chief Constable Gabbitas and Cllr Moore, Commandant of Special Police.' On July 19, 'The stand down of PAMS took place. The ceremony took the form of a march past by 70 boys, at which the Chief Constable, supported by Alderman Wilford, Chairman of the Watch Committee and Inspector Shelvey, took the salute, followed by a supper in St George's Hall. The Chief Constable praised the boys for their loyal service and paid tribute to the men responsible for their success: Inspector Shelvey, Sergeant Jackson, Bandmaster Rogers, SC Ward and PC Brough.'

Leicester CD representatives also attended a national CD Farewell Parade at Serpentine Road, Hyde Park, London, on Sunday, June 10, 1945. The King and Queen, plus the two princesses, reviewed some 3,500 CD members from all over Britain, including NFS and Police. Leicester CD was represented by Warden Section Leader L. Callow; Rescue Party Leader A.J. Harris OBE; Assistant FG Officers R. Garner and J. Halford; WVS Canteen Liaison Officer Mrs A.M. Allen.' The official stand down of Britain's CD occurred on Sunday, July 1, 1945 – a job well done.

On August 26, 1945, a Civic Service of Thanksgiving for Victory against Japan was held in Leicester Cathedral, attended by the Lord Mayor and Lady Mayoress Alderman and Mrs John Minto, who headed a parade of military and civil organisations from sunlit Town Hall Square. 'The parade was dominated by a strong contingent of soldiery, air force and women's services, plus Home Guard, Police, CD and NFS, Red Cross and St John, WVS, British Legion, youth cadets, the Old Contemptibles' and Seaforth Highlanders' Association.'

Although there had been no CD stand down parade in 1945, a year later, there was a national Victory parade in London and a local one in Leicester. The CD Committee recorded: 'A contingent of up to 200 CD personnel shall be supplied for the procession on June 8, 1946, for the Victory Day celebrations. The procession will commence at 11am and follow the route from University Road via London Road, Charles Street and Belgrave Gate to Abbey Park, comprising 70 Wardens, 40 Rescue, 20 Ambulance, 20 Decontamination, 20 FAP personnel and 30 Messengers. Two local CDR members, a warden and two FGs took part in the London Victory Day Parade.'

Souvenir programme for the supper and entertainment event given by Leicester City Transport Committee to members of the Transport Department CD unit at the City Transport Recreation Club on June 21, 1945. It is signed by attendees, including Leicester's Lord Mayor, John Minto. [Valerie Tedder]

The vast CD apparatus was no longer needed. Disposal of CD equipment via public auction continued until 1948.

Many in the CD organisation felt the spirit of goodwill and camaraderie formed during the war years was too valuable to simply cast aside. Some city CD personnel formed social clubs, such as Leicester's 'A' Division Wardens' Old Comrades Association. Leicester CD Association held an AGM on April 25, 1947. Sir John Hodsoll, Inspector General of CD Services, addressed their meeting on June 4, 1947, about 'Future Problems of CD'. LCDA had 14 lectures on CD during 1947. Meetings were well-attended, but petrol rationing and distance discouraged some, plus, it would seem, a general weariness with the war and a desire to move on. It seems Leicester's CD associations did not last for very long.

Members of the CD Services who had served three years or more qualified for the Defence Medal. Due to the number needed to be manufactured and continuing materials shortages, the medal was only distributed after some delay. By July 1948, notice was given of the 'impending issue of Defence Medal to former CD personnel' – three years after the war's end. Records show Leicester's distribution was made from November 1948. Issue was patchy: some long-serving CD personnel did not receive their medal, largely either due to recipients moving or simply, given up waiting. However, in February 2001, the *LM* reported: 'Fighting fires during the Blitz was all in a day's work for Leading Fireman Alfred Vernon. His sterling efforts putting out fires in Leicester, Coventry, Birmingham and US air bases earned him the Defence Medal. Wartime shortages meant he was only presented with the ribbon, with a promise the medal would be issued later. But it never arrived. Now, the 88-year-old great-grandfather, of Dane Hills, can proudly pin his well-earned medal on his chest, thanks to some detective work by Leicestershire Fire and Rescue Service. Personnel adviser Mina Patel took up the case and after months of phone calls and letters, finally located his medal at the Home Office, London. Alfred will be officially presented with his medal at Leicestershire Fire and Rescue Service headquarters.'

In 2001, beaming former Leicester AFS/NFS fireman Alfred Vernon finally received his Defence Medal almost 56 years after the war's end, courtesy of Leicestershire Fire and Rescue Service. [Leicester Mercury]

Civil Defence may have won the battle against the Luftwaffe, but three years after the war, the threat resurfaced as the Cold War developed and our former Russian allies became future foes. On September 13, 1948, CD was reintroduced following the 1948 CD Bill. On November 16/17, 1948, core CD staff undertook a 'theoretical tactical exercise without personnel called 'Resurgam', examining an 'Atomic Bombing Problem on Leicester', at the County Rooms, before an organised local CD service was recruited. Major Storer said it was only the second to be held throughout Britain and its results were sent to the HO. On December 16, 1948, the CD Act received Royal Assent, requiring recruitment, training and planning by local authorities for a new CD Corps. But recruitment was poor – a weak shadow of its successful predecessor. It was apparent to most Britons that against conventional bombing, CD personnel could make a difference – against the overwhelming annihilation of atomic warfare, the helping hands of CD were powerless. Civil Defence was finally disbanded in 1968.

The Reckoning

Published figures recording the Luftwaffe's assault on Leicester vary greatly. In 1944, the *LM* were allowed to publish official statistics: 'Figures show the total number killed in Leicester by enemy raiders is 122, with 284 injured.' Damage to property was reported as:

	Destroyed	Damaged
Shops and houses	172	5,136
Churches and public buildings	1	4
Other property	21	451

An accurate assessment of Leicester's total raid casualties is near impossible, because not all injuries were reported. However, a 2014 count, involving multiple sources, suggests 106 civilians died directly or indirectly due to the Luftwaffe, with 91 on Blitz Night. 28 were killed on CD duties, seven by enemy action, as were twelve RAPC personnel. Approximately 140 HE, 25 UX HE, 4 OB and 6 PM fell on Leicester during 1940-1941.

Conclusion

We now definitively know Leicester *was* deliberately targeted on November 19/20, 1940. Ironically, the Luftwaffe's main objective, London Road LMS station, largely escaped the bombing and it was the surrounding streets that suffered.

Although, technically, Leicester's Blitz was minor compared to some larger cities, 146 Leicester citizens died directly or indirectly due to the Luftwaffe's offensive. Families sheltered together and died together. Luftwaffe bombs didn't discriminate between classes, whether Stoneygate or Wharf Street, nor ages, whether one-year-old Philip Rippon or 79-year-old Emma Pulford: Each death was a tragedy.

Yet, it seems the Luftwaffe's lack of intelligence and appreciation of Leicester's industry meant the city was not bombed more heavily. This was fortunate in the extreme, as Leicester was defenceless when it was most vulnerable. When HAA defences were finally emplaced in 1941, they proved too little, too late.

Whilst Leicester's military defences may have been a failure, it's clear its civil defences were an overwhelming success. Many owed their lives to the praiseworthy deeds of the CD and fire services: many more to the careful planning and precautions taken by local and central ARP authorities.

And, as well as helping the city's citizens, Leicester's CD and AFS/NFS went to aid other British cities, including London, Coventry, Birmingham, Bristol, Liverpool, Manchester, Norwich, Nottingham and Belfast. Leicester also opened its doors to over 30,000 evacuees.

As is often pointed out, it's ironic that more destruction of Leicester's irreplaceable built heritage was carried out not by the Luftwaffe, but by post-war councils and private developers. This destruction continues to this day.

When many talk of Second World War heroes, they commonly focus on daring fighter pilots or machine-gun-brandishing special forces. But, although their bravery is undoubted, elite soldiers faced the enemy armed with weapons – the CD services faced the enemy's bombs and bullets with nothing but their sense of duty.

When I think of Second World War heroes, I think of Dr Garrett and his bomb-blasted St John team tending casualties at the Blitz's epicentre. I think of Group Warden George Emmett injured on duty, or 'unlikely hero' Warden John Higgott GM rescuing two children from a blazing building. I think of Inspector Jesse Weston directing rescue operations as bombs fell all around. I think of AFS and NFS crews fighting fires as bombs and flames threatened to engulf them. I think of nursing staff battling to save lives under an influx of casualties and I think of DS Leonard Norman, DC Brian Hawkes, DC Edwin Trump plus Wardens Bernard Alderson and William Pratt killed by bombs as they went to help others.

In 1972, the *Leicester Mercury* stated: 'Whenever we refer to November 19, 1940, we call it the night there was a hero or heroine in every street. Throughout the city, the men and women of the Civil Defence Services were literally taking their own lives in their hands. They fought fires, tore at mountains of rubble to rescue injured and trapped people, with bombs still falling and before the fires had died down. This was the greatest night in the history of the people of Leicester.' Reading the powerful stories told in this book, it's a claim hard to dispute.

Leicester *was* tested by bomb and flame – and passed its test nobly.

Despite their home being critically damaged by a bomb on August 21, 1940, this Cavendish Road couple still manage a defiant smile as they wave their Union flag at Hitler. [Leicester Mercury]

Appendix A

ARP/CD Awards

George Medal (GM)
HIGGOTT, John	Wardens' Service (1940)
NEALE, Fireman Henry	AFS (1940)

Commander of the British Empire (CBE)
WORTHINGTON, Cllr Charles	CD Controller (1943)

Order of the British Empire (OBE)
HARRIS, Leader A.J.	Rescue Service (1940)
MACDONALD, Dr Ernest Kenneth	Medical Officer of Health (1942)
NICOL, James Lauder	North Midland Regional Information Officer, Min. of Info. (1945)
WESTON, Insp. Jesse	Police (1940)

Member of the Order of the British Empire (MBE)
BRADSHAW, Commandant W.N.	Special Constabulary (1945)
NOEL, Mrs I.B.B.	WVS County Organiser (1945)
PAYNTER, Mrs Diana Alberta	County Director of Leicestershire British Red Cross (1942)
ROBERTS, Column Officer Thomas Bruce	No. 9 (Leicester) Fire Force, NFS (1945)
WINTERINGHAM, Francis	ARP Controller and Chief Fire Officer (1940)

British Empire Medal (BEM)
BARWICK, Divisional Warden Frank	Wardens' Service (1945) 'D' Division
BUCKINGHAM, Divisional Warden R.A.	Wardens' Service (1942) 'G' Division
HELPS, William	Sector Leader, Wardens' Service and Head Fire Guard (1943)
LORD, Miss Rosa	SJAB Nursing Sister (1941)
PARTRIDGE, Divisional Warden S.H.	Wardens' Service (1944) 'D' Division
SARGENT, Third Officer D.	AFS (1941)
SHELVEY, Insp. Frederick	Police (1946)

St. John's Ambulance Certificate of Merit & King's Commendation for Brave Conduct
GARRETT, Medical Officer Dr Ernest B.	SJAB/Casualty Service (1940)
HEFFORD, Mrs Hilda	SJAB/Ambulance Nurse (1940)
LEE, Mr Leonard	SJAB/Ambulance Officer (1940)
MARSH, Miss Ivy	SJAB/Ambulance Nurse (1940)
WELLS, Miss Carrie	SJAB/Ambulance Nurse (1940)

King's Commendation for Brave Conduct
BAYLISS, Leader & Works ARP Officer F.	(1940)
DAWSON, Deputy Sector Leader Kyle	Wardens' Service (1940)
FLEWITT, Mrs W.E.	Report & Control Service (1940)
GARNER, Div. Warden John B.	Wardens' Service (1940)
HANFORD, Mrs M.	WVS Mobile Canteen (1940)
HYDE, Mrs Eva Mary	AFS Mobile Canteen (1941)
LOMAX, Miss A.	Report & Control Service (1940)
MIDGLOW, Squad Leader David	Rescue Service (1943)
PAULSON, Mrs B.	WVS Mobile Canteen (1940)

Appendix B
ARP/CD Roll of Honour

28 Leicester citizens lost their lives whilst serving on ARP/CD duties, seven directly due to enemy action.

They shall grow not old, as we that are left grow old:
Age shall not weary them, nor the years condemn.
At the going down of the sun and in the morning
We will remember them.

AINSWORTH, George Herbert, 56, Warden, of 17 Macdonald Road. Injured November 19, died November 21, 1940. Husband of Agnes Ainsworth.

ALDERSON, Bernard Charles, 33, ARP Telephonist/Warden 158 of 'E' DRC, of 23 Aber Road. Injured by enemy action at Holmfield Avenue, on November 19, 1940, died next day at LGH. Husband of Doris Alderson.

BOOTH, Harry, 28, Warden, of 21 Coventry Street. Died October 4, 1942, at wardens' post, Leamington Street, due to accidental coal gas poisoning. Husband of Dorothy Booth.

BOOTH, William, 48, Fire Guard, of Eaton Street. Accidentally gassed at firewatchers' hut, at Messrs Fergussons builders' yard, in Campbell Street, in February 1944.

BOWN, Ernest Venables, 70; Fire Guard Service, of 85 Walton Street. Suffered burns from electric fire whilst firewatching at Messrs A. Kirkland & Co's Works, Western Road, on April 3, 1944. Died April 18, 1944 at LRI. Husband of Norah Bown. Buried at Welford Road Cemetery.

COE, Fred, 59, of 60 Rendell Road. Killed by enemy action on November 19, 1940, at 40 Rutland Street. Not recovered until August 26, 1941. Husband of Ada Coe.

COWELL, John Thomas, 48, NFS. Died December 16, 1947, at 74 Navigation Street, due to illness contracted on duty. Husband of Betsy Cowell.

GOODBY, Fire Watcher Charles, 42, of 42 Asylum Street. Died July 8, 1941, after falling through skylight at Messrs J.E. Pickard & Sons Dyeworks, Grasmere Street.

HANLEY, Volunteer Fire Watcher Frederick Charles, 21, of 8 Cambridge Street, also a Home Guard, accidentally gassed whilst firewatching, on January 12, 1941, at Messrs Dallow, Lambert & Co. Ltd, Spalding Street.

HAWKES, Brian Mansell, 26, Detective Constable 140, Leicester City Police, of 29 Mickleton Drive, Evington. Died from injuries caused by enemy action, on November 20, 1940, at LRI. Husband of Anne Hawkes.

HULLS, Fire Guard Harry, 61, of Leicester Road, Anstey. Collapsed and died whilst firewatching at Leicester Town Hall, on November 11, 1943.

HURST, Fireman Ernest Alfred, of Leicester NFS, killed by enemy action on March 2, 1944, at Uckfield Road, Lewes, Sussex.

JELLY, William, 44, Rescue Service, of 205 Wigston Lane, Aylestone. Killed in traffic accident on Aylestone Road, on May 11, 1941.

LEVERS, Special Constable William Edward, 56, of 36 Fosse Road South. Collapsed and died whilst on duty in the black-out, on March 29, 1943.

LOCK, Fred, 44, ARP dispatch rider, of 24 Bembridge Close. Killed in a crash whilst motorcycle dispatch riding on October 7, 1940.

LONSLOW, Fire Watcher William Read, about 53, of 8 Carlton Street. Accidentally gassed whilst firewatching, on June 1, 1941, at Messrs Burton's store, Gallowtree Gate.

MARTIN, Leonard Victor, 35, Leicester AFS, of 2 Camville Road. Committed suicide in August 1940, 'while the balance of his mind was disturbed.'

MASON, Ernest Arthur, 51, Rescue Service, of 67 Hill Rise, Birstall. Fell at Melton Road, Leicester, on June 10, 1943 and died at LRI. Husband of Amy Mason.

MAYES, Archibald, 52, Rescue Service, of 8 Conaglen Road, Aylestone. Killed in traffic accident on Aylestone Road, on May 11, 1941.

MORRIS, Fireman Ernest, of Church Gate NFS Sub-station, thrown from bicycle in road accident whilst returning to station, on July 14, 1942.

NORMAN, Leonard Thomas, 34, Detective Sergeant 29, Leicester City Police, of 104 Upper Kent Street. Killed by enemy action on November 20, 1940, at Stoughton Street.

OSBORNE, Alan Charles, 17, Messenger Service, of 26 Melton Road, Leicester. Accidentally killed attempting to black-out a factory ventilator at Messrs Willson's printing works, King Street, on December 16, 1942.

PENN, Fire Guard William, of Percy Road. Taken ill whilst fire watching at Leicester Town Hall, on November 15, 1941 and later died.

PRATT, William Henry, 65, Warden, of 26 Sherrard Road. Killed by enemy action on November 19, 1940, at Grove Road. Body recovered 13 days later, on December 2, 1940. Husband of Lilian Pratt. Buried at Welford Road Cemetery.

PRICE, Joseph Ambrose, 39, NFS, of 45 Gaul Street. Injured December 15, 1943, at Nuneaton, died on January 30, 1945, at 45 Gaul Street. Husband of A. S. Price.

SMITH, Raymond Edward, 20, ARP worker. Died in blackout collision, in June 1940, whilst cycling to his post, after wrong instruction.

TRUMP, Edwin George, 26, Detective Constable 118, Leicester City Police, of 29 Copeland Road, Birstall. Killed by enemy action on November 20, 1940, at Stoughton Street. Husband of Pauline Trump.

WALLIS, Fire Guard Herbert Edward, 46, of 41 Guthlaxton Street. Collapsed and died whilst fire-watching at the Theatre Royal, on January 8, 1942.

Appendix C
Military Roll of Honour

12 RAPC personnel were killed by enemy action on November 19, 1940.

Royal Army Pay Corps badge.

ATTWOOD, Private 7677985 Harry. Killed at 32 Highfield Street. Buried at Kimberworth (St Thomas) Churchyard, Yorkshire.

BRIGGS, Pte 7668065 Harold, 25, of 6 Greenthorpe, Bramley, Leeds. Killed at Lorne Hotel, Highfield Street. Husband of Mrs Gwendoline Briggs. Buried at Bramley Baptist Chapelyard, Yorkshire.

COHEN, Pte 7675381 Lionel Henry, 23, killed at 27 Highfield Street. Son of Abraham and Beattie Cohen, of Leicester. Buried at Jewish section, Gilroes Cemetery, Leicester.

GILES, Pte 7676942 William Ernest, 28, killed at 28 Highfield Street. Husband of Mrs M. Giles. Buried at City of London Cemetery, Manor Park.

HARVEY, Pte 7676958 Frank Edward, of 262 Milkwood Road, London, SE24. Killed at 28 Highfield Street. Buried at Streatham Park Cemetery.

JOHNSON, Pte 7675238 Francis Gordon, Killed at 32 Highfield Street. Buried at Abney Park Cemetery, Stoke Newington.

KIRKPATRICK, Pte 7666044 John, 22. Killed at Upper Tichborne Street. Buried at Liverpool (Kirkdale) Cemetery.

LUESBY, Pte 7674422 Albert Edgar, 24, of 8 Ludgard Lane, Lincoln. Killed at corner of Highfield Street/Tichborne Street. Husband of Mrs Edith Luesby, of Lincoln. Buried at Lincoln (Newport) Cemetery.

SAXTON, Pte 7674449 Sidney Moger, 28. Killed at 28 Highfield Street. Son of Thomas and Amy Saxton, of Nottingham. Buried at Nottingham Church Cemetery.

TINDSLEY, Pte 7671224 Herbert, 26. Killed at 32 Highfield Street. Son of Thomas and Alice Tindsley, of Bolton. Buried at Bolton (Heaton) Cemetery.

WHEELER, Pte 7664667 Frank George Ansell, 22. Killed at 28 Highfield Street. Son of Albert and Jane Wheeler, of Balham. Buried at Arkesden (St. Margaret) Churchyard, Essex.

WILLEY, Pte 7675349 James Conrad, 24. Killed at 32 Highfield Street. Husband of Doris Willey. Buried at Enfield (Lavender Hill) Cemetery

Appendix D

CIVILIAN ROLL OF HONOUR

Compiled from CWGC Register of Civilian War Dead and CWD forms.
*Indicates relatives buried together.

*ALEXANDER, Annie Caroline, 49. Killed November 19, 1940, at 321 Humberstone Road.
*ALEXANDER, Thomas Walter, 13. Killed November 19, 1940, at 321 Humberstone Road. Mother and son buried together at Saffron Hill Cemetery.
ALEXANDER, Walter Charles, 32, of 20 Samuel Street. Killed November 20, 1940, at Southampton Street. Husband of Florence Alexander, of 20 Samuel Street.
BAKER, Alice, 65. Killed November 19, 1940, at 18 Frank Street. Wife of H. Baker.
*BALL, Irene Edith, 27, of 29 Naseby Road. Killed September 14, 1940, at 59 Ireton Road.
*BALL, Louis Jack, 36, of 29 Naseby Road. Killed September 14, 1940, at 59 Ireton Road. Husband and wife buried at Belgrave Cemetery.
*BEREZIN, Isaac, 35. Killed November 20, 1940, at 28 Highfield Street.
*BEREZIN, Sinaida, 30. Killed November 20, 1940, at 28 Highfield Street. Husband and wife buried together.
BIBBY, James, 66. Killed November 20, 1940, at 70 Knighton Drive.
BLASKEY, Isaac, 47, of 32 Highfield Street. Died November 22, 1940, at LRI. Home: 8 Cottesmore Avenue, Walton-on-Thames. Buried in Jewish section, Gilroes Cemetery.
BRAMLEY, Florence Elizabeth, 57, of 2 Darley Street. Killed November 19, 1940, at Jackson's factory shelter, Peel Street. Buried at Welford Road Cemetery.
*BROWN, Ethel Maud, 35, of 31 Severn Street. Killed November 19, 1940, at home.
*BROWN, Frederick Seymour, 7, of 31 Severn Street. Killed November 19, 1940, at home.
*BUNTING (otherwise KIRBY), Cissie, 29, of 27 Upper Tichborne Street. Killed November 19, 1940. Not identified until November 26, 1940, as Mrs Cissie Kirby.
*BUNTING (otherwise KIRBY), Pamela Joyce, 4, of 27 Upper Tichborne Street. Killed November 19, 1940. Mother and daughter buried together at Saffron Hill Cemetery
*CHAFER, Annie, 54, of 8 Saffron Hill Road. Killed August 21, 1940, at home.
*CHAFER, Frederick, 52, of 8 Saffron Hill Road. Killed August 21, 1940, at home. Husband and wife buried together at Saffron Hill Cemetery.
CHANDLER, Margaret, 50. Killed November 19, 1940, at 4 Grove Road. Wife of J.E. Chandler
*COLEMAN, Ada Gertrude, 48, of 30 Latimer Street. Killed November 15, 1940, at home.
*COLEMAN, Gertrude Ada, 23, of 30 Latimer Street. Died November 16, 1940, at LRI. Mother and daughter buried together at Gilroes Cemetery.
*COPSON, Alice Hilda, 36, of 47 Peel Street. Killed November 20, 1940, at Jackson's factory shelter, Peel Street.
*COPSON, John Barry, 6, of 47 Peel Street. Killed November 20, 1940, at Jackson's factory shelter, Peel Street.
*COPSON, Sidney Arthur, 37, of 47 Peel Street. Killed November 20, 1940, at Jackson's factory shelter, Peel Street. Husband, wife and child buried together.
COWIE, Lily Isabella, 37. Killed November 19, 1940, at 28 Highfield Street.
CURTIS, Muriel Edith, age 41, of 31 Severn Street. Killed November 19, 1940, at home.
*FALBER, Jennie, 33, of 51 Dunstan Road, Golders Green, Middlesex. Killed November 20, 1940, at 28 Knighton Road.
*FALBER, Leah, 55, of Vic Lee, Chalgrove Gardens, Finchley, Middlesex. Killed November 20, 1940, at 28 Knighton Road. Wife of Victor Falber.
*FLEMING, Iris, 22, of 30 Highfield Street. Killed November 19, 1940, at home.
*FLEMING, William Alexander, 37, of 30 Highfield Street. Killed November 19, 1940, at home. Husband and wife buried together.
FREEZOR, Frances Edith, 65, of 31 Severn Street. Died November 22, 1940, at LRI.
*GARRATT, Frederick Charles, 55. Killed November 20, 1940, at 17 Saville Street.
*GARRATT, Hetty, 58. Killed November 20, 1940, at 17 Saville Street. Husband and wife buried together.

GELBARD, Samuel, 30, Polish citizen, of Leiszno 6, Warsaw. Killed November 19, 1940, at Lorne Hotel, Highfield Street. Husband of Lucia Gelbard.

*GRIMMITT, Alice, 71, of 43 Peel Street. Killed November 20, 1940, at Jackson's factory shelter, Peel Street.

*GRIMMITT, George, 69, of 43 Peel Street. Killed November 20, 1940, at Jackson's factory shelter, Peel Street. Husband and wife buried together.

HARPER, Sidney, 34, at 58 Saxby Street. Killed November 19, 1940, at home. Husband of Winifred Harper.

HARRIS, Winifred, 30, of 8 Tollemache Avenue. Died November 19, 1940, at home. Wife of Bernard Harris.

HOWELL, William, c.70, of 11 Dorothy Road, died August 28, 1940. Collapsed and died during air raid warning.

HURDELL, Leslie Charles, 30, of 127 Greenway Avenue, Walthamstow, Essex. Killed November 19, 1940, at 32 Highfield Street.

*JAMES, Bryan, 3. Killed November 20, 1940, at 26 Knighton Road. Son of John and Ruth James.

*JAMES, Ruth, 31. Killed November 20, 1940, at 26 Knighton Road. Wife of John James. Sister of Mrs Lankester. Mother and son buried together.

JAMES (otherwise HILL), William John, 34, of 27 Tichborne Street. Died November 22, 1940, at LRI.

*JEWSBURY, Dora, 50, of 27 Highfield Street. Killed November 19, 1940, at home. Buried at Welford Road Cemetery.

*JEWSBURY, Mary Rebecca, 75. Killed November 19, 1940, at 27 Highfield Street. Buried at Welford Road Cemetery. Mother of Gwendolyn Norman

JOHNSON, Mary Jane, 70, of 53 Evington Street. Killed November 19, 1940, at home.

KNEW, Eliza Jane, 76, of 31 Severn Street. Killed November 19, 1940, at home. Buried at Welford Road Cemetery.

*LANKESTER, Janet, 33, of 26 Knighton Road. Killed November 20, 1940, at home. Wife of Dr J.H. Lankester.

*LANKESTER, Robert Allen, 4, of 26 Knighton Road. Killed November 20, 1940, at home. Son of Dr Lankester. Mother and son's ashes scattered at Leicester Crematorium Garden of Remembrance.

*LLOYD, Anthony Frederick, 11, of 98 Sparkenhoe Street. Killed November 19, 1940, at home. Son of Frederick Lloyd.

*LLOYD, Derek James, 8, of 98 Sparkenhoe Street. Died November 22, 1940, at General Hospital. Son of Frederick Lloyd. Mr Lloyd's sons buried together at Goadby.

*LOCK, Dorothy Eliza, 37, of 319 Humberstone Road. Killed November 19, 1940 at home. Wife of Albert C. Lock.

*LOCK, Harold Anthony, 7, of 319 Humberstone Road. Killed November 19, 1940, at home. Son of Albert and Dorothy Lock.

*LOCK, Sylvia, 6, of 319 Humberstone Road. Killed November 19, 1940, at home. Daughter of Albert and Dorothy Lock.

*LOCK, Theresa, 9, of 319 Humberstone Road. Killed November 19, 1940, at home. Daughter of Albert and Dorothy Lock. Locks buried together at Gilroes Cemetery.

MACHIN, Ada Marjorie, 20. Killed August 21, 1940 at 4 Saffron Hill Road. Wife of Private Cecil Machin, Leicestershire Regiment.

MAIN, William George Vearncombe, 38, of St Cryes, Sparkhayes Lane, Porlock, Somerset. Killed November 19, 1940, at Highfield Street.

MARKS, Iris Queenie, 25, of London. Killed November 19, 1940, at 25 Highfield Street. Wife of Alfred Marks of 22a Amhurst Parade, Stamford Hill, N16.

*MARSDEN, Mrs Esther Hilda, 40, of 25 Highfield Street. Killed November 19, 1940, at home. Wife of Nathaniel Marsden, daughter of Rebecca Steinberg.

*MARSDEN, Nathaniel, 40, of 25 Highfield Street. Killed November 19, 1940, at home. Husband of Esther Hilda Marsden. Mother, husband and daughter buried together in Jewish Section, Gilroes Cemetery.

MARTIN, Susan, 60, of 27 Sylvan Street. Died November 20, 1940, at Ingle Street School shelter. Wife of Percy Martin.

MILLER, Lillian Angell, 42, of Woodville, Knighton Park Road. Killed November 19, 1940, at home. Wife of William Spencer Miller.

MOSLEY, Walter, 73. Killed November 19, 1940, at 321 Humberstone Road.

MOTT, Eliza, 63, of 62 Conduit Street. Killed July 19, 1941, at home.

NEWMAN, Connie Doreen, 19, at 70 Knighton Drive. Killed November 20, 1940.

*NORMAN, Christopher John, 12, of 27 Highfield Street. Killed at home, November 19, 1940. Son of Harold and Gwendolyn Norman.

*NORMAN, Gwendolyn, 43, of 27 Highfield Street. Killed at home November 19, 1940. Wife of Harold Norman. Daughter of Mary Rebecca Jewsbury. Father, mother and son buried together.

*NORMAN, Harold John, 43, of 27 Highfield Street. Killed November 19, 1940, at home. Husband of Gwendolyn Norman.

PARDOE, Iris Doreen, 20. Killed November 19, 1940, at 319 Humberstone Road. Wife of J. Pardoe.

PAYNE, Sarah Ann, 76, of 73 Cavendish Road, Killed August 21, 1940, at home.

PEAKE, Frances, 42, of 23 East Street. Killed May 17, 1941, at 11 Webster Road.

PERTZIN, Joseph, 32, of 1 Victoria Terrace. Killed November 19, 1940, at 56 Saxby Street. Husband of Hedwig Pertzin. Buried in Jewish section, Gilroes Cemetery.

PHILLIPS, Bertha Caroline, 60, of Woodville, Knighton Park Road. Killed November 19, 1940, at home.

*PULFORD, Charles William, 79, of 59 Ireton Road. Killed September 14, 1940, at home. Husband of Emma Pulford.

*PULFORD, Emma, 79, of 59 Ireton Road. Killed September 14, 1940, at home. Wife of Charles William Pulford. Husband and wife buried together.

*RIPPON, Jeanette, 25. Killed November 19, 1940, at 27 Upper Tichborne Street. Wife of P. Rippon.

*RIPPON, Philip, 16 months. Killed November 19, 1940, at The Ritz, 27 Upper Tichborne Street. Son of P. Rippon. Mother and son buried at Saffron Hill Cemetery.

*SHEEN, Ivy Beatrice, 40, of 2 Grove Road. Killed November 19, 1940, at 4 Grove Road. Wife of Walter Crowe Sheen.

*SHEEN, Joan, 6, of 2 Grove Road. Killed November 19, 1940, at 4 Grove Road. Daughter of Walter Crowe Sheen and Ivy Sheen. Mother and daughter buried together at Gilroes Cemetery.

SIETZ, Lea, 43. Killed November 19, 1940, at 25 Highfield Street.

SILLS, Edith Nellie, 56, of 7 Quenby Street. Killed November 19, 1940, at home. Buried at Welford Road Cemetery

SKLAR, Alfred Abraham, 35, of 42 Eastfield Road. Died November 23, 1940, at LRI. Husband of Judy Sklar, of 178 Holders Hill Road, Finchley, Middlesex

*SMITH, Dorothy, 32, of 147 Cavendish Road. Killed August 21, 1940, at LRI. Wife of Tom Smith.

SMITH, Eliza, 67, of 319 Humberstone Road. Killed at home November 19, 1940.

*SMITH, Irene, 2, of 147 Cavendish Road. Killed at home on August 21, 1940. Daughter of Tom Smith. Mother and daughter buried together.

SPIRO, Annie Rebecca, 58, of of 31 Queen's Road, Leytonstone, Essex. Killed November 19, 1940, at 25 Highfield Street. Wife of Casper Spiro.

*SPIRO, Gerald, 2, of 31 Queens Road, Leytonstone, Essex. Killed November 19, 1940, at 25 Highfield Street. Son of Mr J. Spiro and Rose Spiro.

*SPIRO, Gordon Beresford, 4, of 31 Queens Road, Leytonstone, Essex. Killed November 19, 1940, at 25 Highfield Street. Son of Mr J. Spiro and Rose Spiro.

*SPIRO, Rose, 35, of Essex. Killed November 19, 1940, at 25 Highfield Street. Daughter of Mr and Mrs J. Weinstein, of 31 Queen's Road, Leytonstone, Essex. Mother and two children buried in Jewish section, Gilroes Cemetery.

STANDEN, Cecilia May, 47, of 33 Tennis Court Drive. Killed November 20, 1940, at 6 Bannerman Road.

STANSFIELD, John Cyril, 28, of 26 Allandale Road. Killed November 20, 1940, at home. Husband of Grace Stansfield.

*STEINBERG, Rebecca/Bella, 70, of 25 Highfield Street. Killed on November 19, 1940, at home. Mother of Esther Hilda Marsden.

STEVENS, Elizabeth, 60, of 25 Highfield Street. Died December 12, 1940, at LRI.

*STUBLEY, Clifford, 28. Killed November 19, 1940, at 18 Frank Street. Found at 28 Frank Street. Son of Edith Stubley, of 28 Frank Street

*STUBLEY, Elsie, 28. Killed on November 19, 1940 at 18 Frank Street. Daughter of Edith Stubley, of 18 Frank Street. Brother and sister buried at Gilroes Cemetery.

TATE, Michael Nathaniel, 7. Killed November 19, 1940, at 25 Highfield Street. Son of Reginald and Rachel Tate, of 18 Bulow Road, Fulham, London.

TAYLOR (otherwise FOWKES), Frances Lillian, 29, of 56 Saxby Street. Killed at home on November 19, 1940.

TAYLOR, Harry (otherwise JOHNSON, William), 48. Killed November 19, 1940, at 56 or 58 Saxby Street.

THOMPSON, Susannah, 73, of 31 Severn Street. Killed November 19, 1940, at home. Buried at Welford Road Cemetery

THORP, Frank Henry, 15, of 35 Kedleston Road. Injured at Sparkenhoe Street on November 19, 1940, died November 20, 1940, at General Hospital.

TILLEY, Kathleen May, 27. Killed November 19, 1940, at 56 Saxby Street. Buried with parents in Cranoe churchyard.

TOWNLEY, Yolande Josephine, 31. Killed November 20, 1940, at 4 Bannerman Road.

WARNER, Mary Emma, 65, of London. Killed November 19, 1940, at 25 Highfield Street.

WATES, Janet Marshall, 42, WVS, of 48 Shirley Road. Killed November 20, 1940, at home.

WILMOTT, Hilda, 42, of 6 Holland Road. Killed November 20, 1940, at 319 Humberstone Road. Wife of Charles Wilmott, of 6 Holland Road.

WOOD, Arthur Knapman, 37, of 289 Higher Heath Lane, Birmingham. Killed November 19, 1940, at 58 Saxby Street. Husband of Charlotte Alice Wood.

Unidentified: Body 85 at 28 Highfield Street, Killed November 19, 1940. Possibly GELBARD, Samuel 30.

On November 26, 1940, grieving tearful relatives stand before Union flag-draped coffins of ten victims of the Luftwaffe raid on Leicester's Blitz Night, at Saffron Hill Cemetery. The Bishop of Leicester, Lord Mayor, Chief Constable and ARP officials stand on the left, whilst FAPy and AFS personnel stand to attention on the right. Meanwhile, a reporter, front right, notes the scene. [Via Terence Burford]

Appendix E
Leicester NFS, July 1942

	Firemen & Leading Firemen		Section Leaders		Column Officers	
	f/t	p/t	w/t	p/t	w/t	p/t

Division A: Leicester

SUB-STATIONS:

Sub Division 1:						
Granby Halls	65	19	3	0	1	0
Lancaster Place	64	1	3	0	1	0
Queens Road	19	30	0	1	1	0
Saffron Lane	15	25	1	0	0	0
Stoneygate Tram Depot	19	31	0	1	0	0
Dover Street	44	9	1	0	1	0
Factory sub-stations	0	32	0	0	0	0
Sub Division 2:						
Danes Hill House	42	0	2	0	0	0
Great Holme Street	32	41	2	1	0	0
Glenfield Road	16	11	0	0	0	0
Winstanley Drive	0	14	0	0	0	0
Factory sub-stations	0	50	0	0	0	0
Sub Division 3:						
Church Gate	79	22	2	2	1	0
Freehold Street	32	16	1	0	1	0
Melton Road	29	27	1	1	0	1
Factory sub-stations	0	113	0	0	0	0
Sub Division 4:						
Conduit Street	42	12	2	0	1	0
Asfordby Street	37	33	1	0	1	0
Gwendolen Road	20	29	1	0	0	0
Humberstone	28	41	1	0	0	1
Factory sub-stations	127	100	5	1	2	0
Totals:	710	659	26	7	10	2

Total Leicester NFS personnel: 1,414

Appendix F

Vulnerable Points in Leicester

List of Vital Factories 1941

(A)= Admiralty
(S)= Ministry of Supply
(P)= Ministry of Aircraft Production

1	(S) Adcock & Shipley, Ash Street
2	(P) Armstrong Siddeley Motors Ltd, Excel Works, Walnut Street
3	(P) Asea Electric Ltd, Erith Road, near Aylestone
4	(S + P) Automotive Products Ltd (Lockheed), Northfield, Narborough Road
5	(S + P) Bentley Engineering Company, Comet Works, New Bridge Street
6	(P) Berridge I.L. & Co. Ltd, Sanvey Gate
7	(A) Booton W.E. Ltd, Wanlip Street
8	(P) B.T.H. Co. Ltd at Hall Earle, Blackbird Road
9	(A) B.T.H. Co. Ltd at Hall & Pincus, Evington Valley Road
10	(P) British United Shoe Machinery Co. Ltd, Union Works, Belgrave Road
11	(S) BSA Guns Ltd, Agency Factory, Abbey Mills, Abbey Park Road
12	(S) BSA Guns Ltd, Agency Factory, CWS, Knighton Fields Road
13	(P) Canon & Stokes Ltd, 9 Orson Street Works, North Evington
14	(P) Canon & Stokes Ltd, 80 Coleman Road
15	(P) Castle Bromwich Aeroplane Factory, Old Skating Rink, Western Boulevard
16	(P) Castle Bromwich Aeroplane Factory, late A.S. Yeats Ltd, Blackbird Road
17	(P) Castle Bromwich Aeroplane Factory at Paton & Baldwins, Westbridge Works
18	(P) Charnwood Engineering Co. Ltd, Abbey Lane
19	(A + S) Coventry Gauge & Tool Co. Ltd, Filbert Street
20	(P) Cascelloid Ltd, Abbey Lane
21	(P) Gent & Co. Ltd, Faraday Works
22	(S) Grieve T. & Co. Ltd, Lancastria Works, French Road
23	(P) Jones A.A. & Shipman Ltd, East Park Road
24	(P) Jones A.A. & Shipman Ltd, Gypsy Lane
25	(P) Lea Francis Engineering (1937) Ltd. at Vaughan & Harborne, Wellington Street
26	(S) Lockheed Hydraulic Brake Co. Ltd (G. Gibbons Ltd), Aylestone Road
27	(A + S) Mellor Bromley & Co. Ltd, Minotaur Works, St. Saviours Road East
28	(A + S) Parmeko Ltd, Percy Road, Aylestone Park
29	(P) Pard F. Ltd, Corona Works, St. Saviours Road
30	(P) Reid & Sigrist Ltd, Braunstone
31	(P) Spencer & Co., 37a Victoria Road East
32	(P) Standard Telephone & Cables at N. Corah
33	(P) Standard Telephone & Cables at Chilprufe
34	(P) Standard Telephone & Cables at Aylestone Dyeworks, Ranby Road, Aylestone
35	(P) Standard Telephone & Cables Laboratories at T.G. Hirst, Abbey Park Road
36	(S) Stibbe G. & Co., Maxim Works
37	(S) S.S. Cars Ltd, premises of J.W. Black Ltd, at Central Eastern [?]
38	(P) Taylorcraft Aeroplanes (England) Ltd, Colmore Road, Frog Island
39	(P) Taylor, Taylor & Hobson Ltd, Stoughton Street Works
40	(P) Taylor, Taylor & Hobson Ltd, Glebe Street
41	(P) Taylor, Taylor & Hobson Ltd, Avenue Road
42	(S) Taylor, Taylor & Hobson Ltd, Byford Road
43	(P) Turner Luke & Co., Deacon Street
44	(P) Wadkin Ltd, Green Lane Works

Waterworks at Bowling Green Street

Gas & Electricity Works
GPO Leicester
Abbey Park Pumping Station, Abbey Park Road
Sub-pumping Station, Belgrave Road
LMS Station/LNER Station, Belgrave Road
LNER Station, Great Central Street
City Transport, Abbey Park Road
The Magazine, Newarkes
HM Prison, Welford Road
Petroleum Board, Parkhurst Street
Petroleum Board, Catherine Street
County ARP HQ, Friar Lane

Vulnerable Points List in Leicester, 1943

Serial No:

A2529:	Armstrong Siddeley, Walnut Street
A2534:	Armstrong Siddeley Motors Ltd, 247 Western Road
A2556:	Colton & Stokes Ltd, Orson Street Works, North Evington
A2632:	Parmeko Ltd, Percy Road, Aylestone Park
A2633:	Parmeko Ltd (Toller & Lankaster), Aylestone Park
A2673:	Bray, Alfred & Sons Ltd, 97 Bridge Road
A2678:	Partridge, Wilson & Co. Ltd, Evington Valley Road
A2314:	Leicester 36 ERD Class 14
E2130:	Leicester Head Post Office
E2131:	Leicester Free Lane Telephone Exchange & Repeater Station
G2005:	Leicester University College
:	University Road 'H' Transmitter
J2111:	Power Station, Aylestone Road
J2230:	Leicester Corporation
J2231:	Leicester Corporation, Belgrave Gate
K2032:	Adcock & Shipley Ltd, Ash Street
K2038:	Bentley Engineering Company
K2043:	BSA Guns Ltd (Rudkin), Laundons Works
K2044:	BSA Guns Ltd (Hirsts Works)
K2055:	BSA Guns Ltd (CWS), Knighton Fields Road
K2068:	Charnwood Engineering Co. Ltd, Abbey Lane
K2072:	Charnwood Engineering Co. Ltd, Yeats Factory, Blackbird Road
K2085:	Coventry Gauge and Tool Co. Ltd, CWS Works, Grace Road
K2214:	Grieve T. & Co. Ltd, Lancastria Works, French Road
K2253:	Mellor Bromley & Co. Ltd, St. Saviours Road East
K2312:	Stibbe G. & Co. Ltd, Maxim Works
K2319:	Taylor, Taylor & Hobson Ltd, Byford Road
K2322:	Taylor, Taylor & Hobson Ltd, Stoughton Street Works
K2902:	British Thomson Houston RDF [*radar*] Test Site
L2008:	British United Shoe Machinery Co. Ltd, Swan Works
L2010:	British United Shoe Machinery Co. Ltd, Union Works
L2050:	Gent & Co. Ltd, Faraday Works
L2091:	Standard Telephone & Cables Ltd, Granby Road
L2092:	Standard Telephone & Cables Ltd, Archdeacon Lane
L2098:	Wadkin Ltd, Green Lane Works

Primary Sources

Dr E.K. MacDonald file
ARP/CD Handbooks, Memoranda, Training Bulletins, Industrial Bulletins, Manuals, Pamphlets, Circulars (1935-1945)

Illustrated Leicester Chronicle 1939-1945
Leicester Evening Mail 1939-1945
Leicester Mercury 1939-2014

London Gazette 1940-1945

Kelly's *Directory of Leicestershire & Rutland* 1938 & 1941

www.wartimeleicestershire.com
www.raf.mod.uk

Bundesarchiv, Germany

RL7/93

Record Office for Leicestershire, Leicester & Rutland, Wigston Magna

7 D 69: Civilian War Deaths Book 1940-41
10 D 58: Chief Fire Officer's Letters
15 D 70: Files on Leic. civilian air raid deaths 1940 (restricted access)
21 D 64: Leic. Fire Service records to 1945
CM 42/33: Watch Committee Minutes 14.11.1939-21.10.1941
DE 1850/1-29: Miscellaneous Leic. CD material
DE 2013/63: Miscellaneous Leics. CD file 1940-1944
DE 2013/81: General file of Leics. CD instructions 1941-1945
DE 2013/82: North Midlands Region CD Intelligence Bulletins 1941-1945
DE 2013/83: Minutes of Leics. Heads of CD Services Meetings 1941-1946
DE 2013/89: File of general Leics. CD admin and operational correspondence 1941-1945
DE 2372: Leics. Mortuary Office List of killed 1940-1941
DE 3277/36-41: Leicester ARP/CD Committee Minutes 1939-1952
DE 4591/1: ARP documents on Leicester 12.7.1935-1.12.1937
DE 4591/2: ARP documents on Leicester 2.12.1937-19.10.1938
DE 6362: Log Book of ARP Messenger Mr A.C. Hebb of Braunstone
L355P: Report of the CD Committee to Leicester Corporation 31/10/1944
M336: ARP Scheme for Leicester 1937

National Archives, Kew, London

HO 45/25557: Looting: disparity of sentencing by courts 1940-1944
HO 186/2145: CD Reserve Nottingham Regional Mobile Column: Willingham House, 1942-45
HO 186/2953: Regional Organisation: History of CD, No.3 Region 1939-1945
HO 187/505: Admin. and Organisation: Layout of Fire Force areas: No.9 (Leicester) 1941-1942
HO 198/216: MoHS Research & Experiments Dept: Statistical Records: Region 3
HO 199/47: MoHS: Intelligence Branch: Aylestone, Leicester, 21 Aug 1940
HO 199/54: MoHS: Intelligence Branch: Leicester 19/20 Nov 1940
HO 203/5: MoHS: Home Security Daily Intelligence Reports Sept 1940-Dec 1940
HO 207/1129: Region No.3: Leicester: Reports on CD Scheme 1939-1948
HW 5/719: Govt Code & Cypher School: German Section: 'Brown' Reports 5.9.1940-25.3.1941

WO 166/1225: War diary HQ East Mids Area Aug 1940-Feb 1941
WO 166/2117: War diary HQ 2nd AA Div. Sep-Dec 1940
WO 166/2118: War diary HQ 2nd AA Div. Jan-Aug 1941
WO 166/2256: War diary of HQ 32 AA Brig Aug 1939-Dec 1941
WO 166/3995: War diary of No. 3 Bomb Disposal Company RE, Sep 1940-Dec 1941
WO 166/4037: War diary of 42 Bomb Disposal Section, No. 3 Coy RE Nov 1940-Dec 1941
WO 166/11206: War diary of 32 AA Brig Jan-Dec 1943
WO 166/14516: Leicester Sub-Area War Diary Jan 1944-Oct 1944

Via Malc Tovey: Unpublished 1968 MS by Edward Doughty and unpublished 1974 MS by Arthur Cramp, plus photos

Secondary Sources

Adam, R. (2009): *Jewish Voices: Memories of Leicester in the 1940s and 50s*, Writing School Leicester Ltd
Balke, U. (1997): *Der Luftkrieg in Europa 1939-1941: Die Einsatze des Kampfgeschwaders 2…*, Bechtermuz Verlag, Germany
Beazley, B. (2001): *From Peelers to Pandas: An Illustrated History of Leicester City Police*, Breedon Books, Derby
Beazley, B. (2004): *Wartime Leicester*, Sutton Publ., Gloucestershire
Blandford, E. (1997): *Target England: Flying With the Luftwaffe in World War II*, Airlife, Shrewsbury
Bonser, R. (2001): *Aviation in Leicestershire and Rutland*, Midland Publishing Ltd, Leicestershire
Bowyer, M.J.F. (1986): *Air Raid! Enemy Air Offensive Against East Anglia, 1939-1945*, Patrick Stephens Ltd, Cambridge
Bowyer, M.J.F. (1990): *The Battle of Britain: 50 Years On*, Patrick Stephens Ltd, Northamptonshire
Boynton, H. (2000): *The History of Victoria Park, Leicester*, privately published, Leicester
Brooksbank, B.W.L. (2011): *Damage and Disruption on the Railways of Great Britain During World War Two*, Noodle Books, Hants
Bungay, S. (2009): *The Most Dangerous Enemy: A History of the Battle of Britain*, Aurum Press, London
Carswell, J. et al (1989): *Ours To Defend… Leicestershire People Remember the Home Front*, Leicester Oral History Archive, Leicester
Cartwright, T.C.C. (1998): *Birds Eye Wartime Leicester*, TCC Publ., Leicester
Cartwright, T.C.C. (2002): *Birds Eye Wartime Leicestershire*, TCC Publ., Leicester
Cole, J.A., (1964): *Lord Haw-Haw and William Joyce*, Faber & Faber, London
Doherty, M.A. (2000): *Nazi Wireless Propaganda*, Edinburgh University Press, Edinburgh
Dover, D. (200?): *Leicester: Our War*, Reprint UK, Leicestershire
Duncan, J. & Webb, E. (1990): *Blitz Over Britain*, Spellmount Ltd, Kent
Dunn, C.L. (1952 & 1953): *Emergency Medical Services – Vol. I & Vol.II*, HMSO, London
Fleischer, W. (2004): *German Air-Dropped Weapons to 1945*, Midland Publ., Leicestershire
Goodrum, A. (2005): *No Place For Chivalry*, Grub Street, London
Goss, C. (2010): *The Luftwaffe's Blitz: The Inside Story November 1940-May 1941*, Crecy Publ., Manchester
Hickin, W. (2013): *Fire Force: The NFS 1941-1948*, WFH Publ., London
Hinton, J. (2002): *Women, Social Leadership, and the Second World War*, OUP, Oxfordshire
Ingles, G.H. (1945): *When The War Came To Leicester*, C. Brooks & Co., Leicester
Jopp, K. (1965): *Corah of Leicester 1815-1965*, Newman Neame
Lee, L. (1983): *A Short History of 100 Years Service by the St John Ambulance Brigade Leicestershire 1882-1982*, St John Ambulance, Leicestershire
Leicester Mercury (1976 & 1989): *Leicester at War: Supplements, 1-3*, Leicester Mercury, Leicester
Leicester Promotions Ltd (1996): *Leicester at War Guided Walk Information Pack*, Leicester Promotions Ltd

Malcolmson, P. and R. (2013): *Women At The Ready: The Remarkable Story of the WVS on the Home Front*, Little, Brown, London
Mason, F.K. (1969): *Battle Over Britain*, McWhirter Twins, London
McDougall, J. (1979): *Civil Defence in Leicestershire 1939-1945*, privately published
Middlebrook, M. (1980): *The Battle of Hamburg*, Allen Lane, London
Mills, J. (1993): *A People's Army*, Wardens Publ., Kent
Nash, D. & Reeder, D. (Eds) (1993): *Leicester in the Twentieth Century*, Sutton Publ., Gloucestershire
O'Brien, T.H. (1954): *Civil Defence*, HMSO, London
Penny, J. (1995): *Luftwaffe Operations Over the Bristol Area, 1940-44*, Fishponds Local History Society, Bristol
Price, A. (2000): *Blitz on Britain 1939-45*, Sutton Publ., Gloucestershire
Radtke, S. (1990): *Kampfgeschwader 54: Eine Chronik Nach Kriegstagebuchern, Dokumenten und Berichten 1935-1945*, Schild-Verlag, Germany
Ramsey, Ed. W. (1987): *The Battle of Britain: Then & Now: MkV*, Battle of Britain Prints International, London
Ramsey, Ed. W. (1987, 1988, 1990): *The Blitz: Then & Now: Vols.1-3*, Battle of Britain Prints International, London
Rothnie, N. (1992): *The Baedeker Blitz: Hitler's Attack on Britain's Historic Cities*, Ian Allan Publ., London
Ruddy, A.J. (2007): *To The Last Round: The Leicestershire & Rutland Home Guard 1940-1945*, Breedon Books, Derby
Seaton, D. (2004): *Leicester's Town Hall: A Victorian Jewel*, Leicester City Council, Leicester
Spick, M. (2001): *Luftwaffe Bomber Aces*, Greenhill Books, London
Taghon, P. (2004): *Die Geschichte des Lehrgeschwaders 1: Band 1 1936-1942*, UDM Heinz Nickel, Germany
Taylor, L. (2010): *Luftwaffe Over Scotland*, Whittles Publ., Caithness
Tedder, V. (1994): *The Pantry Under the Stairs*, Leicester City Libraries, Leicester
Titmuss, R.M. (1950): *Problems of Social Policy*, HMSO, London
Wakefield, K. (1999): *Pfadfinder*, Tempus Publ., Gloucestershire
Wakeling, Lt Col. E.E. (1998): *The Lonely War*, B.D. Publ., Buckinghamshire
Warburton, S. (1946): *Chingford at War 1939-1945*, Chingford Borough Council, Essex
Wood, D. and Dempster, D. (1969): *The Narrow Margin*, Arrow Books, London
Wright Process Engraving Co. (c.1946): *Leicester Blitz Souvenir*, Wright Process Engraving Co., Leicester

The alarming cover of Leicester Blitz Souvenir *(c.1946), showing Leicester's crest in an explosion, under a hail of German bombs. [Author]*